CRITICAL INSIGHTS

Great Expectations

CRITICAL INSIGHTS

Great Expectations

by Charles Dickens

Editor
Eugene Goodheart
Brandeis University

Salem Press
Pasadena, California   Hackensack, New Jersey

Cover photo: The Granger Collection, New York

Published by Salem Press

© 2010 by EBSCO Publishing
Editor's text © 2010 by Eugene Goodheart
"The *Paris Review* Perspective" © 2010 by Elizabeth Gumport for *The Paris Review*

∞ The paper used in these volumes conforms to the American National
Standard for Permanence of Paper for Printed Library Materials, Z39.48-1992
(R1997).

Library of Congress Cataloging-in-Publication Data
Great expectations, by Charles Dickens / editor, Eugene Goodheart.
   p. cm. — (Critical insights)
Includes bibliographical references and index.
ISBN 978-1-58765-614-9 (alk. paper)
1. Dickens, Charles, 1812-1870. Great expectations. I. Goodheart, Eugene.
PR4560.G689 2009
823'.8—dc22

                                                2009026312

PRINTED IN CANADA

Contents

Resources

About This Volume

Eugene Goodheart

Here is a collection of lively and diverse essays—prefaced by commentaries on context, the novelist's life and the critical reception—on plot symbolism, class, gender, and sexuality in Dickens's great and perhaps most popular novel, *Great Expectations* (1860-1861).

In focusing on the workings of plot, Eiichi Hara, Peter Brooks, Samuel Sipe, and Elizabeth MacAndrew address themselves to the question of the moral character of Pip, the protagonist, as it emerges in his narrative of events. Sipe and MacAndrew share the view that Pip achieves moral autonomy and peace at the end; in contrast, Brooks and Hara see him as the incorrigible and hapless victim of the plotting of others (Magwitch, Miss Havisham, and Estella) and of the irrational demons of his own character. (For Brooks, it should be noted, *Great Expectations* is an opportunity for a sophisticated psychoanalytic interpretation.) Caroline Levine reads *Great Expectations* as a detective story, in which the suspense and doubt generated by the plot serve the pursuit of truth and reality. Calum Kerr employs a mythic-structural approach, based on Joseph Campbell's narrative model of the hero's journey, in tracing Pip's progress in the novel. These different, vigorously and incisively argued, readings of plot should provide students with an opportunity to take sides or formulate their own views.

MacAndrew and John Cunningham demonstrate the richly symbolic structure of the novel. MacAndrew addresses the ways in which "abstract views of social institutions [e.g., church and prison] and spiritual states [e.g., weather] are symbolized." Cunningham has a keen eye for Christian imagery and shows how in the early episodes, rituals such as baptism are perverted in the service of death, only to be restored at the end to their true life-giving Christian significance. In a tour de force, William A. Cohen, in perhaps the most controversial essay in the collection, finds a sexual subtext, a theme of pervasive masturbation. It remains for the reader who is persuaded by the argument to connect the theme with the more open themes of the novel, such as Pip's social ambition or his love of Estella. In the concluding essay, Peter Scheckner provides a lively account of Dickens's treatment of gender and class in which the novelist reveals himself at different times as liberal, conservative, and radical. Scheckner comprehends the contradictoriness of Dickens's politics, whereas most critics, whom he cites, tend to fix Dickens in one or another political position.

The hope is that students will be stimulated by this cornucopia of approaches to make their own individual readings of the novel.

THE BOOK
AND
AUTHOR

On *Great Expectations*

Eugene Goodheart

Fear is the first emotion in the story Pip, the protagonist and narrator of *Great Expectations* (1860-1861), experiences; it is also the emotion that awakens an awareness of his identity. "The small bundle of shivers growing afraid of it all and beginning to cry, was Pip." His fear of the wilderness, river, and "the distant savage lair from which the wind was rising" will turn into terror when confronted by the chained criminal Magwitch, who emerges from the landscape, threatens to cut his throat if he cries out, and demands that he steal a file and "wittles" from his sister's house. Pip performs the task, and the emotions of fear and terror turn into a sense of guilt that will govern his life and the telling of it. Orphaned as an infant, he is raised "by hand" by a cruel sister. With the exception of his sister's benevolent husband Joe Gargery, his early life is a nightmare of guilt-inducing child abuse by family and family friends.

Pip is both victim and apparent beneficiary of circumstance, for he is given the chance to escape the squalor and oppression of childhood by being invited to Satis House, the home of Miss Havisham and her ward, the beautiful Estella with whom he falls in love. He will soon learn that he is heir to a substantial fortune from an anonymous source. The triumphant trajectory of his career, however, proves illusory. Estella fails to requite Pip's love, indeed she is incapable of love, having grown up as a product of Miss Havisham's insatiable desire to avenge herself on men for having been abandoned by her lover. Estella, a starry name, recalls the desirable women in courtly love poems who put their knightly lovers to the test in deeds on the battlefield or in the making of verse before they condescend to their lovers. In Dickens's version, the beloved is the instrument of sadism, the object of unattainable desire; the lover, the subject of insurmountable masochism. Nothing that he learns about Estella can dissuade him from loving her. As for his legacy, that too is an inheritance of grief, for its source, as Pip learns, is the grateful criminal Magwitch, whom he had helped on the marsh. After being apprehended by the authorities, Magwitch had been exiled to Australia, the dumping ground of England's criminals, where he had made a fortune as a sheep farmer. Pip's fairy-tale expectations turn into nightmare.

His love for Estella and Magwitch's gift are two facets of a single theme, his desire to become a gentleman. In a novel of significant coincidences, Magwitch turns out to be Estella's father. In the mid-Victorian period (the novel was published in 1861), the ambition to rise above one's class has the encouragement of the extraordinary social and economic changes occurring as a result of the industrial revolution. The status of gentleman entails money, superior manners, and social power. The relationship between Pip's love for Estella and his desire to become a gentleman turns into a question raised by Pip's childhood friend, Biddy.

> "Do you want to be a gentleman, to spite her or to gain her over?" Biddy quietly asked me, after a pause.
>
> "I don't know," I moodily answered.
>
> "Because if it is to spite," Biddy pursued, "I should think—but you know best—that might be better and more independently done by carrying nothing for her words. And if it is to gain her over, I should think—but you know best—she was not worth gaining over."

Is Estella cause or effect in Pip's ambition to become a gentleman? A clue to the answer is the fact that his love for Estella survives his disillusionment with the idea of becoming a gentleman and its vanities, suggesting that the desire for Estella is not exhausted by his ambition. For much of the narrative, however, ambition and desire are inextricably combined. We might see an American parallel of Pip's unreciprocated love for Estella in Jay Gatsby's yearning for Daisy Buchanan, in whose voice he hears "the sound of money."

Great Expectations, I am not the first to say, is a bildungsroman, a novel of the education and development of a young man. On the surface at least, Pip achieves moral and spiritual maturity. Fearful and guilt-ridden in childhood, he "escapes" into a corrupt world of snobbery, greed, and cruelty. Bentley Drummle, whom Estella marries, is its embodiment. (Trabb's boy's pantomime of Pip's gentlemanly pretensions is superb satire.) If we are to trust Pip's account, his conversion to a life of Christian charity and kindness should provide us with a satisfying sense of closure. But for many readers, myself included, the novel does not achieve closure. For that matter, I suspect that this was the case with Dickens himself as a reader of his own work. There is evidence for this view in the two endings that he provided for the novel. In the first ending, the one that Dickens wanted, Pip and Estella part ways (an unhappy ending at a time when fiction was supposed to supply happy endings); in the second, urged upon Dickens by Edward Bulwer-Lytton, who feared reactions of readers to the unhappy ending, there is the suggestion of a future for the lovers. The second ending is a travesty of the novel's narrative logic. Her capacity for love eviscerated by Miss Havisham, Estella is no more than Pip's wishful fantasy.

The question that remains is why Pip should persist in loving her even after his moral transformation. Having learned about the empty pretensions of being a gentleman (the novel transvalues the term, conferring the status Christian gentleman on the kindly blacksmith Joe Gargery), why would he remain attached to the illusion of Estella as an object worthy of love? Pity and compassion for what she had been turned into yes, but as a lover? That is the mystery. Estella is a hollow shell of a character with a beautiful and elegant surface, and yet Pip persists in trying to endow her with the possibility of an inner life of which she is incapable. Eiichi Hara, in an essay in this collection, speaks of "the madness" and "irrationality" of his love for Estella. But at the end of the novel, Pip, apparently morally transformed and self-possessed, communicates nothing of madness and irrationality. Both Peter Brooks in his essay and Hara argue that though Pip is the narrator, he is not the author of his own story, which is really the achievement of the plotting of other characters: Magwitch, Pumblechook, Miss Havisham, and Estella. In their reading Pip remains a victim of circumstance and abuse to the every end. There is no emergence into spiritual maturity.

There is truth and excess in this reading. The excess is in the refusal to accept the evidence of the changes that occur in Pip. He is not the completely unreliable narrator such a reading makes him out to be. Pip's acknowledgment of the humanity of Magwitch, the risks he takes in helping him escape, his reconciliation with Joe Gargery, and his anonymous generosity to his friend Pocket are real moral achievements. The truth in the reading, however, lies in Pip's insurmountable obsession with Estella. The demon of irrational desire possesses Pip, despite his moral transformation. The source of Pip's obsession lies, I believe, in a powerful and characteristic tendency in Dickens's imagination. Obsession to the point of caricature defines the Dickensian character in all his novels. Characters are fixed in rituals of behavior and language. The lawyer Jaggers cannot speak without pointing an accusatory finger. His associate Wemmick, whether in the public space of the law or the private space of home, acts or speaks as if he were a puppet made of wood. Time has stopped in Satis House and Miss Havisham remains forever arrested in her passion for revenge. Pumblechook and Wopsle are caricatures that Pip may find in life. And think of Mr. Micawber (in *David Copperfield*), who ritualistically repeats the statement that "he will never leave Mrs. Micawber," and the unctuous and hypocritical Uriah Heep (also in *David Copperfield*), who ritualistically caresses the palm of his hand. It is the rare character, usually the protagonist of a novel, who has the complexity and capacity for change and development. Pip is such a character, but he cannot entirely escape the obsessiveness that pervades the gallery of Dickensian characters. That Pip partakes of this condition may be a failure in Pip, but not in Dickens, whose imagination refuses to accept the diplomatic assumption (diplomatic, because we all want to believe it of ourselves) that human beings are potentially complex and capable of growth and change. Dickens is saying in effect that most people are dominated by passions and fixed in their obsessions without knowing it, the effect of which is both comic and tragic. Even Pip, who has the capacity for self-awareness and change, cannot completely free himself from this condition. Dickens's "caricatures" are not distortions of human reality, but rather the creations of a great psychological realist.

Biography of Charles Dickens_____

Charles E. May

Early Life

Charles John Huffam Dickens was born at Portsmouth, England, on February 7, 1812, the second of eight children. His father, John Dickens, a clerk in the Naval Pay Office, was always hard-pressed to support his family. Because his father's work made it necessary for him to travel, Dickens spent his youth in several different places, including London and Chatham. When he was only twelve years old, his father's financial difficulty made it necessary for the young Dickens to work in a shoeblacking warehouse while his father was placed in a debtor's prison at Marshalsea—an event that was to have a powerful influence on Dickens throughout his life. Oliver Twist's experience in the workhouse is one of the best-known results of what Dickens considered to be an act of desertion by his parents.

After his father was released from prison, Dickens was sent to school at an academy in London, where he was a good student. When he was fifteen, he worked as a solicitor's clerk in law offices and two years later became a shorthand reporter of parliamentary proceedings and a freelance reporter in the courts. In 1829, he fell in love with Maria Beadnell, the daughter of a banker, but broke with her in 1833. At age twenty-one, he began publishing his *Sketches by Boz* and joined the *Morning Chronicle* as a reporter. His first collection of *Sketches by Boz* appeared in 1836, the same year he began a series of sketches titled *Pickwick Papers* (1836-1837). Also in 1836, he married Catherine Hogarth, the daughter of a journalist. As *Pickwick Papers* became a strikingly popular success in serial publication, the Dickens phenomenon began, putting the author well on his way to becoming the most powerful and widely read author in nineteenth century England.

Life's Work

With Dickens's sudden fame came offers of more literary work. He began editing a new monthly magazine for which he contracted to write another serial story, which he called *Oliver Twist* (1837-1839) and which began to appear while *Pickwick Papers* was still running. Thus, Dickens started the breakneck speed of writing which was to characterize the energy of his work throughout his life. While *Oliver Twist* was still running in serial form, Dickens also began publishing *Nicholas Nickleby*, another great success, first in serial form (1838) and then as a book (1839). Immediately thereafter, he began the serialization of *The Old Curiosity Shop* (1840-1841) in a weekly publication, followed soon after by *Barnaby Rudge: A Tale of the Riots of '80* (1841).

Dickens paused from his writing between 1836 and 1841 to travel in the United States, the result of which was *American Notes* (1842) and, more important, the serialization of *Martin Chuzzlewit* (1843-1844), which outraged many American readers with its caricature of life in the United States. During the Christmas season of 1843, Dickens achieved one of his most memorable successes with *A Christmas Carol*, which gave the world the character of Ebenezer Scrooge. The poor circulation of *Martin Chuzzlewit* was cause enough for Dickens to cease his writing once again for an extended visit to the Continent. Yet the poor reception of *A Christmas Carol* was not enough to prevent Dickens from publishing two more Christmas stories—*The Chimes* (1845) and *A Cricket on the Hearth* (1845).

Returning from Italy in 1845, Dickens began editing a new daily newspaper, *The Daily News*, but resigned from that job after only three weeks. He began instead the serialization of *Dombey and Son* (1846-1848), only to begin the serialization of *David Copperfield* (1849-1850) the following year. During this time, Dickens began working with amateur theatricals as an actor and a director, mostly to benefit literature and the arts. He then began editing the periodical *Household Words* and writing what many call his most ambitious work, *Bleak House*, in 1852, which ran for a year and a half.

In 1854 *Hard Times* was published serially in order to boost the failing circulation of *Household Words*, and soon thereafter, Dickens began serialization of *Little Dorrit* (1855-1857). At this time, Dickens purchased a home at Gad's Hill, on the road between London and Dover, but his home life was not to be that of country tranquility. In 1858 he separated from his wife amid much bad publicity.

Also in 1858, Dickens began another major aspect of his professional life—a series of public readings from his own work. Although he published *A Tale of Two Cities* in 1859, the public readings in London did not abate. In 1860, he began writing *Great Expectations* (1860-1861) to increase the circulation of a new weekly, *All the Year Round*. London readings continued through 1863, when he went to Paris for another series of readings there. Although he was experiencing poor health, Dickens wrote *Our Mutual Friend* (1864-1866) and performed public readings in London until 1868, when he made his last trip to the United States for a tour of readings which brought him much money but also taxed his already failing health.

When Dickens returned to England after several months in the United States, he took up readings again in London, Scotland, and Ireland, in addition to beginning his last work (which he did not live to finish), *The Mystery of Edwin Drood* (1870). In 1870, on June 8, after working all day, Dickens suffered a stroke while at his Gad's Hill home and died the next day. He was buried in Westminster Abbey.

From *Great Lives from History: The 19th Century.* Pasadena, CA: Salem Press, 1999. Copyright © 2007 by Salem Press, Inc.

Bibliography

Ackroyd, Peter. *Dickens*. London: Sinclair-Stevenson, 1990. The author, a major English novelist, writes a biography of Dickens that warrants the characterization of being Dickensian both in its length and in the quality of its portrayal of the nineteenth century writer and his times. In re-creating that past, Ackroyd has produced a brilliant work of historical imagination.

Butterworth, R. D. "*A Christmas Carol* and the Masque." *Studies in Short Fiction* 30, no. 1 (Winter, 1993): 63-69. Discusses how Dickens's famous Christmas story embodies many of the characteristics of the masque tradition. Considers some of the implications of this tradition for the story, such as the foreshortening of character development.

Carey, John. *The Violent Effigy: A Study of Dickens' Imagination.* London: Faber and Faber, 1979. The number of works about Dickens and the various aspects of his career is enormous. Carey, in one insightful Dickens study, focuses on Dickens's fascination with various human oddities as a spur to his artistic inspiration.

Connor, Steven, ed. *Charles Dickens.* London: Longman, 1996. Part of the Longman Critical Readers series, this is a good reference for interpretation and criticism of Dickens.

Coolidge, Archibald C., Jr. *Charles Dickens as Serial Novelist.* Ames: Iowa State University Press, 1967. A helpful study of a very important aspect of Dickens's work: The fact that his writing first appeared in serialization had a great influence on the nature of his narrative.

Davis, Paul B. *Charles Dickens A to Z: The Essential Reference to His Life and Work.* New York: Facts on File, 1998. An excellent handbook for the student of Dickens.

Epstein, Norrie. *The Friendly Dickens: Being a Good-Natured Guide to the Art and Adventures of the Man Who Invented Scrooge.* New York: Viking, 1998. An interesting study of Dickens. Includes bibliographical references, an index, and a filmography.

Erickson, Lee. "The Primitive Keynesianism of Dickens's *A Christmas Carol.*" *Studies in the Literary Imagination* 30, no. 1 (Spring, 1997): 51-66. A Keynesian reading of Dickens's story that shows how Scrooge is an economic hoarder because of his fear of the financial future and his need for complete financial liquidity. Claims that Dickens correctly diagnoses the economic depression of Christmas 1843.

Flint, Kate. *Dickens.* Brighton, England: Harvester Press, 1986. Looks at paradoxes within his novels and between his novels and his culture. Includes a select bibliography and an index.

Ford, George H., and Lauriat Lane, Jr., eds. *The Dickens Critics.* Ithaca, NY: Cornell University Press, 1961. This collection consists of more than thirty essays concerned with various aspects of Dickens's literary life. Represented are notables such as Edgar Allan Poe, Henry James, Anthony Trollope, George Bernard Shaw, T. S. Eliot, Aldous Huxley, George Orwell, Graham Greene, and Edgar Johnson.

Hawes, Donald. *Who's Who in Dickens.* New York: Routledge, 1998. The Who's Who series provides another excellent guide to the characters that populate Dickens's fiction.

Hobsbaum, Philip. *A Reader's Guide to Charles Dickens.* Syracuse, NY: Syracuse University Press, 1998. Part of the Reader's Guide series, this is a good manual for beginning students.

Jacobson, Wendy S., ed. *Dickens and the Children of Empire*. New York: Palgrave, 2000. A collection of fourteen essays focusing on child images and colonial paternalism in the work of Dickens.

Johnson, Edgar. *Charles Dickens*. 2 vols. New York: Simon & Schuster, 1952. Subtitled "His Tragedy and Triumph," this work was perhaps the first major scholarly biography of Dickens. The author integrates into his study an excellent discussion and analysis of Dickens's writings. It remains a classic.

Jordan, John O., ed. *The Cambridge Companion to Charles Dickens*. New York: Cambridge University Press, 2001. From the Cambridge Companions to Literature series. Includes bibliographical references and an index.

Kaplan, Fred. *Dickens: A Biography*. New York: William Morrow, 1988. Published a generation later than Edgar Johnson's study of Dickens, Kaplan's biography is more forthright about Dickens's family life and personal qualities, especially his relationship with the actress Ellen Ternan. An interesting and well-written work.

Leavis, F. R., and Q. D. Leavis. *Dickens the Novelist*. London: Chatto & Windus, 1970. Focuses on the novels from *Dombey and Son* through *Great Expectations*; excellent criticism by two highly respected British critics.

Newlin, George, ed. and comp. *Every Thing in Dickens: Ideas and Subjects Discussed by Charles Dickens in His Complete Works—A Topicon*. Westport, CT: Greenwood Press, 1996. A thorough guide to Dickens's oeuvre. Includes bibliographical references, an index, and quotations.

Newsom, Robert. *Charles Dickens Revisited*. New York: Twayne, 2000. From Twayne's English Authors series. Includes bibliographical references and an index.

Newton, Ruth, and Naomi Lebowitz. *The Impossible Romance: Dickens, Manzoni, Zola, and James*. Columbia: U Missouri P, 1990. Discusses the impact of religious sensibility on literary form and ideology in Dickens's fiction.

Reed, John Robert. *Dickens and Thackeray*. Athens: Ohio University Press, 1995. Discusses how beliefs about punishment and forgiveness affect how Dickens and William Makepeace Thackeray told their stories. Discusses Dickens's major fiction in terms of moral and narrative issues.

Smiley, Jane. *Charles Dickens*. New York: Viking, 2002. A Dickens biography by a noted American novelist. Includes bibliographical references.

Smith, Grahame. *Charles Dickens: A Literary Life*. New York: St. Martin's Press, 1996. A strong biography of Dickens.

Tytler, Graeme. "Dickens's 'The Signalman.'" *The Explicator* 53, no. 1 (Fall, 1994): 26-29. Argues that the story is about a man suffering from a type of insanity known in the nineteenth century as lypemania or monomania; discusses the symptoms of the signalman.

Wilson, Angus. *The World of Charles Dickens*. New York: Viking Press, 1970. The author, an Englishman, has been a professor of literature, published a major work on Rudyard Kipling, and written several novels. This relatively brief study is enriched by many period illustrations ranging from George Cruikshank to Gustave Doré.

the PARIS
REVIEW

The *Paris Review* Perspective_____
Elizabeth Gumport for *The Paris Review*

When the first chapters of *Great Expectations* appeared in December of 1860, Charles Dickens was already an internationally celebrated author. Readers in England and abroad eagerly awaited each new installment of his novels, which originally appeared in serial form. When *The Old Curiosity Shop* was first published, fans in New York gathered at the docks to await the arrival of its final pages, calling to the ships, "Is Little Nell dead?" She was, but Dickens's career was never more alive.

Great Expectations followed a number of successful novels—*David Copperfield, Bleak House*, and *A Tale of Two Cities* among them—and thus anticipation ran high. "The very title of this book indicates the confidence of a conscious genius," quipped *The Atlantic Monthly* in an early review. "The most famous novelist of the day," it went on, "watched by jealous rivals and critics, could hardly have selected it, had he not inwardly felt the capacity to meet all the expectations he raised." And meet them he did: "Altogether we take great joy in recording our conviction that *Great Expectations* is a masterpiece."

Who was the master behind this novel? In 1822, when he was ten years old, Dickens and his family moved to London. Two years later, after his father was sent to debtors' prison, Dickens left school to work at Warren's Blacking Factory, pasting labels on jars of shoe polish. This early labor, Edmund Wilson argued, profoundly influenced Dickens, serving as the origin of a deep sense of humanity that allowed him to create "superhuman art." In the warehouse on the Thames, Dickens the artist was made, and the lessons he learned at Warren's are evident in *Great Expectations*: to be a child is to be powerless; parents are at once absent and omnipresent, their abdication of responsibility a kind of despotic power; and home is not a haven—at best it is unreliable shelter, and at worst it is hell.

Pip, raised by a sister who beats him and surrounded by adults who cannot stand him, lives an orphan's precarious existence. During Christmas dinner at the Forge (the name suggests fire and brimstone, a burning hole at the center of the home), the adults compare Pip to the pork they are consuming. "If you want a subject, look at Pork!" Pumblechook declares. "'Swine,' pursued Mr. Wopsle, in his deepest voice, and pointing his fork at my blushes, as if he were mentioning my Christian name; 'Swine were the companions of the prodigal. The gluttony of Swine is put before us, as an example to the young. . . . What is detestable in a pig is more detestable in a boy.'" Pumblechook proceeds to elaborate the manner in which Pip, had he been born a pig, would have been butchered. The men and women charged with Pip's protection then gorge themselves on pork as a sort of Pip surrogate. Grown-ups! They either desert you or devour you.

So the story begins: escape the cannibals. Pip embarks on a search for a home to replace the Forge, but it doggedly eludes him throughout the story. The first of these possible substitutes—Satis House, home to the terminally unsatisfied Miss Havisham—is a monument to youth and fertility gone to waste. But Miss Havisham also introduces Pip to Estella; winning her love is the other great, unconsummated quest in the novel. She not only drives Pip's journey, she becomes his lodestone, the source of all meaning in the scattershot events of his life. When, late in the book, Estella tells Pip about her impending marriage to Drummle, he cries, "You are part of my existence, part of myself. You have been in every line I have ever read, since I first came here, the rough common boy whose poor heart you wounded even then." Pip's declaration—"you have been in every line I have ever read"—knits together romantic desire and the desire that impels us to read.

To be a reader, Dickens suggests, is to be like a lover, transfixed and tugged ceaselessly forward in pursuit of fulfillment. In this regard, the nineteenth century might have something on the twenty-first: where the serial reader's pleasure in the novel was intensified, pulled taut by the long gaps between installments, we have only instant gratification, the bound book held fast in our hands. "We have read it," the reviewer for *The Atlantic* wrote of *Great Expectations*, "as we have read all Mr. Dickens's previous works, as it appeared in installments, and can testify to the felicity with which expectation was excited and prolonged." Prolonged excitement: the state of suitors, and the state of readers. All good things come to those who wait, and expectations are always great: we stand at the dock, looking for the ship that bears our beloved—or the next chapter of a novel—toward our waiting arms.

Bibliography

Dickens, Charles. *Great Expectations*. New York: Penguin Books, 1996.
"*Great Expectations*, by Charles Dickens." *The Atlantic Monthly*. September 1861.
Smiley, Jane. *Charles Dickens*. New York: Viking, 2002.
Wilson, Edmund. *The Wound and the Bow*. Athens: Ohio University Press, 1997.

CRITICAL CONTEXTS

Great Expectations in Context_____

Gurdip Panesar

Charles Dickens's novel *Great Expectations*, which he completed in 1861, has enjoyed considerable critical acclaim since its first publication. George Newlin puts it thus: "*Great Expectations* is special. Commentators have almost universally rated it very highly, if not the highest, among the works of Charles Dickens, who is generally considered the greatest of English novelists" (1). Newlin also goes on to remark that while lacking in the 'exuberance or manic humour' of earlier novels and his last completed work *Our Mutual Friend*, it is fashioned, as are all Dickens's works, from a "rich, subtle, and diversified palette" (1).

The lack of "exuberance" and obvious comedy is one feature which strongly marks out *Great Expectations* in the Dickens canon. Of course, in many other ways it is a typical Dickens work, exhibiting familiar Dickensian traits, with a strong plot, melodrama, and touches of sentimentalism and also of the grotesque. It also employs many of his favorite themes. One of these is child cruelty; the main character, Pip, bereft of both parents at an early age, suffers daily oppression while being brought up by his much older sister. Another favorite Dickens theme in this novel is crime and the law, a particular focus here being on transportation, as shown through the fate of convicts like Magwitch and Compeyson. However, Dickens does not engage with social and political issues and institutions of his day on quite the same level as in some other novels, where his journalistic bent is in far greater evidence. Nor are there any characters that loom quite as large in the imagination as those in other Dickens works. There is no comic creation to rank alongside a Micawber or a villain as memorable as a Fagin or a Quilp—although there is the unforgettable, twisted, demented figure of Miss Havisham, the inscrutable and seemingly all-knowing lawyer Jaggers, and the odious Pumblechook. However, the character that remains at the fore throughout is Pip, who is also the narrator; his consciousness infuses the whole novel, and his is a troubled, questing, self-doubting voice, which gives *Great Expectations* a distinctive flavor among Dickens's novels. It is, perhaps, something that initially is not too apparent; it would certainly be absurd to claim that Dickens is trying for any radically experimental technique. Indeed, at first glance the narrative method in this novel would not appear to be even as sophisticated as that of another of Dickens's own works, *Bleak House*, with its much-debated "double" structure. Yet Pip, both as character and as narrator, is problematic; it is because of this, most of all, that post-nineteenth-century readers are left with the impression that *Great Expectations* is, in fact, something of a modern novel behind an old-fashioned "Victorian" façade. For many observers, this is what renders it especially significant.

On the simplest level, *Great Expectations* is a bildungsroman, a narrative that depicts the growth of its protagonist, charting his or her intellectual, emotional, and spiritual development and coming to self-knowledge and knowledge about the world. Indeed, several of the most famous and acclaimed Victorian novels—Charlotte Brontë's *Jane Eyre*, George Eliot's *The Mill on the Floss* and Dickens's own *David Copperfield*—are of this type. And, as in *David Copperfield*, there are recognizable elements included from Dickens's own life. Pip's move from the marsh country of Kent to London during his formative years mirrors the relocation of the Dickens family, when Charles was about ten. It was a move that turned nightmarish as his father lost all his money and was imprisoned for being unable to pay his debts, forcing his young son to work for a period in a blacking factory, which, as critics have always noted, was one of the worst, and also one of the most defining, periods in his life.[1] The horror of his own experience of child labor and the financial disgrace that befell his family never quite left him; the intense revulsion from manual labor is also reflected in Pip's reaction to the prospect of a lifetime working in the forge like his sister's husband, Joe Gargery: "There have been occasions in my later life . . . when I have felt for a time as if a thick curtain had fallen on all its interest and romance, to shut me out from anything save dull endurance any more. Never has that curtain dropped so heavy and blank, as when my way in life lay stretched out straight before me through the newly-entered road of apprenticeship of Joe" (Dickens 107).

In discussing the autobiographical elements of the work, attention should also be drawn to some of the most important characters: Joe, Pip's sister, and Estella. Joe may be modeled on Dickens's father, a kindly and rather ineffectual man, while Pip's sister recalls the emotional neglect of his own mother. Estella, too, may be based on Maria Beadnell, with whom Dickens fell in love as a young man but who did not return his feelings. Thus in the novel we get a glimpse into the emotions of Dickens's early years, as recorded in Pip's responses to certain crucial figures in his life.

However, although Dickens works these autobiographical elements into the novel, its significance goes deeper than this. Dickens uses his own experiences as a starting point to explore an important aspect of Victorian society: the phenomenon of social mobility. Pip's removal to London is a case not just of physical but also of social dislocation. Dickens experienced this in his own life when he rose from humble beginnings to become the most lionized writer of his day. The social rise of Pip is rather different in nature. Born into the lower-middle class, lacking any kind of social prestige, he is first propelled into the higher echelons of society by the machinations of his sister and Uncle Pumblechook, who arrange for him to go to the wealthy Miss Havisham's as they entertain hopes of his social advancement, less from a desire for his happiness than for mercenary motives of their own. Then, having met Miss Havisham's ward, the beautiful, remote Estella—whom he naturally, if erroneously, assumes to be high-born—he is fired with even greater aspirations. In order to become worthy of her, he feels, he must become a gentleman, and through the unexpected intervention of his secret benefactor he appears to gain his chance. His yearning for social status reflects an important social reality of the Victorian age. The growth of a mercantile merchant class, earning their fortune through trade and commerce rather than inheriting it like the upper classes, had been in evidence since at least Renaissance times and reflected in the work of such writers as Daniel Defoe, but it was a process that was undoubtedly accelerated in the wake of the great changes wrought by the Industrial Revolution, the formation of new industrial and economic centers and new opportunities for capitalist enterprise. Sally Mitchell has remarked that "the concept of a distinctly middle way of life developed early in the Victorian period" (21). Throughout the nineteenth century the power of the middle class continued to grow at the expense of the old landed gentry, traditionally the bastions of power and influence. For many, the dream of making one's own fortune, and gaining social prestige as a result, had become a realistic goal. Of course in Pip's case it is still a matter of inheriting wealth rather than earning it, but his ideal of setting up as a profitable, well-to-do, cultivated urban businessman is the same. Thus *Great Expectations* is not just based on the fairy-tale paradigm of rags to riches (or rather on an ironic reversal of it, as it all goes awry for Pip); it also functions as a document of a vital, ongoing process in Victorian society.

The novel takes a distinctly dim view of Pip's aspirations to wealth, however, as in his case he will not achieve it through the much-vaunted middle-class principle of earnest hard work. In his edition of *Great Expectations*, David Trotter notes Pip's unspoken fear that "there is no such thing as clean money" (Dickens xiv). Wealth throughout the novel is associated with guilt, an idea reinforced by the pervasive figure of the convict Magwitch, Pip's secret benefactor. Furthermore, the novel draws attention not only to the dubious morality of money-making but also to the essentially precarious nature of capitalist enterprise; the brewery at Miss Havisham's has long since fallen into disuse, leaving behind only "a wilderness of casks" (Dickens 63); while in London, Herbert Pocket is forever looking about him in the vague hope that some business venture will eventually take off, leading his friend Pip to reflect "what a difficult vision to realize this. . . . Capital sometimes was" (Dickens 252).

London itself, the heart and hub of financial dealings and so often prominent in Dickens's work, is presented in unflattering terms, with the sordid Barnard's Inn and Jaggers's seedy office (presided over by the two grim shrunken casts). There is a general atmosphere of unwholesomeness, as underlined by the newly arrived Pip's visit to the Smithfield Meat Market: "that shameful place . . . all asmear with filth and fat and blood and foam" (Dickens 164). Even worse is his first glimpse of Newgate Prison. Portrayals of prisons are famous, or infamous, in Dickens, for example in *Oliver Twist* and *Little Dorrit*; here, the "dreadful portal" known as the Debtors' Door gives Pip "a sickening idea of London" as he witnesses those hapless prisoners soon "to be killed in a row" (Dickens 165). The Debtors' Door may be taken as an economic metaphor: the weak, or the less fortunate, in the game of wealth accumulation go to the wall. Of course it was a place that had particular unhappy resonance for the author, in light of his father's experiences, and it nearly claims Pip himself, as in the course of the story he incurs all manner of debt while his great expectations fail to materialize.

Pip, therefore, is left wholly chastened by his London experiences and ends up homeless there, both literally and figuratively (Dickens 451); he is saved only by the intervention of the truly good people in his life, Herbert and his fiancée Clara, Joe and Biddy. As in so many Victorian novels, a moral is evident; Pip has to learn to value those who truly care about him and to discard his vain social ambitions. He—and Estella—have to learn harsh lessons about the essential falsity of social distinctions. Those in the higher echelons of society are generally seen in an unfavorable light, for instance the minor nobleman Bentley Drummle, who eventually marries Estella and treats her brutally, while those further down the social scale—most notably Joe—are seen as truly noble in nature, if not in name. And Pip is punished for his ungratefulness to Joe, his snobbery and extravagance. The worthlessness of his great expectations are finally and starkly revealed; it is said that they have "dissolved like the marsh mists before the sun" (Dickens 470). It is a wholesome and purifying image, and Pip goes on to reveal, with conscious Biblical echoes, that subsequently he "sold all he had" (Dickens 480) to go abroad and take up his post as inferior but hard-working clerk in Herbert's business. He comes to recognize the value of duty, thrift, and honest industry. Moreover, he also gains real satisfaction from the one good deed that, in retrospect, he sees himself as having achieved in life: secretly helping his friend Herbert to set up in business (although discouraged from so doing, from a practical point of view, by Wemmick). The good characters are rewarded, like Biddy and Joe, who find happiness with each other; the evil Orlick and Compeyson are justly served, while Miss Havisham and Magwitch are redeemed through forgiveness.

It is certainly tempting, in this light, to read *Great Expectations* as a kind of homily, as indeed it is. But if there were little more to it than this, it would be unlikely that it could continue to have much impact in modern times as it has done. It is clear, on any close reading of the text, that Pip's journey of self-discovery and eventual moral enlightenment is not altogether a straightforward business. Although he returns to his childhood home with a sense of newfound appreciation, he does not—cannot—remain there. There is no simple dichotomy here (as there is, for example, in *Oliver Twist*) between London and outlying rural areas. London becomes a place of torment for Pip, but the marsh country of his birth is hardly an idyllic one. The view of this country that first imprints itself on the consciousness of the young Pip is unrelievedly grim:

> My first most vivid and broad impression of the identity of things, seems to me to have been gained on a memorable raw afternoon towards evening. At such a time I found out for certain, that this bleak place overgrown with nettles was the churchyard; and that Philip Pirrip, late of this parish, and also Georgiana, wife of the above, were dead and buried; and that Alexander, Bartholomew, Abraham, Tobias, and Roger, infant children of the deceased, were also dead and buried; and that the dark flat wilderness beyond the churchyard, intersected with dykes and mounds and gates, with scattered cattle feeding on it, was the marshes; and that the low leaden line be-

yond, was the river; and that the distant savage lair from which the wind was rushing, was the sea; and that the small bundle of shivers growing afraid of it all and beginning to cry, was Pip. (Dickens 3)

This scene, powerfully rendered in David Lean's acclaimed 1948 film adaptation, is fittingly crowned with the image of the tombstones of Pip's parents and five brothers, "who gave up trying to earn a living exceedingly early in that universal struggle" (Dickens 3). This striking use of the phrase, "universal struggle" has strong Darwinian overtones.[2] In keeping with this—and unlike so much of Dickens's other work—there is in the rest of the novel little sense of any overarching divine order. The phrase sets the tone for themes of hardship and suffering, and this opening scene is also notable for the advent of the hunted fugitive Magwitch. Criminality and squalor do not make their first appearance in the city but in this backwater, and there is also the dark, brooding image of the prison ships, the "hulks," moored on the river, a reminder of the grim realities of hard labor and transportation for convicts in this period. Other figures in this landscape, notably Joe and Biddy, may be idealized, but life in Pip's native marsh country is not. Rather, it appears bleak and primitive. Joe's trade as a blacksmith may enable him to earn an honest living, but it is also very hard, physically demanding work. There are also frank references to Biddy's initial state of wretched poverty and work as a "drudge," teaching in "a miserable little noisy evening school" (Dickens 126). Education in this place is of a haphazard and extremely rudimentary nature. Similarly, churchgoing appears to be in the nature of a penitential trial for the likes of Pip and Joe (Dickens 23) and seemingly offers little comfort of any kind.

In view of all this, it is not surprising that on the eve of his departure to London Pip entertains notions of improving his native community when he should come into his fortunes. Although such philanthropic concern on Pip's part is presented as an instance of his misguided sense of superiority and "condescension" (Dickens 147) as he dreams of becoming a gentleman, the novel does little elsewhere to dispel generally negative impressions of this marsh country. Indeed the marshes are explicitly used as a metaphor by Pip for the bleakness of his prospects when contemplating a lifetime of working in the forge: "I used to stand about the churchyard on Sunday evenings when night was falling, comparing my own perspective with the windy marsh view, and making out some likeness between them by thinking how flat and low both were" (Dickens 107). Later, when trapped by the villain Orlick and in fear of his life, he envisages his own physical dissolution among the marsh mists (Dickens 427). In this chilling image the marsh country becomes more or less synonymous with the extinguishing of life itself. If London is seen to be a noisome, stressful environment, the marsh country appears backward and almost stultifying. In this way the novel mirrors the actual social conditions of the day, the protracted agricultural depression which sped the movement of much of the population to the big towns. Like Thomas Hardy's novels decades later, *Great Expectations* serves as an edifying reminder to the modern-day reader that, whatever the problems associated with rapidly increasing urbanization in the wake of the Industrial Revolution, life away from the big towns also had its fair share of hardships throughout the nineteenth century.

The novel, however, provides a degree not only of social realism but also of psychological realism in its portrayal of Pip's upbringing. It gives us Pip's thoughts and feelings as he comes to maturity, generally filtered through the critical lens of his older and wiser self but retaining all the vividness of deep emotion. This continual, indeed relentless, insight into Pip's mind lends an intense psychological dimension to the novel, more so than in any other of Dickens's works. Other Victorian writers, notably George Eliot, were also capable of adopting a psychological approach in their novels, and Dickens does not abandon conventional linear narrative methods and language use for any startling experimental style, such as the "stream-of-consciousness" technique of much self-avowed modernist fiction. Generally speaking, however, the psychological preoccupations of *Great Expectations* do make it somewhat more akin to twentieth-century novels than many other literary works of his own day. This close psychological scrutiny encompasses all aspects of Pip's life—notably his love for Estella. Although completely spellbound by her, he is never under any illusions as to her lack of feeling and the nature of his own feelings for her. He remarks that "according to [his] experience, the conventional notion of a lover cannot always ring true," and goes on: "The unqualified truth is, that when I loved Estella with the love of a man, I loved her simply because I found her irresistible. Once for all: I knew to my sorrow . . . that I loved her against reason, against promise. . . . I loved her none the less because I knew it, and it had no more influence in restraining me, than if I had devoutly believed her to be human perfection" (Dickens 232).

The novel thus acknowledges the reality of sexual desire, divested of romantic idealizing; and Estella is not like the usual run of sentimentalized, sanctified heroines found in Dickens and in the work of other Victorian writers. Biddy is more obviously a candidate for such a role, but in Pip's eyes she can only ever be second best to Estella. It is Estella who helps determine the course of his life by first awakening social ambitions in him, and he goes on hopelessly desiring her even though she continually and clearly repulses him. His love can, indeed, be counted obsessive. Dickens makes of their relationship an effective platform from which to explore the psychological realities of sexual love, in a way that perhaps finds greater approval with modern audiences than his rather more simplistic treatment of the subject in other works.

The psychological strain in *Great Expectations* runs deeper than the delineation of sexual desire, however. One feature of the novel that has always intrigued critics is Pip's pervasive sense of guilt. There may be several reasons for this, but the kernel of the matter appears to lie in the nature of his upbringing at the hands of his much older sister and similar harsh treatment by other odious characters, such as Uncle Pumblechook. The abused child is a familiar figure in Dickens's fiction.

Jaggers, when outlining the miserable conditions of Estella's illegitimate birth among the working class, expatiates solemnly upon the subject, remarking that all he has ever seen of children, in his particular line of work, is "their being generated in great numbers for certain destruction . . . tried at a criminal bar. . . . [i]mprisoned, whipped, transported, neglected, cast out, qualified in all ways for the hangman, and growing up to be hanged" (Dickens 413). Essentially, however, Dickens's handling of the theme in *Great Expectations* is rather different from his more sensationalist treatment in other novels (the orphan Oliver Twist or the maltreated little crossing-sweep Jo in *Bleak House* being classic examples). Pip does not have to endure slum conditions or the workhouse, but he suffers from being in a dysfunctional family, although Joe does in some measure alleviate Pip's misery by providing as much emotional support as he can. Pip himself is acutely aware of the deleterious effects of his sister's harsh child-rearing methods on his character and outlook:

> Within myself, I had sustained, from my babyhood, a perpetual conflict with injustice. I had known, from the time when I could speak, that my sister, in her capricious and violent coercion, was unjust to me. . . . Through all my punishments, disgraces, fasts and vigils, and other penitential performances, I had nursed this assurance; and to my communing so much with it, in a solitary and unprotected way, I in great part refer the fact that I was morally timid and very sensitive. (Dickens 63)

Doris Alexander observes that "Dickens knew that early circumstances shape character and that character, in turn, shapes reactions to later circumstances" (3). Dickens, indeed, goes further than any other Victorian writer in his focus on childhood experiences, particularly negative experiences. This is attractive to modern scientific thought, stemming from early twentieth-century psychology and Freud's theories about the fundamental importance of an individual's early years and the damage caused by the repression of longstanding desires and fears. Pip, in short, has no outlet; and in a Freudian reading of the novel his constant state of guilt arises from his secret fantasies of revenge on those who wrong him, which come unexpectedly true in the case of his sister, at least, who is struck down with a weapon—the convict's leg iron—which he himself helped to provide.

However far one may or may not wish to go in any "psychological" reading of the work, there is no doubt that Pip's early abusive treatment by adults, by members of his own family, leaves him with a severe lack of confidence from the first. He is unsure of himself, of his place in society, of just who he is and what he should become. Indeed, with the character of Pip, more so than with any other major Dickens character, we get something of the sense of a fluidity of self. Of course, a bildungsroman aims to trace the change and development of its protagonist, but *Great Expectations* seems to go even further than this. Christopher D. Morris, in a deconstructionist analysis of the work, observes that "some very probing questions have been asked about the depiction of [Pip's] moral character, even about his self" and questions whether he actually has "an autonomous, continuous, achieved, created self" (Bloom 197). With this apparent lack of a readily identifiable core or center to the hero's character, *Great Expectations* appears to eschew some of the ready-made conventions of the Victorian novel, with its categories of broadly good and bad characters. Of course it can be said that Pip is, essentially, good of heart, but this appears to be a rather vague quality in him rather than a truly positive and proactive one—the author himself notes that his setting up Herbert in business is really the only good act he performs (Dickens 512). Rather than projecting any strongly defined, positive traits of his own, Pip appears worked on by his circumstances and the influence of others, whether the fear of a Magwitch or the allure of an Estella, to such an extent that he appears in a constant state of flux. There is a strong sense that he is continually being molded by his circumstances, and his actions seem largely to stem from this. Dickens draws on the Frankenstein story to represent this idea of "molding" (or, one might say, "forging," in keeping with the blacksmithing theme of the work). Pip, on first learning that Magwitch is his benefactor, laments that "[t]he imaginary student pursued by the creature he had made, was not more wretched than I, pursued by the creature who had made me" (Dickens 339).[3] Estella's character, too, is shaped, to her detriment, by Miss Havisham from the beginning of her life. All of this is in line with the behavioral sciences of modern times and theories about the importance of the influence of one's environment throughout life and how one's character and very sense of being are constructed by others' ideas and views and opinions. In a similar vein, we might note how Pip is also greatly influenced by the idea of his "great expectations," which keep him continually fretting, in a state of "chronic uneasiness" (Dickens 272). The title of the work is wholly ironic, in a way more common perhaps to modern writing than to classic Victorian fiction.

This "modern" feeling is underscored by the ending of the novel. Dickens famously provided two endings to this work, both of which continue to be much debated. In the original ending, which appeared in proof while the novel was still being serialized, Pip makes his peace with Estella but retains no hope of marrying her, as she has married again (following the death of her first husband, Bentley Drummle), but the revised ending, which is the one which appears in all publications of the book, holds out this possibility. Dickens made the change at the insistence of fellow writers, notably Edward Bulwer-Lytton, in order to placate readers. However, the second ending remains ambiguous: although Pip and Estella have come together, seemingly without any remaining encumbrances, their union is still not assured. The manner of the novel's conclusion has caused dissatisfaction to many observers, for instance George Bernard Shaw who, as Jerome Meckier remarks, went to the length of devising a third ending because he felt that Dickens had "made a mess" of the first two, the first one being psychologically appropriate and the second being more aesthetically pleasing (Bloom 167).

The note of inconclusiveness on which the novel ends, its lack of a clear resolution, is certainly unusual among Victorian novels and more common to modern fiction. However, it can be taken as representative of Dickens's strategy as a whole in this work. He does not make any radical break with the novelistic traditions of his day; in many respects *Great Expectations* is a typical Victorian narrative, with a strong plot (as its original serial format demanded), melodrama, one-dimensional villains, and amazing coincidences (as when Estella, the great love of Pip's life, turns out to be the daughter of his mysterious benefactor Magwitch). Like other Dickens novels, it provides a broad view of the Victorian social landscape, of life both within and without the big towns, giving us a picture of everything from the urban legal profession to the rustic and centuries-old trade of blacksmithing. Also, like other Dickens novels, it depicts struggles within, and between, different social classes, and readers continue to value its insights into Victorian society. However, in the twenty-first century it is probably enjoyed less as a period piece than some other of Dickens's novels, and more for a certain sensibility that appeals to the modern age. It is more private, more individualistic, more concerned with the inner life than with outward events and issues than his other works, and it displays a greater all-around sense of uncertainty. Even more noteworthy is the way in which it seems to incorporate a slew of modern ideas, from scientific theories such as Darwinism and psychology (which developed greatly as a science from the beginning of the twentieth century onward) to new ways of shaping the novel—most notably in the ambiguity of the ending. Of course, all this is not to suggest that Dickens was actively and self-consciously aiming to write a novel in any kind of "modern" fashion. One cannot deny, however, that there is in *Great Expectations* a wealth of material that critics and readers in the post-Victorian age have found fruitful to unpack according to post-nineteenth-century designs. This has led to the persuasion that the novel's strongest significance is its congeniality with the modern day and age, and that— arguably more so than almost any other single Victorian novel–*Great Expectations* has a special relevance for our own times.

Notes

1. See, for example, Kaplan 41-43.

2. See Morgantaler for a Darwinian reading of the novel. Darwin's *The Origin of Species* was first published in 1859, two years before the completion of *Great Expectations*.

3. This *Frankenstein* imagery is also used earlier, in a humorous way, in relation to the manservant Pip acquires when he first sets himself up as a gentleman in London: "after I had made the monster (out of the refuse of my washerwoman's family) and had clothed him . . . I had to find him a little to do and a great deal to eat; and with both of those horrible requirements he haunted my existence" (Dickens 218).

Works Consulted

Ackroyd, Peter. *Dickens*. London: Minerva, 1991.

Alexander, Doris. *Creating Characters with Charles Dickens*. University Park: Penn State University Press, 1991.

Bloom, Harold, ed. *Charles Dickens's Great Expectations*. Philadelphia: Chelsea House, 2000.

Dickens, Charles. *Great Expectations*. Ed. David Trotter and Charlotte Mitchell. Harmondsworth, Middlesex, England: Penguin, 1996.

Kaplan, Fred. *Dickens: A Biography*. Baltimore: Johns Hopkins University Press, 1998.

Mitchell, Sally. *Daily Life in Victorian England*. Westport, CT: Greenwood Press, 1996.

Morgantaler, Goldie. "Meditating on the Low: A Darwinian Reading of *Great Expectations*." *Studies in English Literature 1500-1900* 38 (1998): 701-721.

Newlin, George. *Understanding Great Expectations: A Student Casebook to Issues, Sources, and Historical Documents*. Westport, CT: Greenwood Press, 2000.

Paroissien, David. *A Companion to Charles Dickens*. Oxford: Blackwell, 2008.

Thompson, F. M. L. *The Rise of Respectable Society: A Social History of Victorian Britain, 1830-1900*. Cambridge: Harvard University Press, 1988.

Walsh, Susan. "Bodies of Capital: *Great Expectations* and the Climacteric Economy." *Victorian Studies* 37 (1993): 73-99.

The Critical Reception of *Great Expectations*_____

Shanyn Fiske

In mid-September 1860, Charles Dickens wrote to his longtime friend and future biographer, John Forster, that he had conceived of "a very fine, new, and grotesque idea" for a story. "It so opens out before *me* that I can see the whole of a serial revolving on it, in a most singular and comic manner," he continued (*Letters* 310). The inspiration came at a critical moment, for sales of Dickens's weekly journal *All the Year Round* had begun to plummet as readers lost interest in its current serial—Charles Lever's *A Day's Ride*. "[T]here is no vitality in it," Dickens commented of Lever's effort, "and no chance whatever of stopping the fall; which on the contrary would be certain to increase" (*Letters* 320). Hastening to prevent a further drop in sales, Dickens wrought his "grotesque, tragi-comic conception" (*Letters* 325) into his third to last novel, *Great Expectations*. Tapping into his own childhood and youth for inspiration—as he had done with *David Copperfield* some ten years earlier—Dickens dashed off the first eight chapters of his new novel within a month's time (Rosenberg 397). On December 1, 1860, the novel's first installment was published in *All the Year Round*, and the journal's readership quickly rose back to 100,000, where it had stood for Dickens's first contribution, *A Tale of Two Cities* (Paroissien 1). We might measure this statistic against the sales numbers of other mid-century periodicals: Dickens's first journal, *Household Words* (1850-1859), averaged a readership of 40,000 in its best years, as did *Punch*, a weekly satirical magazine, in 1854; the *Cornhill Magazine*, another weekly miscellany begun in 1860, averaged 84,000 in its first two years; *Englishwoman's Domestic Magazine* and *Boy's Own Magazine* averaged 60,000 and 40,000 respectively in 1862 (Altick 395). Enthusiasm for *Great Expectations* did not diminish when it was published in three-volume book form on July 6, 1861, and it ran through five editions in the same number of months (Rosenberg 398). A century and a half later, *Great Expectations* remains one of the most widely taught of

Dickens's works and is without doubt the most canonical of the novels to have been published originally in *All the Year Round*, which also ushered into the world Wilkie Collins's *The Woman in White* (1859-1860) and Charles Reade's *Hard Cash* (1863). Between Dickens's time and our own, attitudes toward *Great Expectations* have ranged from lavish praise to skepticism and dismissal as the novel provided a platform for debates over such issues as the nature and value of Dickens's realism, Dickens's political stance, the relevance and effects of his traumatic childhood on his fiction, and his attitude toward women. Indeed, a review of the novel's critical reception offers ample testimony to the pronouncement of early 20th-century critic and literary historian George Saintsbury that "no author in our literary history has been both admired and enjoyed for such different reasons; by such different tastes and intellects; by whole classes of readers unlike each other" (Saintsbury 256).

Publishing serial novels in periodicals became common practice for authors in the mid to late nineteenth century. Rising literacy rates and increased leisure time along with the repeals of the newspaper stamp tax (1855) and paper duty (1861) (known as "taxes on knowledge") made this form of publication lucrative and expedient for authors, publishers, and printers while providing the public with a relatively cheap form of entertainment that could be enjoyed in short spurts of time. In 1858, the sensation novelist and Dickens's close friend Wilkie Collins estimated the total readership of periodical fiction in England at three million (Altick 357). By 1864, records show that journals containing novels were the most popular of all weekly periodicals, averaging a million and a half copies sold per month (Altick 358). Writing for serial publication posed considerable challenges for novelists, who had to adhere to tight deadlines, conceive of their novels in segments aimed at maintaining readers' interest between installments, settle for little or no revision time, and face criticism for a novel before its completion. Some critics regarded these challenges as ultimately beneficial for the craft of fiction. Reviewing *Great Expectations* in 1861, the *Times* commented that serial publication—of which it acknowledged Dickens as a founding father—was initiating a positive change in novel writing. "The periodical publication of the novel . . . has forced English writers to develop a plot and work up the incidents. Lingering over the delineation of character and of manners, our novelists began to lose sight of the story and to avoid action. Periodical publication compelled them to a different course" (Collins 431). Some novelists resisted this change in course, feeling the challenge of writing for deadlines too difficult, and both George Eliot (aka Marian Evans) and Elizabeth Gaskell declined Dickens's invitation to contribute to *All the Year Round*. Their reluctance—and the failure of Charles Lever's novel—was one catalyst for *Great Expectations*'s appearance in the journal.

Dickens was well aware of the many drawbacks to serial publication, lamenting in the Postscript to *Our Mutual Friend* that the reader of the serial cannot "until they have [the novel] before them complete, perceive the relations of its finer threads to the whole pattern which is always before the eyes of the story-weaver at his loom" (Postscript 162). Nevertheless, despite the admitted difficulties of planning a novel in short allotments of space and time, Dickens enjoyed the challenges that serial publication posed. (Indeed, he had little experience writing novels in any other way.) John Butt and Kathleen Tillotson note that one of the attractions of the form for Dickens lay in the intimate relationship formed between storyteller and audience as the novel developed in response to its readers' reactions. Serial publication, write Butt and Tillotson, "meant a larger public, but also a public more delicately responsive, who made their views known during the progress of a novel both by writing to him and by reducing or increasing their purchases" (16). To maintain this dialogue with his readers, Dickens never got too far ahead of them in his writing. Archibald Coolidge relates in *Charles Dickens as Serial Novelist* that "Dickens wrote his novels as he published them, in monthly or weekly installments. He rarely completed a monthly number much more than ten days before it was to be printed and considered being four weeks ahead of the printer his customary advance in the weekly serials" (50). The writing of *Great Expectations* started off with a bang, but ill health seized Dickens shortly after he finished the first month's installment. In his 1990 biography of Dickens, Peter Ackroyd attributes the darker aspects of the novel to Dickens's sickness during composition, but from Dickens's letters, it is apparent that writing had a restorative effect. "A certain allotment of my time when I have that story-demand upon me, has, all through my Author life, been an essential condition of my health and success," he confessed in a letter on Dec. 4, 1860. "I have just returned here [to his home at Gad's Hill] to work so many hours every day for so many days. It is really impossible for me to break my bond" (*Letters* 345). It is possible that Dickens's bond to his writing was particularly important at this time in providing a form of stability to compensate for his separation in 1858 from Catherine, his wife of 22 years.

Reviews immediately following the publication of *Great Expectations* were concerned primarily with comparing Dickens's newest novel to his previous works. Many critics welcomed what appeared to be a return to the light-heartedness and humor that had been absent from his last three works. "After passing under the cloud of *Little Dorrit* and *Bleak House*. . . . [Dickens] has written a story that is new, original, powerful and very entertaining," commented the *Saturday Review*. "*Great Expectations* restores Mr Dickens and his readers to the old level. It is in his best vein, . . . quite worthy to stand beside *Martin Chuzzlewit* and *David Copperfield*" (Collins 427). The *Atlantic Monthly* echoed this sentiment and deemed the plot of *Great Expectations* to be "the best that Dickens has ever invented" (Collins 428). It further commented on the skill with which Dickens manipulated the serial form, testifying "to the felicity with which expectation was excited and prolonged, and to the series of surprises which accompanied the unfolding of the plot of the story" (Collins 428). The *Times* similarly welcomed the novel's lighter tone but did so more cautiously: "Mr Dickens has in the present work given us more of his earlier fancies than we have had for years. *Great Expectations* is not, indeed, his best work, but it is to be ranked among his happiest. There is that flowing humour in it which disarms criticism and which is all the more enjoyable because it defies criticism" (Collins 431). The *Dublin University Magazine*, however, felt neither disarmed nor dissuaded from criticism and attributed the humor, which others had praised, to a decline in the aging author. "The favourite of our youth still stands before us, in outline but little changed, the old voice still sounding pleasantly in our ears, the old humour still peeping playfully from lip to eye; but time, flattery, and self-indulgence have robbed his phrases of half their whilom happiness; the old rich humour shines wan and watery through an ever-deepening film of fancies farfetched or utterly absurd; while all the old mannerisms and deformities that once seemed to impart a kind of picturesque quaintness to so many neighbour beauties, have been growing more and more irredeemably ungraceful and pitilessly obtrusive . . ." (Collins 434-435). The note of disappointment was likewise sounded by Margaret Oliphant in her famous *Blackwood's Magazine* article on "Sensational Novels," which found in *Great Expectations* all the "strange, dangerous, and exciting" incidents of the new genre but deemed the overall work to be "feeble, fatigued, and colourless" (Collins 439). In Mrs. Oliphant's view, Dickens was betraying all his "genius and natural power" (442) by stooping to adopt sensational techniques that ultimately failed to create the desired effect on his readers. "Mr Dickens," concludes Mrs. Oliphant, "is the careless, clever boy who could [write a novel] twice as well as [Mr Wilkie Collins] but won't take the pains" (Collins 442).

Critics in the late nineteenth and early twentieth centuries seemed largely to concur with Mrs. Oliphant's view that Dickens had misapplied—or failed to apply—his obvious genius. The very sensationalism and humor that had endeared him to early and mid-Victorian readers became the grounds for dismissal by highbrow, Modernist critics. "Dickens had no university education, and the literary men from Oxford and Cambridge, who have lately been sifting fastidiously so much of the English heritage, have rather snubbingly left him alone," Edmund Wilson commented in 1965 of Dickens's decline in the critical eye during the decades immediately following his death. "The Bloomsbury that talked about Dostoevsky ignored Dostoevsky's master, Dickens. . . . [He has been] made into one of those Victorian scarecrows with ludicrous Freudian flaws—so infantile, pretentious, and hypocritical as to deserve only a perfunctory sneer" (3). While the formation of The Dickens Fellowship in 1902 and their founding of *The Dickensian* in 1905 proved that Dickens still maintained a loyal following of readers, these same years saw heated debates arise among scholars and critics over Dickens's importance to literary history. Dickens's caricature, sensationalism, sentimentality, and leavening humor found little support in a critical atmosphere that favored social realism and philosophical sobriety. "Mr Dickens is a great observer and a great humorist, but he is nothing of a philosopher," Henry James noted in an 1865 review of *Our Mutual Friend* for *The Nation*. "[The novelist] must know *man* as well as *men*, and to know man is to be a philosopher" (Wall 168). George Eliot's paramour, George Henry Lewes, praised Dickens's imagination, genius, and vision in the *Fortnightly Review* in 1872 but noted that his characters were "merely masks—not characters, but personified characteristics, caricatures and distortions of human nature" (Wall 195). In the eyes of cultivated readers, Lewes continues, Dickens's "drawing is so vivid yet so incorrect, or else so blurred and formless, with such excess of effort . . . that the doubt arises how an observer so remarkably keen could make observations so remarkably false, and miss such very obvious facts . . ." (Wall 198). Lewes's reflection on Dickens ultimately transpires into a criticism of an unreflective mass readership all too willing to accept Dickens's unreal, impossible, mechanistic figures for reality. His call for a tightening of critical standards and a clear distinction between literature and popular fiction was certainly answered judging from Dickens's dismissal by a number of influential critics in later years. Virginia Woolf's father, Leslie Stephen, wrote Dickens's entry in the *Dictionary of National Biography* in 1888: "If literary fame could be safely measured by popularity with the half-educated, Dickens must claim the highest position among English novelists. . . . The criticism of more severe critics chiefly consist in the assertion that his merits are such as suit the half-educated" (Stephen 221). Perhaps F. R. Leavis sums up best the reason for Dickens's critical disfavor in the early twentieth century when he excludes Dickens from *The Great Tradition* (1948), a text that largely helped to shape the literary canon as we now know it (though he would later amend his stance). "The reason for not including Dickens in the line of great novelists is [that his] genius was that of a great entertainer, and he had for the most part no profounder responsibility as a creative artist than this description suggests" (31-32).

Dickens was not, however, without some influential supporters during the late nineteenth and early twentieth centuries, and these often cited *Great Expectations* in their defense of the author's skill and insight. The novelist George Gissing argued in his 1898 book *Charles Dickens: A Critical Study* that those who thought Dickens's characters were types and abstractions rather than real individuals did not know the reality of lower middle-class life in Dickens's London: "Sixty years ago, grotesques and eccentricities were more common than nowadays; . . . nowadays he would have to search for them amid the masses drilled unto uniformity, but there they are—the same creatures differently clad" (14-15). Dickens's subjects, Gissing asserts, lived a different reality than the upper-class, fin-de-siècle critics who dismissed his works as mere fantasy. Of *Great Expectations*, Gissing writes that "nothing [is] related, as seen or heard, which could not have been seen or heard by the writer" (67). He cites Joe Gargery as an exemplar of realism who "lives in a world, not of melodrama, but of everyday cause and effect" (107). Admitting that Dickens's imagination did occasionally run away with him, Gissing stresses that the author's ability to create real characters must not be denied simply because these characters sometimes occupied impossible circumstances: "Pip is so thoroughly alive that we can forget his dim relations with Satis House" (107). A. C.

Swinburne also wrote favorably in Dickens's defense in 1902, citing *Great Expectations* as one of "the highest landmarks of success ever reared for immortality by the triumphant genius of Dickens" (Swinburne 252). Others, like G. K. Chesterton, writing in 1906, saw in Dickens an influential social reformer and humanitarian and called Gissing to task for failing to acknowledge the hope and optimism of Dickens's time. Dickens, according to Chesterton, "was the voice in England of this humane intoxication and expansion, this encouraging of anybody to be anything. . . . His work has the great glory of the Revolution, the bidding of every man to be himself . . ." (14). For Chesterton, *Great Expectations*, coming at the end of Dickens's career, begins to reflect some of the pessimism and loss of hope that colors the later part of the century. However, the novel still remained true to what Chesterton considered to be Dickens's understanding of "permanent and presiding humanity" (228). According to Chesterton, Pip's "vacillations . . . between the humble life to which he owes everything, and the gorgeous life from which he expects something, touch a very true and somewhat tragic part of morals; for the great paradox of morality . . . is that the very vilest kind of fault is exactly the most easy kind. . . . Dickens has dealt with this easy descent of desertion, this silent treason, with remarkable accuracy in the account of the indecision of Pip" (233-234). For writers like Gissing and Chesterton, the disconnect between Dickens and his Modernist critics must be attributed not to problems with the former's realism but with the latter's inability to appreciate the social milieu of mid-Victorian England and to perceive transcendent human truths.

Many of Dickens's defenders from the first decades of the twentieth century rested their arguments on the author's sympathy for and support of the lower and working classes. In 1908, the novelist and critic Edwin Pugh claimed in *Charles Dickens: The Apostle of the People* that Dickens was a "Socialist without knowing it" (315), and in 1938, Thomas A. Jackson read Dickens through a Marxist lens (as does Raymond Williams later in 1970). According to Jackson, *Great Expec-*

tations is Dickens's indictment of modern, Capitalist society. "Self-satisfied, mid-Victorian, British society buoyed itself up with as great 'expectations' of future wealth and glory as did poor, deluded Pip. If it had but known, its means of ostentation came from a source (the labour of the depressed and exploited masses) to which it would have been as shocked to acknowledge indebtedness as Pip was to find he owed all his acquired gentility to the patronage of the transported felon" (Jackson 197). Magwitch, according to Jackson, represents the monstrous image of the working man created by and looming in the minds of respectable society. But the exposure of Pip's indebtedness to the convict reveals the reality of respectable society's dependence on the laboring classes. While later criticism tarnished Dickens's image as a Revolutionary writer, contemporary critics like Jeremy Tambling and Susan Walsh have used Marxist approaches productively to understand the role of mid-Victorian economic conditions on the novel's configurations of class and gender.

The 1930's and 1940's witnessed a protest to the image of Dickens as a Revolutionary and Socialist. In contrast to earlier scholars who criticized Dickens's populist appeal, Socialist critics emphasized Dickens's snobbery and apologist stance toward aristocratic values. George Bernard Shaw's 1937 foreword to the Edinburgh limited edition of *Great Expectations* suggested that Pip's snobbery toward Magwitch must be seen as a reflection of Dickens's own attitudes toward the lower classes. Shaw notes that Dickens "never raises the question why Pip should refuse Magwitch's endowment and shrink from him with such inhuman loathing. Magwitch no doubt was a Warmint from the point of view of the genteel Dickens family and even from his own. . . . I am afraid Pip must be to this extent identified with Dickens—[he] could not see Magwitch as an animal of the same species as himself or Miss Havisham. His feeling is true to the nature of snobbery; but his creator says no word in criticism of that ephemeral limitation" (296). Shaw, erroneously, predicted the novel's lack of self-awareness in this regard would limit its appeal to later generations "as our social conscience expands and makes the intense class snobbery of the nineteenth century seem less natural to us" (296).

George Orwell expanded on Shaw's suggestions in his 1940 essay on Dickens. Orwell criticizes Dickens for attacking "the law, parliamentary government, the educational system and so forth, without ever clearly suggesting what he would put in their places. . . . There is no clear sign that he wants the existing order to be overthrown, or that he believes it would make very much difference it if *were* overthrown" (Orwell 297-8). Far from being a Socialist, Dickens, in Orwell's estimation, exhibited pro-capitalist sentiments and a reprehensible complacency with his current political situation: "It seems that in every attack Dickens makes upon society he is always pointing to a change of spirit rather than a change of structure. . . . A 'change of heart' is in fact the alibi of people who do not wish to endanger the *status quo*" (299). In contrast to critics like Gissing, Orwell suggests that Dickens knew nothing about the lives of the working people he portrayed and for whom he seemed to evoke sympathy. His ignorance is evidenced by the fact that few of his novels show people at work. "Pip, for instance, 'goes into business' in Egypt: we are not told what business, and Pip's working life occupies about half a page of the book. . . . As soon as he has to deal with trade, finance, industry or politics he takes refuge in vagueness, or in satire" (301). Orwell goes on to point out the upper-class pretensions of Dickens's supposedly working-class characters. "The vivid pictures that he succeeds in leaving in one's memory are nearly always the pictures of things seen in leisure moments, in the coffee-rooms of country inns or through the windows of a stage-coach" (303). Noting that Dickens has been "stolen" for various causes—Marxism, Catholicism, Conservatism—Orwell doubts Dickens's appropriateness for any of these social agendas: "The question is, What is there to steal? Why does anyone care about Dickens? Why do *I* care about Dickens?" (306). The answer, Orwell concludes, is that Dickens has become an institution: "Whether you approve of him or not, he is *there*, like the Nelson Column" (307). The comment is telling of Dickens's tenacious hold on the minds and imaginations of a diverse population of readers, despite the attempts of prominent critics to evict him from the literary canon.

Humphry House's *The Dickens World* (1941) has often been credited with lifting Dickens back into critical favor. Using Dickens's works as lenses into Victorian London, House argued that Dickens's novels could serve as documents recording the events, tempers, and tones of their age with the accuracy and perceptiveness of Dickens's journalistic eye. In stark contrast to earlier critics who had refuted the reality of Dickens's portraits, House stated that "many readers who would be bored by the reports of the Poor Law Commissioners or Garratt's *Suggestions for a Reform of the Proceedings in Chancery* can look in *Oliver Twist* and *Bleak House* for pictures of their times, and contributions to the cure of the evils they describe" (9). House deemed *Great Expectations* to be "the perfect expression of a phase of English society: it is a statement, to be taken as it stands of what money can do, good and bad; of how it can change and make distinctions of class; how it can pervert virtue, sweeten manners, open up new fields of enjoyment and suspicion. The mood of the book belongs not to the imaginary date of its plot, but to the time in which it was written; for the unquestioned assumptions that Pip can be transformed by money and the minor graces it can buy, and that the loss of one fortune can be repaired on the strength of incidental gains in voice and friends, were only possible in a country secure in its internal economy, with expanding markets abroad: this could hardly be said of England in the 'twenties and 'thirties" (159). House's idea that Dickens's novels could be used as journalistic testimonials to his time was taken up by Dickens scholars like Philip Collins and Ivor Brown in the 1960's, and House's approach still exerts undeniable influence over current New Historical approaches to the novel.

Emerging almost simultaneously with House's work, Edmund Wilson's essay "Dickens: The Two Scrooges" (first published in the *Atlantic Monthly* in 1940) brought Dickens criticism in a very different but equally influential direction. Determining Dickens's childhood work in the blacking factory to be "a trauma from which he suffered all his life" (7), Wilson introduced a psycho-biographical approach that allowed for more complex interpretations of characters and their motives. For Wilson, "the work of Dickens' whole career was an attempt to digest [his childhood] shocks and hardships, to explain them to himself, to justify himself in relation to them, to give an intelligible and tolerable picture of a world in which such things could occur" (8-9). This assumption informs his reading of *Great Expectations*, which, for Wilson, occupies an important transitional moment in Dickens's opus. In *Great Expectations*, Wilson claims, Dickens moves out of the melodramatic dualism upon which his earlier works had turned as he tries to combine good and bad qualities in a single character, thereby allowing for more psychological complexity: "In *Great Expectations* we see Pip pass through a whole psychological cycle. At first, he is sympathetic, then by a more or less natural process he turns into something unsympathetic, then he becomes sympathetic again. Here the effects of both poverty and riches are seen from the inside in one person. This is for Dickens a great advance; and it is a development which, if carried far enough, would end by eliminating the familiar Dickens of the lively but limited stage characters, with their tag lines and their unvarying make-ups" (54). Wilson is recognized as blazing the way for a branch of Dickens criticism that focused, in Lyn Pykett's words, on the "social construction of the writer's psyche and in his fictional representations of the complex interdependence of psychological and social organization" (475). Certainly, Wilson's work has allowed for the application of psychoanalytic apparatus as interpretive tools, as evidenced by the works of Peter Brooks and Michal Peled Ginsburg, both whom borrow Freudian terminology to understand the novel's structural and thematic issues.

The mid-twentieth century saw both an integration and rejection of previous critical approaches as Dickens settled firmly into the literary canon. Among the two most influential books on Dickens to come out in the 1950's were Dorothy Van Ghent's *The English Novel: Form and Function* (1953) and J. Hillis Miller's *Charles Dickens: The World of His Novels* (1958). Both critics focused on the significance of Pip's isolation from his family and society, but while the former incorporated elements of Wilson's psychological criticism and Marxist readings, the latter formed itself on an explicit rejection of Wilson's and House's approaches. Van Ghent's analysis of *Great Expectations* focuses on the soliloquizing quality of characters' spoken language and the failure of communication that results from their solipsism. Dickens's world, Van Ghent argues, is one "of isolated integers, terrifyingly alone and unrelated" (Van Ghent, 127). Borrowing from Marxist readings of the novel, she suggests that *Great Expectations* reflects a world where "people were becoming things, and things (the things that money can buy or that are the means for making money or for exalting prestige in the abstract) were becoming more important than money. People were being de-animated, robbed of their souls, and things were usurping the prerogatives of animate creatures—governing the lives of their owners in the most literal sense" (Van Ghent, 128). Pip, as a child, is treated as a thing (by Magwitch, Mrs. Joe, and Miss Havisham), is surrounded by people who have lost their humanity, and subsequently learns to exploit others as an adult. Pip's snobbery, Van Ghent asserts, "is a denial of the human value of others" (Van Ghent 136). In contrast to Van Ghent's interweaving of previous approaches to the novel, J. Hillis Miller, who would later become a leading member of the Yale School of Deconstruction, argued for reading Dickens's works not as products of the author's psychological conditions or of his environment but as means of self-apprehension and self-creation. Novels, Miller asserts, must be regarded as "autonomous works of art" that do not act as transparent lenses into the real world but rather transform the real world through the distortive lens of the author's imagination as he tries to understand the world and find his place in it. Miller regarded *Great Expectations* as "the most unified and concentrated expression of Dickens' abiding sense of the world" and Pip as "the archetypal

Dickens hero" (249) who is separated from nature, orphaned, holds no status in his community, desires possession, and is conscious of deprivation. "At the center of Dickens's novels is a recognition of the bankruptcy of the relation of the individual to society as it now exists, the objective structure of given institutions and values. Only what an individual makes of himself, in charitable relations to others, counts. And this self-creation tends to require open revolt against the pressures of society. Human beings are themselves the source of the transcendence of their isolation" (254). Thus, while Van Ghent sees Pip's isolation as an indictment of a dehumanized, mechanized, and tragically fragmented society, Miller views this same isolation as the source of heroic action and self-realization.

In his recent book, *The Dickens Industry: Critical Perspectives 1836-2005*, Laurence Mazzeno asserts that "by the 1960's [Dickens] was accorded primacy of place among Victorian novelists both as an artist and a chronicler of society" (119). Erasing doubt about the author's rightful place in literary history, a number of critical retrospectives appeared, including Ford and Lane's *The Dickens Critics* (1961), Gross and Pearson's *Dickens and the Twentieth Century* (1962), and Martin Price's *Dickens: A Collection of Critical Essays* (1967). Published on the centenary of Dickens's death, F. R. and Q. D. Leavis's *Dickens the Novelist* (1970) exemplifies the shift in tone toward Dickens from skepticism to celebration. F. R. Leavis, who had rejected Dickens from the Great Tradition, and his wife, Q. D. Leavis, who had voiced similar dismissal in her *Fiction and the Reading Public* (1932), now claimed in the preface that "Our purpose is to enforce as unanswerably as possible the conviction that Dickens was one of the greatest of creative writers; that with the intelligence inherent in creative genius, he developed a fully conscious devotion to his art, becoming as a popular and fecund, but yet profound, serious and wonderfully resourceful practicing novelist, a master of it; and that, as such, he demands a critical attention he has not had" (ix). Rejecting the approach of Edmund Wilson and his followers as "wrong-headed, ill-informed . . .

and essentially ignorant and misdirecting" (ix), the Leavises attempted to redeem Dickens's literary genius by extricating his work from psychoanalytical, Marxist, and "other ideologically-slanted interpretations of Dickens's achievement" (xiii). Q. D. Leavis's chapter, "How We Must Read *Great Expectations*" operates under the assumption that Dickens "worked schematically by translating ideas into characters and their relations to each other, and by choosing or arranging illustrative settings for this . . ." (289). These ideas, Leavis suggests, allowed Dickens to deduce "a coherent and compelling analysis of what was *fundamentally* amiss with his society. . . . [In *Great Expectations*] it is seen as a society that first makes and then executes criminals, with a quite arbitrary conception of justice, a society in which all are therefore guilty inescapably—there are no innocent, only those more or less aware of guilt, ranging from the blindly self-righteous to the repentantly self-accusing" (290). Through close readings of the novel, Leavis attempts to convey to contemporary readers the homogeneity of tone and the logic of events and actions in the novel as they stem from Dickens's profound understanding of human motivations and conduct. For Leavis, *Great Expectations* not only testifies to Dickens's mature style but provides an exemplary text for demonstrating an interpretive strategy that is able to compensate for the historical gap between Dickens and modern readers without resorting to pop psychology and anachronistic political biases.

In counterpoint to centenary celebrations of Dickens, the 1970's also saw the blossoming of feminist readings, most of which objected to Dickens's treatment of women as hopelessly sentimentalizing. Kate Millett's important work *Sexual Politics* (1970) condemned Dickens for his reduction of female characters to "insipid goodies" (90). With its cast of manipulative, cruel, and downright creepy women, *Great Expectations* hardly falls guilty under this particular accusation, but it doesn't escape the indictment that Dickens's women are even more caricatural and unreal than his male characters. Even Margaret Oliphant, writing in 1862, labels Dickens's portrayal of Miss Havisham as "fancy run mad" (Collins 440) and deems "the entire connection between Miss Havisham, Pip, and Estella" a failure (Collins 441). In 1983, Michael Slater admitted in his *Dickens and Women* that *Great Expectations* "is a novel without a heroine to love and admire" (282), but he attempted to attribute Dickens's negative portrayals of women to the author's own traumatic encounters with the opposite sex. The portrayal of Mrs. Joe stemmed, suggests Slater, from the author's ambivalence and resentment toward his mother; Estella was a representation of the actress Ellen Ternan, the late object of Dickens's affections; and Miss Havisham's original was determined to be Maria Beadnell, Dickens's early crush who abruptly broke off their love affair. Slater's attempt to explain Dickens's fraught relationships with women left feminist critics largely unmoved. One example of continued feminist indictment of Dickens is Monica Cohen's *Professional Domesticity in the Victorian Novel: Women, Work, and Home* (1998), whose chapter on *Great Expectations* faults Dickens for endorsing and reinforcing the separation between home and the public sphere of work. Cohen's reading of the novel reveals that for Dickens, home is only a good home when the women are enclosed within their proper domestic sphere: "The novel appears to place a premium on establishing and maintaining the distinction between home and work in order to mark good homes, like the Castle, from the flawed homes scattered about the rest of the novel's terrain" (77). Some feminist critics have been more forgiving, seeing Dickens's portrayal of women as a reflection of the attitudes of his society. Linda Raphael, for instance, asserts that "the characterization of Miss Havisham provides a model of the power of repressive forces" (Raphael 705). She outlines Miss Havisham's repression by the circumstances of her engagement to Compeyson and her subsequent adoption of a male (and thus powerful) role in her relationship with Pip. Estella, Raphael argues, might end up being portrayed as "the angel in the house," but "the reversal of her character remains unconvincing in contrast to the representation of her as an abused and abusing female" (709). Raphael cites Estella's failed transformation into redemptive angel of the house as indication of Dickens's acknowledgement of but inability to escape a society that forces women into vicious cycles of abuse, repression, domination, and cruelty. In contrast, Elizabeth Campbell's *Fortune's Wheel: Dickens and the Iconography of Women's Time* (2003) calls on antique and medieval iconography to argue for Dickens's empowerment of female characters in *Great Expectations*. In Campbell's reading of the novel, Miss Havisham becomes "Dickens's strangest and most symbolically suggestive Fortune" (198), a goddess-like figure playing alternately the roles of witch and fairy godmother. In Campbell's analysis, Dickens uses the material of folklore and fairy-tale to lift his female characters beyond the constraining reality of their male-dominated society.

Post-colonial criticism is a relatively new approach to Dickens that has seized on *Great Expectations* as a launching point for studying England's relations with Australia. While the novel postdates the abolition of convict transportation to New South Wales, Dickens was intensely fascinated with this aspect of England's history. Various critics have begun to explore the symbolic function of Magwitch's Australian exile. Grace Moore, for example, sees Magwitch's geographic dislocation as symbolic of social exile and its consequences: "As a returned convict who has been forcibly expelled, Magwitch in *Great Expectations* occupies a more complex position than mere 'outsidedness' and becomes a tool for a critique of contemporary British society. He is both insider and exile; one who has been abused by the social system and as a result come to abuse that same system" (15). Grahame Smith's "Suppressing Narratives: Childhood and Empire in *The Uncommercial Traveller* and *Great Expectations*" argues on similar lines, suggesting that Magwitch is the "'black slave' of the British class system, brutalized to such an extent by the body politic that its only solution is to eject him to a grotesque mirror image of itself . . ." (51). Post-colonial perspectives are still relatively new contributions to the work on *Great Expectations* and hold considerable potential for future scholars of the text.

It would be impossible to conclude a critical history of *Great Expec-*

tations without mentioning one major point of the novel that has exercised critics from the late nineteenth century to the present day, a point which all scholars of the novel must wrestle with at one moment or another: the multiple endings to the novel. A brief history of these endings runs something like this: Dickens originally concluded the novel on June 11, 1861, with Pip and Estella meeting by chance in London after the former's return from an eleven-year absence in the East. Pip leaves Estella with reflection that, after suffering abuse at the hands of her deceased husband, she now had "a heart to understand what my heart used to be" (Dickens 492). The ending suggests rather conclusively that this casual encounter is the last time Pip and Estella meet. When Dickens allowed his friend and fellow-writer Bulwer-Lytton to read the proofs of the ending, however, the latter objected strongly. "Bulwer was so very anxious that I should alter the end of *Great Expectations* . . . and stated his reasons so well, that I have resumed the wheel, and taken another turn at it," Dickens wrote to Wilkie Collins on June 23, 1861. "Upon the whole I think it is for the better. You shall see the change when we meet" (*Letters* 428). In the revised and extended conclusion, Pip is away in the East for eight years and meets with Estella again on the grounds of Satis House. The novel concludes with the sentence: "I saw the shadow of no parting from her" (Dickens 358). The original ending of the novel was first discovered in Forster's biography of Dickens in 1874, and since then critics have focused extraordinary attention on the significance of the change and debated the appropriateness of one ending over the other. Early critics—like Forster, Charles Dickens Jr., Gissing, and Chesterton—tended to favor the first ending (Rosenberg 511). Humphry House feels that the marriage to Estella is "artistically wrong" (157) and Tillotson and Butt see the new ending as inappropriate. On the other hand, many others, including Q. D. Leavis, prefer the revised ending. Leavis writes: "The preference of critics generally for the originally-planned ending to the novel instead of the one printed seems to me incomprehensible. . . . Dickens's second thoughts produced the right, because the logical, solution to the problem of how to end without a sentimental 'happy ending' but with a satisfactory winding-up of the themes. This he has done with dignity and economy" (329). Edgar Rosenberg offers an excellent summary of the debate as it currently stands as well as an account of the controversial changes Dickens made to the last sentence of the novel. Since modern editions of the novel now conventionally include both endings, the debate will undoubtedly continue and yield more new readings of the text as a whole.

The open-endedness of *Great Expectations* and its many narrative and interpretive gaps have stirred the minds not only of critics but of novelists and screenwriters. Contemporary novelists seem to be particularly attracted to the character of Magwitch and his years of absence in Australia. Australian novelist Michael Noonan's book *Magwitch* (1982) explores Pip's later life as he travels around Sydney, uncovering Magwitch's history during his absence from England. Peter Carey's novel *Jack Maggs* retells Magwitch's return from his own point of view. Multiple film adaptations of the novel include David Lean's 1946 version, a five-hour 1981 television movie, and the 1998 Hollywood adaptation starring Gwyneth Paltrow and Ethan Hawke. Indeed, the continued circulation of *Great Expectations* both in critical arenas and the mass media seems to answer earlier debates over the novel's proper sphere of influence. Ultimately, time has proven that Dickens belongs not to scholars or to casual readers but to both even as his legacy continues to challenge the divisions between high culture and popular entertainment.

Works Cited

Ackroyd, Peter. *Dickens*. New York: HarperCollins, 1990.

Altick, Richard D. *The English Common Reader: A Social History of the Mass Reading Public, 1800-1900*. Columbus: Ohio State University Press, 1957.

Brooks, Peter. "Repetition, Repression, and Return: The Plotting of *Great Expectations*" in *Great Expectations*, ed. Edgar Rosenberg. New York: W.W. Norton, 1999. 679-689.

Brown, Ivor. *Dickens in His Time*. London: Nelson, 1963.

Brown, James M. *Dickens: Novelist in the Market-Place*. Totowa, NJ: Barnes & Noble Books, 1982.

Butt, John, and Kathleen Tillotson. *Dickens at Work*. Fairlawn, NJ: Essential Books, Inc., 1958.

Campbell, Elizabeth. *Fortune's Wheel: Dickens and the Iconography of Women's Time*. Athens: Ohio University Press, 2003.

Chesterton, G. K. *Charles Dickens*. New York: Schocken Books, 1965.

Cohen, Monica F. *Professional Domesticity in the Victorian Novel: Women, Work, and Home*. New York: Cambridge University Press, 1998.

Collins, Philip, ed. *Dickens: The Critical Heritage*. London: Routledge and Kegan Paul, 1971.

_____. *Dickens and Crime*. London: Macmillan, 1962.

_____. *Dickens and Education*. London: Macmillan, 1963.

Coolidge, Archibald C., Jr. *Charles Dickens as Serial Novelist*. Ames: Iowa State University Press, 1967.

Cotsell, Michael, ed. *Critical Essays on Charles Dickens's Great Expectations*. Boston: G. K. Hall and Co., 1990.

Dickens, Charles. *Great Expectations*, ed. Edgar Rosenberg. New York: W.W. Norton, 1999.

_____. Postscript to *Our Mutual Friend*. Reprinted in *Charles Dickens: A Critical Anthology*, ed. Stephen Wall. New York: Penguin, 1970. 162-164.

Ford, George. *Dickens and His Readers: Aspects of Novel-Criticism Since 1836*. Princeton, NJ: Princeton University Press, 1955.

Ford, George, and Lauriat Lane, Jr., eds. *The Dickens Critics*. Ithaca, NY: Cornell University Press, 1961.

Ginsburg, Michal Peled. "Dickens and the Uncanny: Repression and Displacement in *Great Expectations*" in *Great Expectations*, ed. Edgar Rosenberg. New York: W.W. Norton, 1999. 698-704.

Gissing, George. *Charles Dickens: A Critical Study*. New York: Dodd, Mead, and Co., 1904.

Gross, John, and Gabriel Pearson, eds. *Dickens and the Twentieth Century*. Toronto: University of Toronto Press, 1962.

House, Humphry. *The Dickens World*. Oxford: Oxford University Press, 1941.

Jackson, Thomas A. *Charles Dickens: The Progress of a Radical*. New York: Haskell House Publishers, 1971.

Jordan, John O., ed. *The Cambridge Companion to Charles Dickens*. New York: Cambridge University Press, 2001.

Kaplan, Fred. *Dickens: A Biography*. Baltimore, MD: Johns Hopkins University Press, 1988.

Leavis, F. R. *The Great Tradition*. Garden City, NY: Doubleday and Co., Inc., 1954.

Leavis, F. R., and Q. D. Leavis. *Dickens: The Novelist*. New Brunswick, NJ: Rutgers University Press, 1970.

Mazzeno, Laurence. *The Dickens Industry: Critical Perspectives 1836-2005*. Rochester, NY: Camden House, 2008.

Miller, J. Hillis. *Charles Dickens: The World of His Novels*. Cambridge: Harvard University Press, 1958.

Millett, Kate. *Sexual Politics*. Garden City, NY: Doubleday, 1970.

Moore, Grace. *Dickens and Empire: Discourses of Class, Race and Colonialism in the Works of Charles Dickens*. Burlington, VT: Ashgate, 2004.

Orwell, George. "Charles Dickens" in *Inside the Whale and Other Essays* (1940). Reprinted in *Charles Dickens: A Critical Anthology*, ed. Stephen Wall. New York: Penguin, 1970. 297-313.

Paroissien, David, ed. *The Companion to Great Expectations*. Westport, CT: Greenwood Press, 2000.

Price, Martin. *Dickens: A Collection of Critical Essays*. Englewood Cliffs, NJ: Prentice-Hall, 1967.

Pugh, Edwin. *Charles Dickens: The Apostle of the People*. New York: Haskell House Publishers, 1971.

Pykett, Lyn. "Dickens and Criticism" in *The Companion to Charles Dickens*, ed., David Paroissien. Malden, MA: Blackwell, 2008. 470-485.

Raphael, Linda. "A Re-Vision of Miss Havisham: Her Expectations and Our Responses" in *Great Expectations*, ed. Edgar Rosenberg. New York: W.W. Norton, 1999. 705-709.

Rosenberg, Edgar. "Launching *Great Expectations*" in *Great Expectations*, ed. Edgar Rosenberg. New York: W.W. Norton, 1999. 389-426.

_____. "Putting an End to *Great Expectations*" in *Great Expectations*, ed. Edgar Rosenberg. New York: W.W. Norton, 1999. 491-527.

Sadrin, Anny. *Great Expectations*. London: Unwin Hyman, 1988.

Saintsbury, George. "Dickens," *The Cambridge History of English Literature*, vol. 13, no. 2, chapter 10, 1916. Reprinted in *Charles Dickens: A Critical Anthology*, ed. Stephen Wall. New York: Penguin, 1970. 255-256.

Shaw, George Bernard. Foreword to the Edinburgh limited edition of *Great Expectations* (1937). Reprinted in *Charles Dickens: A Critical Anthology*, ed. Stephen Wall. New York: Penguin, 1970. 284-297.

Slater, Michael. *Dickens and Women*. Palo Alto: Stanford University Press, 1983.

Smith, Grahame. "Suppressing Narratives: Childhood and Empire in *The Uncommercial Traveller* and *Great Expectations*" in *Dickens and the Children of Empire*, ed. Wendy S. Jacobson. New York: Palgrave, 2000. 43-53.

Stephen, Leslie. "Dickens" in the *Dictionary of National Biography*. Vol. 15, 1888. Reprinted in *Charles Dickens: A Critical Anthology*, ed. Stephen Wall. New York: Penguin, 1970. 221-222.

Story, Graham, ed. *The Letters of Charles Dickens*, vol. 9. Oxford: Clarendon Press, 1997.

Swinburne, A. C. *Charles Dickens* (1913). Reprinted in part in *Charles Dickens: A Critical Anthology*, ed. Stephen Wall. New York: Penguin, 1970. 250-253.

Tambling, Jeremy. "Prison-Bound: Dickens and Foucault" in *Critical Essays on Charles Dickens's Great Expectations*, ed. Michael Cotsell. Boston: G. K. Hall and Co., 1990.

Van Ghent, Dorothy. *The English Novel: Form and Function*. New York: Harper & Row, 1961.

Wall, Stephen, ed. *Charles Dickens: A Critical Anthology*. New York: Penguin, 1970.

Walsh, Susan. "Bodies of Capital: *Great Expectations* and the Climacteric Economy," *Victorian Studies* 37.1 (1993): 73-98.

Williams, Raymond. *The English Novel from Dickens to Lawrence*. London: Hogarth Press, 1970.

Wilson, Edmund. *The Wound and the Bow: Seven Studies in Literature*. New York: Oxford University Press, 1965.

Worth, George John. *Great Expectations: An Annotated Bibliography*. New York: Garland, 1986.

From Sham to "Gentle Christian Man" in *Great Expectations*

Mary Ann Tobin

Charles Dickens believed that his society wrongly valued economic transactions over natural human interactions, which resulted in a ruinous transference of commercial interests from the public sphere into the private. Among the middle classes, this inhumane, mercantile manner of assigning social status was born, as Walter E. Houghton suggests, from the Victorian "passion for wealth [that] was closely connected with another, for respectability": part and parcel of an "economic struggle . . . focused less on the comforts and luxuries which had hitherto lain beyond their reach than on the respect money could now command" (184). Repeatedly in his novels, Dickens berates his readers for conflating the family home with the counting house in their quests for respectability, whereby human worth is no longer measured by one's capacity for sympathy, affection, and moral integrity, but by one's ability to climb the social ladder through self-interest, artifice, and simple greed.

In *Great Expectations* (1860-1861), Dickens delivers a powerful example of what he feels to be the prime evil of his time: the power of money and its role as a prime indicator of status in the social system. The novel's protagonist, Philip Pirrip, or Pip, rejects his original place in the social system and seeks an entirely new station to which he has no claim other than the size of his pocketbook, over which he has no actual control. In doing so, he eventually learns how to reject snobbery and how to be a "gentle Christian man" who practices what Robert R. Garnett calls "the usual Dickens Virtues" that are "domestic and child-like rather than heroic" (26). Once Pip discovers that his life as a gentleman is a sham, he sees the social system itself as a sham and learns to live in it without sacrificing his integrity. Thus, Dickens insists, even more forcefully than he had done in *David Copperfield* (1849-1850), that true respectability can be found in all levels of society and has less to do with prideful wealth than with humble compassion.

Before he began work on *Great Expectations*, Dickens reread *David Copperfield*, partially in fear of repeating himself in another story of a boy growing into a man (Forster 734). Despite those efforts to avoid duplication, many similarities exist between *Great Expectations* and *David Copperfield* beyond those of plot and theme; the most obvious point of comparison is that both novels are semiautobiographical works in the form of memoirs delivered by first-person narrators. Additionally, both Pip and Copperfield are orphans and consequently lack verifiable social status until they forge their own roles in society as adults. Although the basic plot elements of the bildungsroman—"a novel of all-around self-development" (Hader par. 1)—exist in both novels, Dickens's treatment of Pip's growth into manhood and his search for a place in society is radically different from his treatment of Copperfield. As Robin Gilmour argues, "Pip's story stands in ironic relation to that of David Copperfield, reversing or subverting the motifs of the earlier novel" (*Novel in the Victorian Age* 101). In comparison to Dickens's evident complicity with the social system in *David Copperfield*, in *Great Expectations* Dickens highlights and renounces the prejudices and injustice of that system. For example, Copperfield seeks to regain his birthright to his nonlaboring, middle-class station; in contrast, Pip rejects his laboring-class roots and seeks an entirely new station to which he has no claim beyond his mere expectations of bestowed, not earned or even inherited, wealth. Like Copperfield, Pip tries to live in a manner outside that of his true class; however, whereas Copperfield places great importance on his past history and relationships, Pip takes to it wholeheartedly, completely rejecting the life he had led and the people with whom he had lived. Furthermore, both Copperfield and Pip dream of raising themselves to an even higher social status through marriage, but Copperfield succeeds in marrying Dora Spenlow, while Pip fails either to woo or to win Estella.

Indeed, Pip's failure to marry Estella marks a definitive departure from *David Copperfield*, wherein Dickens complies with social expectations of gentlemanly behavior by rewarding Copperfield for living up to those expectations. For covering up his time in the blacking (shoe polish) factory, Copperfield reaps the rewards of a flourishing career as an author and its subsequent riches, just as his creator had done. Pip, on the other hand, eventually discovers that his life as a gentleman and the social system itself are shams and leaves England altogether. In refusing Pip the fruition of his great expectations, Dickens exposes the potentially disastrous result of distancing oneself from a laboring past and signals his rejection of the social system.

Dickens himself was conflicted about his right to respectability, and many of his characters suffer the strain of not knowing where or how they fit in. Dickens's father, John, was perpetually in debt, which led to Dickens's brief employment in Warren's Blacking Factory at the age of twelve (Ackroyd 69-74). Dickens was so ashamed of having been forced to leave school and do manual labor that he never told anyone in his own family about the incident (1057). After his father's debts were cleared and Dickens grew to manhood, he worked his way up the social ladder, initially applying his skills as a shorthand writer at the various courts of law in London and as a journalist. His nearly overnight success as a fiction writer began with the serialization of *The Pickwick Papers* (1836-1837). No matter how famous or wealthy he became, however, Dickens never truly reconciled his early social setbacks with his later successes. Undoubtedly, this is why he chose to show his heroes and heroines in a similar light, always striving to be respectable while justifying their right to be considered as such. Anny Sadrin notes that *Great Expectations*, in particular, "expresses how difficult it was for Dickens to reconcile the meritocratic ideals of men of his generation and social class and their attachment to more romantic images of success" (70) and "is in many respects Dickens's final and very critical statement on Dickens the novelist as much as on the boy or the man Dickens" (72). In other words, the novel manifests Dickens's inability to mesh the actual and the ideal both within and beyond the pages of a novel.

Pip's tale begins with the chaotic depiction of life at the forge with his ever-watchful sister, referred to only as "Mrs. Joe" or "Mrs. Joe Gargery," and her husband Joe Gargery. Despite being raised "by hand" by Mrs. Joe, Pip seems stoically content in his station because he knows no better—as though he assumes his is the life that all children lead. Upon entering Satis House, however, his views radically change as Miss Havisham and Estella initiate Pip into the rites of class ideologies and abuses, informing him of his inferior class status by calling him "a common laboring-boy" (55). Grahame Smith explains the dynamic of Pip's relationship with Estella: "having inspired him with a sense of his own inferiority, he sees her as the exquisite representation of a higher kind of life" (176). Pip quickly internalizes Estella's opinions about him and the importance of station, bemoaning his state to Joe: "[S]he . . . said I was common, and that I knew I was common, and that I wished I was not common" (65). By accepting Estella as a superior being of sorts, Pip signals his willingness to comply with her ideal social hierarchy both within and without Satis House.

Estella's opinions are quickly reinforced at home, where Mrs. Joe and Mr. Pumblechook discuss Miss Havisham's intentions toward Pip, planting seeds of self-deceit in the boy that will later produce his class prejudices. Only Joe, who as a "gentle Christian man" represents the ideal of unprejudiced morality that supersedes class boundaries, knows the danger involved in filling Pip's head with such fantasy, as well as the perils of the classes mixing so freely. Joe warns, "common ones as to the callings and earnings . . . mightn't be the better of continuing for to keep company with common ones, instead of going out to play with oncommon [sic] ones" (66). Although Joe agrees with Estella on the necessity of separation between the laboring and nonlaboring classes, thus implying complicity in the status quo, his warning proves apt, as Pip will later learn. In this manner, Joe acts as the voice of reason throughout the novel.

Miss Havisham also helps Pip to formulate his class identity, as J. Hillis Miller asserts: "Miss Havisham and her house are the images of a fixed social order, the power which can judge Pip at first as coarse and common, and later as a gentleman" (267). Simply by being brought in to Miss Havisham's home, as dilapidated as it is, Pip grows ashamed of his own humble surroundings at the forge. When Miss Havisham pays for Pip's indentures to be apprenticed to Joe, she unwittingly intensifies that shame by dashing the lad's hopes for something better. Pip no longer considers blacksmithing to be a noble profession, saying, "I had liked it once, but once was not now" (99). Echoing Copperfield's complaints about having to labor for his own upkeep, Pip recalls, "There have been occasions in my later life . . . when I have felt for a time as if a thick curtain had fallen on all its interest and romance, to shut me out from anything save dull endurance any more" (100). Pip sees his indenture to Joe as the end of any hopes he had for a better position in society, as well as his aspirations toward Estella.

Pip's transferring onto Joe his own feelings of inferiority as well as his desires to eradicate their outward appearances signal the young man's first step toward adopting an immoral and inhumane ideal of respectability. Previously, in their joint sufferings under the "tickler" of Mrs. Joe, Pip admitted that he and Joe were "equals," while simultaneously "looking up to Joe in [his] heart" (45). This apparent equality between the comrades changes radically when Joe and Miss Havisham meet for the first time and Pip compares his two guardians in relation to their class, with Estella looking on. Joe appears completely uncomfortable in this new situation, and Pip offers him little aid. He recalls, "I am afraid I was ashamed of the dear good fellow—I *know* I was ashamed of him—when I saw that Estella stood at the back of Miss Havisham's chair, and that her eyes laughed mischievously" (95). Whether Estella is laughing at Joe or at Pip is irrelevant. The fact that she is laughing, and that Pip recognizes the cause and feels ashamed because of it, shows Pip to have completely subscribed to Estella's notions and prejudices of class. Garnett goes one step further, arguing that Pip's "desideratum"—his desire for Estella—"is virtually his identity" (33).

Just as Pip tries to better himself through education, he attempts at various times to improve Joe's manners and appearance in the hope of making the blacksmith more respectable. Pip explains his reasons for doing so rather clearly and unreservedly: "I wanted to make Joe less ignorant and common, that he might be worthier of my society and less open to Estella's reproach" (102). This admission highlights some of the motives driving Pip's desires to improve Joe. First, now that Pip is nominally in the society of the upper classes, he is no longer comfortable around the likes of Joe, who is even more "common" than he is; second, the major impetus of Pip's life is pleasing and winning Estella, not Joe. Therefore, he must adopt her opinions and manners in order to unite with her in class and marriage. He will later make this startlingly evident when he tells Biddy, "I want to be a gentleman on [Estella's] account" (122). This confession illustrates Gilmour's claims that, for the Victorian gentleman-in-the-making, "The impulse to improve oneself was likely to be inspired by social, and even more, sexual ambitions" (*Idea of the Gentleman* 100). For Pip, winning Estella constitutes both a sexual and a social ambition.

Pip's shame over Joe increases with his access to ready cash, which instantly confers a heightened social status—the first indication of which occurs during a conversation with Joe in which Pip bemoans the blacksmith's lack of an education. Pip had hoped to "do something for Joe" but admits, "it would have been much more agreeable if [Joe] had been better qualified for a rise in station" (140). In other words, Pip believes that doing "something for Joe" would be a waste of time and money because Joe lacks the wherewithal to be a proper gentleman, namely wealth. When Pip explains himself to Biddy, the other voice of reason in the novel, she chastises him. Biddy knows, even if Joe will not admit it, that Pip's relationships to the blacksmith and herself must change drastically. Although Pip insists that things will remain the same and that he will always be candid with her, Biddy responds, "Till you're a gentleman" (123). Later, Biddy continues to frustrate Pip with her insistence on calling him "sir" and "Mr. Pip," by which she reminds him of his roots and censures his acquired biases.

Pip's education about how a gentleman should and should not behave begins, appropriately, at school. Michael C. Kotzin argues that Pip's classmate Herbert Pocket can be seen as a "double" for Pip (96). More important, however, Pocket is Pip's example of proper gentlemanly behavior, as Tommy Traddles is for Copperfield. Pocket displays the moral qualities that every true gentleman should possess and actively guides Pip into the proper gentlemanly channels. The most obvious instance occurs during their first dinner together, when Pocket corrects Pip's table manners (169). Aside from the rudiments of genteel eating habits, Herbert continually offers comments and suggestions in regard to Pip's love of Estella. Although Pocket has no claim to a title, he does fit Pip's perceptions of gentlemanly behavior and manners. Thus Pip is willing to accept Pocket's teachings and philosophies, whereas he refuses to take such an education from Joe.

In contrast to Pocket's positive example of the gentleman, Bentley Drummle exhibits those characteristics that Pip must avoid to be considered the gentle Christian man that Dickens envisions. A titled gentleman whose wealthy appearance disguises his immoral and brutal nature, Drummle is described as

> idle, proud, niggardly, reserved and suspicious. He came of rich people . . . who had nursed this combination of qualities until they made the discovery that it was just of age and a blockhead . . . half a dozen heads thicker than most gentlemen. (192)

Having accepted society's definition of respectability, Pip instinctively bows to Drummle's lead as he has done with Estella, and Drummle replaces her as Pip's arbiter of taste. This substitution is evinced in Pip's spending the interval before Joe's visit in "considerable disturbance, some mortification, and a keen sense of incongruity," having "the sharpest sensitiveness as to [Joe's] being seen by Drummle" (206). Earlier, Pip was embarrassed to have Estella see him with Joe; now, he is concerned that Drummle will think less of him for his association with the blacksmith. Moreover, Pip's fear of Drummle's discovering his former, poorer life reflects a social phenomenon among the rising middle classes in the Victorian era. As Walter Houghton describes it, "There were . . . social worries which were inseparable from the ambition to move up the social ladder. Many a self-made man dreaded the fatal exposure of his humble origins or . . . of some dubious cutting of corners on the way up" (61). Just as Dickens feared such discoveries in his own life, so did Pip. Initially, Pip fears only the discovery of being related to a blacksmith, but later he fears the ramifications of having been made a gentleman by a criminal.

Like Herbert Pocket, Abel Magwitch serves as a double—or, more precisely, a foil—for Pip, especially since they share orphan status and opinions of class based on appearances alone, although each reached those conclusions through very different life experiences. Unlike Pip, who has socially sanctioned, respectable role models to follow as he becomes a man, Magwitch comes to his understanding of class the hard way, through victimization at the hands of the escaped convict Compeyson and the legal authorities. Seeking vengeance, Magwitch hopes to live vicariously through Pip the life of luxury that was denied him. While completing his sentence, Magwitch deliberately sets out to "make a gentleman" *for* himself, since he could never *be* one himself. Magwitch explains as much to Pip:

> [I]t was recompense to me . . . to know in secret that I was making a gentleman. The blood horses of them colonists might fling up the dust over me as I was walking; what do I say? I says to myself, "I'm making a better gentleman nor ever you'll be!" When one of 'em says to another, "He was a convict, a few year ago, and is a ignorant common fellow now, for all he's lucky," what do I say? I says to myself, "If I ain't a gentleman, nor yet ain't got no learning, I'm the owner of such. All on you owns stock and land; which on you owns a brought-up London gentleman?" (306)

Magwitch knows that no matter how rich he became during his exile in Australia, he would never be considered a gentleman, because of his lack of education, his criminality, and his outward appearance. He takes pride and pleasure, however, in the accomplishment of taking a low orphan boy from a forge, without rank in his own right, and producing a gentleman by outfitting and educating him properly, that is, by giving Pip what he himself never had. For Carolyn Brown, Magwitch's "displaced desires for gentility make it clear that Pip's wishes are not an isolated and eccentric desire, but a widespread social phenomenon" (69). Similarly, Ewald Mengel sees Magwitch as "a representative of contemporary society as Dickens saw it, because [Magwitch] believes in its materialistic value system, and because his ultimate goal in life is to turn Pip into a gentleman" (191). Magwitch's desire to gain status through Pip is also another reason to consider him as Pip's double, because both desire a status to which they were not originally entitled.

Pip is mortified by Magwitch's confession and is immediately concerned for his position and the inevitable effect of this news on his chances of winning Estella. Pip recalls his reception of the confession: "All the truth of my position came flashing on me; and its disappointments, dangers, disgraces, consequences of all kinds, rushed in" (303). Gilmour argues, "In discovering the sources of his great expectations, Pip discovers the tangled roots from which the artificial class divisions of the nineteenth century have grown" (*Novel in the Victorian Age* 102). Furthermore, Pip knows that if the truth were known, regardless of his appearance and education, he would be an outcast like Magwitch. The possibility of Pip's losing Estella is his first concern; however, his feelings of regret over abandoning Joe become stronger, as well. Pip says, "But, sharpest and deepest pain of all—it was for the convict, guilty of I knew not what crimes, and liable to be taken out of those rooms where I sat thinking, and hanged at the Old Bailey door, that I had deserted Joe" (307-308). Before this discovery, Pip could rationalize his shunning Joe. Now that Pip knows the truth of his situation—that his respectability is a complete sham—he is finally struck with the error of his ways and refuses Magwitch his one wish of seeing his "gentleman spend his money *like* a gentleman" (313). Instead, Pip desires to work for his own keep. However, he is unfit for any specific vocation because, in his own words, he has "been bred to no calling, and [is] fit for nothing" (324). He has become another Bentley Drummle, idle and proud, as the prevailing notion of respectability demands.

Pip's personal social revolution begins with Magwitch's description of his own betrayal by the sham-gentleman Compeyson, which occurred primarily because Magwitch bought into the social constructs of the day and accepted Compeyson on his appearance as the genuine article. Magwitch describes Compeyson as "set up fur a gentleman . . . he'd been to a public boarding-school and had learning. He was a smooth one to talk, and was a dab at the ways of gentlefolks. He was good-looking too" (329). Compeyson was genteel enough not only to fool Magwitch and Miss Havisham, but also to convince a jury of his innocence of the crimes for which Magwitch would be transported (332-333). Here, Dickens warns readers that the appearances they value so highly are untrustworthy and potentially damning.

Over time, Pip comes to recognize Magwitch as a human being with emotions and the right to be treated in a decent, humane manner. However, Pip does not completely transfer the compassion he learned during his own sickness from Joe to Magwitch until the convict is once again arrested, that is, at the point of no return. Pip consoles and holds the convict's hand, realizing his "place henceforth while he lived" was "by Magwitch's side" (456). In establishing his own rightful place in society—one that relies not on cash values but on humane, Christian values—Pip admits,

[M]y repugnance to him had all melted away, and in the hunted wounded shackled creature who held my hand in his, I only saw a man who had meant to be my benefactor, and who had felt affectionately, gratefully, and generously, towards me with great constancy through a series of years. I only saw in him a much better man than I had been to Joe. (423)

This admission demonstrates Pip's ultimate rejection of Drummle's and Miss Havisham's false models of respectability and his internalization of Joe's (and Dickens's) ideal of the gentle Christian man.

With this new understanding of his self-determined role in society, Pip repents his snobbery and wishes to reestablish himself at home, but that desire is frustrated when he discovers that Joe and Biddy have married, in essence having moved on without him. Instead, Pip and Pocket head to India, where their firm allows them a comfortable, but not expansive, income. Pip humbly explains, "I must not leave it to be supposed that we were ever a great House, or that we made mints of money. We were not in a grand way of business, but we had a good name, and worked for our profits, and did very well" (455-456). Now that Pip can see the true value of money and, more important, the benefits of being a self-made man, he can take pride in the fact that he works for his living and is a burden to no one. He can also be comfortable in his new life, having witnessed firsthand the abuses of power and corruption that wealth without work can cause and the fallacy of station based on appearances alone.

Since Pip completely rejects artificial class divisions and no longer subscribes to the belief systems inherent in them, it would seem apt if Pip had nothing whatsoever to do with Estella in his reformed state, since her great social expectations led him down that dangerous path in the first place. Dickens had originally planned such an ending. However, at the suggestion of Edward Bulwer-Lytton, Dickens created a "softer" ending (Ackroyd 902) in which Pip meets Estella on the grounds of Satis House and, at the conclusion of their interview, "saw no shadow of another parting from her" (*Great Expectations* 460). Although it appears that Pip and Estella marry, the phrasing leaves sufficient room for doubt, especially when coupled with the dialogue that appears immediately before the conclusion. Pip says, "We are friends," to which Estella replies, "And will continue friends apart" (460). Taking this exchange into consideration, I believe that they do not marry, but part and never meet again. Such an interpretation suggests that once Pip discovers the sham of both his own and Estella's respectability, they cannot be so easily brought together and live happily ever after, as Mr. and Mrs. Copperfield do.

Copperfield, in fact, marries not once but twice: first he woos and wins Dora Spenlow, who dies an early death; then he marries Agnes and settles down into a comfortable, middle-class life. Both of Copperfield's marriages can be seen as rewards for living up to society's ideals of respectability. More important, at the end of his memoir, Copperfield is a self-made man who regains his birth status by practicing humble compassion and living guilt-free. On the contrary, at the conclusion of Pip's story, he finds little reward beyond personal satisfaction only after he rejects his great expectations along with the class consciousness proffered at Satis House and starts living up to the ideal of Joe, the gentle Christian man who never leaves the forge. Furthermore, Pip becomes acutely aware of the corruption that often accompanies wealth. The possibility of marriage to Estella, then, is a cheat and a sham.

Works Cited

Ackroyd, Peter. *Dickens*. New York: HarperCollins, 1990.

Brown, Carolyn. "'*Great Expectations*': Masculinity and Modernity." *English and Cultural Studies*. Ed. Michael Green. London: Murray, 1987. 40, 60-74.

Dickens, Charles. *David Copperfield*. Oxford: Oxford University Press, 1987.

_____. *Great Expectations*. Oxford: Oxford University Press, 1987.

Forster, John. *The Life of Charles Dickens*. New York: Doubleday, 1928.

Friedman, Stanley. "Estella's Parentage and Pip's Persistence: The Outcome of *Great Expectations*." *Studies in the Novel* 19, no. 4 (1987): 410-421.

Garnett, Robert R. "The Good and the Unruly in *Great Expectations*—and Estella." *Dickens Quarterly* 16, no. 1 (1997): 24-41.

Gilmour, Robin. *The Idea of the Gentleman in the Victorian Novel*. London: Allen & Unwin, 1981.

_____. *The Novel in the Victorian Age: A Modern Introduction*. London: Edward Arnold, 1986.

Hader, Suzanne. "The *Bildungsroman* Genre: *Great Expectations, Aurora Leigh*, and *Waterland*." 1996. *Victorian Web*. 19 September 2008. http://victorian.lang.nagoya-u.ac.jp/victorianweb/genre/hader1.html.

Houghton, Walter E. *The Victorian Frame of Mind, 1830-1870*. 1957. New Haven, CT: Yale University Press, 1985.

Kotzin, Michael C. "Herbert Pocket as Pip's Double." *Dickensian* 79, no. 2 (1983): 95-104.

Mengel, Ewald. "Portrait of the Artist as a Grown Man: Dickens's *Great Expectations* as Autobiographical Fiction." *Proceedings of the Conference of the German Association of University Professors of English.* Tübingen: Max Neimeyer Verlag, 1990. 184-194.

Miller, J. Hillis. *Charles Dickens: The World of His Novels.* Cambridge: Harvard University Press, 1958.

Sadrin, Anny. "The Trappings of Romance in *Jane Eyre* and *Great Expectations.*" *Dickens Quarterly* 14, no. 2 (1997): 69-91.

Smith, Grahame. *Dickens, Money, and Society.* Berkeley: University of California Press, 1968.

Van Ghent, Dorothy. *The English Novel: Form and Function.* New York: Harper-Torchbook, 1961.

CRITICAL
READINGS

Stories Present and Absent in
*Great Expectations*_____

I

In the plethora of criticism on *Great Expectations* one central issue, although it has been recognized and referred to implicitly by many critics, has not yet been discussed substantially: the problem of authorship. By author I mean not the actual writer of the novel but the one "implied" in the text, an entity quite different from the real author.[1] For Pip, as for David Copperfield, the novel is a kind of autobiography or memoir. But when the peculiar narrative situation in *Great Expectations* is considered the other way round, from the side of the narrated story, it seems to present Pip's "authorship" as something hollow and void. If one takes the enigma of Pip's secret benefactor to be the central axis of the novel, as it indeed is, it is clear that the author of the story is not Pip but Magwitch, who has been devising, plotting, and writing Pip's story. Magwitch is a character representing the double meaning of "author": the writer and the father.[2] He is both the author of Pip's story and the father who has secretly adopted him as his son, begetter of the text and its hero at the same time. Thus the central axis of the novel poses the problem of authorship, providing a clue to other layers of the novel where story and its authors stand in ambiguous and sometimes quite incompatible relationships with each other. When Pip, urged by some inner compulsion, strives to write the story of his own life, just as David had done before him, his pen constantly fails him; for, as he writes, the written text slips out of his hand and is instantly transformed into stories written by strange authors. The problem of authorship is in fact the problem of writing or the failure of writing.[3] Pip fails to write his life story; the novel is never to be written by this "author." As Magwitch's writing of Pip's story suggests, Pip can never be the writer nor the independent hero of his own story; rather, the novel is structured around the central story of Pip as written by Magwitch, with

---

other stories, also of Pip, encircling this central axis. Just as the Magwitch story destroys all Pip's false hopes, decomposes itself, the structure of these stories in the novel is to be seen as a self-destroying process, an unwriting, a structure that is nonstructure. Because the stories of Pip are always written by other authors, they collapse by their alienation from the hero. Pip, always a passive object to be written, fails to be the "hero of my own life": unlike David Copperfield, he fails to be the novelist, the writer of his own life story. But when presence of stories gives way to absence of stories, a story that is absent in *Great Expectations* emerges whose absence will guide us to the innermost depth of Pip's failed narrative. It is this structure of presence and absence, of author and story, that I would like to elucidate in the following argument.

II

Poetics of narrative fiction is perhaps the facet of literary studies that has profited most from the structuralist enterprise. Although such rigorously structuralist systems as Genette's *Narrative Discourse* or Todorov's *Poetics of Prose* will come to be seen with some misgivings in the wake of deconstruction, there is no doubt that they have clarified the workings of a fictional text and supplied useful terms and concepts for the discussions of narrative fiction. Among the most fundamental and useful of concepts is the distinction between "story" and "plot" bequeathed by the Russian Formalists. Here story means "the story in its most neutral, objective, chronological form—the story as it might have been enacted in real time and space, a seamless continuum of innumerable contiguous events" and plot is "the actual text in which this story is imitated, with all its inevitable (but motivated) gaps, elisions, emphases and distortions."[4] As this definition indicates, story is the hypothetical construct that could be reassembled and arranged in chronological order from the often confused texture of actual narrative, with a beginning, a middle and an end neatly arranged as a completed whole.

It is an assumed primal text or metatext that the reading process recovers and reconstructs, though the paradox is that it is to be recuperated *a posteriori*, only after the plot is worked out in narrative fiction. Of the two aspects that comprise narrative it is plot that has generally been the object of aesthetic studies since plot is what a novelist actually writes and is primarily present to the reader. Thus studies of the basic structure of *Great Expectations* have been concerned mainly with its plot.[5] In a recent and important essay, for example, Peter Brooks describes the novel as "concerned with finding a plot and losing it, with the precipitation of plottedness around its hero, and his eventual 'cure' from plot" (Brooks uses the word "plot" in a somewhat different sense from the one defined above as he considers it "not only design but intentionality as well").[6] Without questioning the validity of studies of plot, however, I would like to call attention to the presence—indeed the predominance—of *story* in the novel. Story, normally reconstructed almost as an afterthought from the actual narrative text, is in *Great Expectations* a presence *a priori*. It is already there, written by some writer other than the hero-narrator Pip, with its beginning, middle and end all complete even before the plot begins. My description of the novel would be that Pip does not find any plot but that story finds and traps him, plot as intentionality remaining always outside him. He is not "cured" from plot; story or stories collapse and become absent, leaving him in the vacuum created by this absence.

That intentionality is outside Pip, that he is not the writer of his own story, is indicated in the novel's opening scene, in which he is a being poised in the space of ontogenetic ambiguity with an insignificant monosyllable for a name. His actual name is given in the text only as an appellation designated his by some alien agency: "I give Pirrip as my father's family name on the authority of his tombstone. . . ."[7] Here the double meaning of author as father and writer as well as the pure textuality of Pip's existence come to the fore. Pip's father is dead, he has become a text, the inscription on the tombstone that locates Pip in a fixed space-time; and the contours of Pip's being begin to flesh out only after this textual location. He takes his being from the text of his absent father, whose authority is symbolically represented by Magwitch who starts up, like an apparition of the real father, "from among the graves at the side of the church porch" (2). Magwitch establishes complete control over the terrified child immediately; he turns him upside down, threatens him with cannibalism (". . . what fat cheeks you ha' got. . . . Darn Me if I couldn't eat em"), orders him to bring a file and "wittles," and extracts a pledge of strict silence. Thus, from the very beginning, Pip becomes involved in the world of criminality where crime, guilt and bad faith torment him. Though this criminality is to be the primal text in which he is caught, we would be mistaken to regard Pip as a guilty being who carries the burden of some transcendental original sin. The guilt here does not belong to him; it is something that is imposed upon him by outside authority. The helpless orphan boy is placed in an atmosphere of criminality by a force over which he has no control.

The otherness of the taint of criminality in Pip, the alienation of essence from being, is manifest in the fact that he is always regarded as a boy with criminal propensities by the adults around him who, like Magwitch, have incontestable authority over him. These adults are possessed with the idea that the young are "naterally wicious," Pip especially so. With this preconception they treat him as if his life were already written and finished as a story, the plot of which Pip is going to follow as a predestined, assigned path. As authors of the story of Pip's criminal career, Wopsle and Pumblechook are more adept in writing stories than Mrs. Joe, who uses only her hand and occasional applications of the Tickler. For example, at the Christmas dinner at Joe's house, they are quite aware of the nature of the novel's semiotic universe, in which one can write a story even in a word:

Mr Pumblechook added, after a short interval of reflection, 'Look at Pork alone. There's a subject! If you want a subject, look at Pork!'

'True, sir. Many a moral for the young,' returned Mr Wopsle; and I knew he was going to lug me in, before he said it; 'might be deduced from that text.'

('You listen to this,' said my sister to me, in a severe parenthesis.)

Joe gave me some more gravy.

'Swine,' pursued Mr Wopsle, in his deepest voice, and pointing his fork at my blushes, as if he were mentioning my christian name; 'Swine were the companions of the prodigal. The gluttony of Swine is put before us, as an example to the young.' (I thought this pretty well in him who had been praising up the pork for being so plump and juicy.) 'What is detestable in a pig, is more detestable in a boy.' (57-8)

Here a seemingly innocent word "pork" undergoes radical transformations with an ever increasing semantic density. What is merely a thing to be eaten becomes a "text" and the biblical reference brings forth "swine," with its connotations of gluttony and sensuality, and "prodigal," inevitably associated with the story of the Prodigal Son.[8] Thus a sign, a word, is transformed into a story, a finished tale with a beginning, a middle and an end, which becomes a story of Pip as Pumblechook immediately transforms Pip into Swine with his pompous authority: "If you'd been born a Squeaker . . . would you have been here now? Not you. . . . You would have been disposed of for so many shillings according to the market price of the article, and Dunstable the butcher would have come up to you as you lay in your straw, and he would have whipped you under his left arm, and with his right he would have tucked up his frock to get a penknife from out of his waistcoat pocket, and he would have shed your blood and had your life" (58). The story of Pip the Prodigal Son is thus present, written by these authors, even before any plot development could be introduced.

The story written by Wopsle and Pumblechook may seem an incomplete realization of the story of Pip the Criminal since the story of the

Prodigal Son does not include any criminal act, though, of course, the son is guilty of a moral crime against his father. Pumblechook's reference to the butchering of Pip the Swine, however, recalls the gallows and the execution of criminals. In the popular tradition, a story depicting the life of a criminal ends in his execution or suicide. Dickens, who had an avowed interest in crime and criminals, faithfully follows this tradition. Bill Sykes, Ralph Nickleby, Jonas Chuzzlewit and Mr Merdle all meet violent deaths at the end of their careers of crime. Pip's story as written by Pumblechook and Wopsle must also include the hero's death in total misery and wretchedness as the morally plausible outcome of a criminal life. The story will become complete when a plot that will realize it in a particular circumstantial context is established. For Wopsle and Pumblechook, there is no need to work out the story in all its squalid details since they have only to choose a text that fits into the prescribed pattern from the stock-in-trade of the popular criminal literature. Wopsle discovers a pertinent text in a bookshop: "the affecting tragedy of George Barnwell," George Lillo's *The London Merchant*. As it is his inevitable fate to come across authoritarian figures, Pip is seized by Wopsle in the street and made to listen to the recitation of the drama in the Pumblechookian parlor. The story of George Barnwell who, seduced by a harlot called Millwood, robbed his master and murdered his uncle, so alien to the innocent child, is turned into the story of Pip the Criminal. The transformation is so complete that Pip speaks of Barnwell as himself:

> What stung me, was the identification of the whole affair with my unoffending self. When Barnwell began to go wrong, I declare that I felt positively apologetic, Pumblechook's indignant stare so taxed me with it. Wopsle, too, took pains to present me in the worst light. At once ferocious and maudlin, I was made to murder my uncle with no extenuating circumstances whatever; Millwood put me down in argument, on every occasion; it became sheer monomania in my master's daughter to care a button for me; and all I can say for my gasping and procrastinating conduct on the fa-

tal morning, is, that it was worthy of the general feebleness of my character. Even after I was happily hanged and Wopsle had closed the book, Pumblechook sat staring at me, and shaking his head, and saying, 'Take warning, boy, take warning!' as if it were a well-known fact that I contemplated murdering a near relation, provided I could only induce one to have the weakness to become my benefactor. (145)

Identified with Barnwell, it is only natural that Pip believes he "must have had some hand in the attack upon my sister" that happened just at the time. Orlick is wrong, however, to see Pip's guiltiness here as metaphysical ("It was you as did for your shrew sister"),[9] because the Pip who feels guilt is the Pip defined by Pumblechook and Wopsle and written into the story of Pip the Criminal, not the actual Pip who is perfectly innocent. As he is not the author of the story of Barnwell, begetter of the criminal Pip, he has no authority even over the feelings he has or the narrator says that he has. He feels guilt only because subjectivity, the "I," has become unstable, because the story of Barnwell, which actually can never be the story of Pip, envelops him.

III

But George Barnwell, for all his difference from Pip, shares a significant factor with him. When criminality is removed from the story of Barnwell, it comes nearer to Pip's story: they are both apprentices torn by agonizing desire for a worthless woman. Here again, as in the case of "pork," the word "apprentice" contains in it a complete story (or stories) that is present *a priori*, before plot is conceived and actualized. Moreover, the Barnwell story is only one aspect of a dualistic structure. There is another side, a positive story paired with the dark, negative story of the criminal apprentice. The duality of the apprentice story is best exemplified in William Hogarth's series of engravings *Industry and Idleness*, by which Dickens was no doubt greatly influenced.[10] Hogarth presents two apprentices whose contrasting careers have almost exact parallels in the apprentice stories in *Great Expectations*. The story of the Industrious Apprentice, modeled on the legend of Dick Whittington, presents Francis Goodchild, who gains his master's confidence through his industry and honesty. He becomes partner in his master's business, marries his master's daughter, and finally attains the highest rung of the middle-class social ladder by becoming the Lord Mayor of London. The Idle Apprentice, Tom Idle, modeled apparently on George Barnwell (who had been a subject of popular ballads as early as the second half of the seventeenth century[11]) goes astray through his idleness and association with bad companions. Committing one crime after another, he is betrayed by his whore, arrested and brought before Goodchild who as magistrate must condemn him. Tom Idle is finally executed at Tyburn. For Dickens the dual story of the apprentice was the source of many characters and stories. The good apprentice appears as such heroes as Oliver Twist, Walter Gay, and in the references to Dick Whittington in *Dombey and Son* and *Barnaby Rudge* that indicate their origin.[12] The idle apprentice is presented in those villains who obstruct the hero's progress in life; Noah Claypole in *Oliver Twist*, Simon Tappertit in *Barnaby Rudge*, Uriah Heep in *David Copperfield* and Dolge Orlick in *Great Expectations* are typical examples. Again the explicit references to George Barnwell in *Barnaby Rudge* and *Great Expectations* reveal the origin of this recurring type.[13] For Dickens, to be an apprentice is to choose between the two poles of a story, each of which will lead to a course of life fundamentally incompatible with the other. But the uniqueness of *Great Expectations* among Dickens's novels consists in the fact that these two poles have been combined into one. For, if we follow the argument of critics like Julian Moynahan, the bad apprentice, Orlick, might be a psychological double, an alter ego, of Pip the good apprentice.[14] But, in Orlick's view at least, the disparity between the two is very marked because, as he tells Pip in the lime-kiln, Pip was the favored, petted one who was always in Orlick's way; Pip, according to him, even came between him and "a young woman" he liked (435). Pip will succeed Joe

Critical Insights

some day in his profession and marry Biddy, frustrating all the expectations of the other apprentice. While the story of the criminal apprentice has been written by other authors, the story of the good apprentice Orlick describes might be the one that Pip can virtually be author and hero of. However much he deviates from the path of honesty, no one can deny his innate goodness, and as a Dickens hero he has qualifications enough to be another Francis Goodchild.

In fact, to pursue the course of the Industrious Apprentice, to live the story of Goodchild, is undoubtedly the life most natural to Pip. He is accustomed to the life at the forge and to his master Joe, who is both a father and best friend to him. With his unfailing goodness and kindness Joe will be an ideal master and companion to the orphan boy. Joe himself looks forward with genuine delight and expectation to the day when Pip will be his apprentice; he tells Pip that when Pip is apprentice to him, "regularly bound," they will "have such Larks! . . ." (48). For Pip, however, this natural state of life, the life of an apprentice to Joe, is suddenly transformed into something strange and unnatural, a story written by an alien hand, in Satis House.

The encounter with Miss Havisham is of great importance in Pip's life because she is expected to be the donor of both wealth and the beautiful maiden. But the encounter with Estella carries far greater weight, not only for the hero but for the overall structure of the novel. Estella is not only—and melodramatically—Magwitch's daughter, but she also plays a role essentially identical with her father's, the role of an author with dictatorial authority over his subject. Magwitch, as we know, is the anonymous author of Pip's fortunes; Estella also drastically changes the meaning of life for Pip when, with queenly disdain and cruelty, she ridicules his low birth and commonness. Pip, who has lived (albeit not very happily) with serenity and modest hopes, is compelled by Estella to look at his existence from an entirely new angle. Playing "beggar my neighbour" with her, he is called "a common labouring-boy"; his language, his limbs and his attire all become the objects of her spiteful attacks:

'He calls the knaves, Jacks, this boy!' said Estella with disdain, before our first game was out. 'And what coarse hands he has! And what thick boots!'

I had never thought of being ashamed of my hands before; but I began to consider them a very indifferent pair. Her contempt for me was so strong, that it became infectious, and I caught it.

She won the game, and I dealt. I misdealt, as was only natural, when I knew she was lying in wait for me to do wrong; and she denounced me for a stupid, clumsy, labouring-boy. (90)

As Pip cannot be anything other than a future blacksmith, Estella's ridicule is directed against that state of existence which is most natural to him. A blacksmith's hands are coarse and black from work, the thickness of his boots is proper in the forge, and his language, as Joe demonstrates, is often capable of sustained dignity. There is no need for Pip to be ashamed of himself in front of this spoilt and proud girl. But he smarts, smarts terribly, because Estella, who is the erotic symbol of the great expectations, is not only proud but very beautiful; by virtue of her beauty she has power, irresistible authority over him. Pip is caught less in the magic web of Miss Havisham than in the text of an apprentice story that becomes thralldom not because of the class system but because Estella has rewritten the natural state of Pip's existence into a story alienated from himself. Suddenly his hands and boots, which have "never troubled" him before, do trouble him; now he is "much more ignorant than" he has considered himself so far and is "in a low-lived bad way" (94). Thus Estella becomes the author of the story of Pip the Apprentice which, though a presence from the beginning of the novel, becomes a hollowness, an absence when Pip, trapped in Estella's authority, becomes aware of his alienation from it. It is a story written and imposed upon him by others, by the social system or by Estella, a story he himself can never be the author of. But Pip has been caught in this story from the beginning. There is no way out; he is tightly "bound" there by society and its institutions. Here the contrasting stories of Tom Idle and Francis Goodchild are synthesized through the catalyst of the hero's alienation; he is alienated from both aspects of the dualism. When the time comes for Pip to be apprenticed to Joe, it is no longer the moment of fulfillment, the moment of "larks," but the moment of execution in which to be bound apprentice is tantamount to being bound in the halter:

> The Justices were sitting in the Town Hall near at hand, and we at once went over to have me bound apprentice to Joe in the Magisterial presence. I say, we went over, but I was pushed over by Pumblechook, exactly as if I had that moment picked a pocket or fired a rick; indeed, it was the general impression in Court that I had been taken red-handed, for, as Pumblechook shoved me before him through the crowd, I heard some people say, 'What's he done?' and others, 'He's a young 'un, too, but looks bad, don't he?' One person of mild and benevolent aspect even gave me a tract ornamented with a woodcut of a malevolent young man fitted up with a perfect sausage-shop of fetters, and entitled, TO BE READ IN MY CELL.
>
> The Hall was a queer place, I thought, with higher pews in it than a church. . . . Here, in a corner, my indentures were duly signed and attested, and I was 'bound,' Mr Pumblechook holding me all the while as if we had looked in on our way to the scaffold, to have those little preliminaries disposed of. (132-33)

It is quite fitting that Pumblechook, the prime author of the story of Pip the Criminal, is present as custodian in the scene where Pip is "bound" in the story of Pip the Apprentice, a story now no more his own than the story of George Barnwell. Pip reflects: "I . . . had a strong conviction on me that I should never like Joe's trade. I had liked it once, but once was not now" (134).

IV

After three years of apprenticeship to Joe, during which Pip works at the forge with forced industry much "against the grain," nursing deep dissatisfaction, anguish and burning passion for Estella in his bosom, Jaggers, the dark lawyer, comes to him with the "great expectations," the gift from an anonymous benefactor. The gift lifts Pip out of the apprentice story and, this time with his willing acceptance, places him in another story, the story of *Great Expectations*. Harry Stone and Shirley Grob, among others, have pointed out the strong presence of the fairy tale in *Great Expectations*. Viewed as a structuring principle, the fairy tale provides the basic materials of this new story in which Pip is henceforth to live.[15] Miss Havisham may be regarded as the fairy godmother, Estella as the beautiful princess, and Jaggers as the wizard who looks sinister at first but will prove, perhaps, benevolent in the end. The hero is Pip, of course, the knight errant who will rescue the princess caught in the magic castle, Satis House. As this arrangement of basic elements suggests, the story of *Great Expectations* has its origin in and follows, or seems to follow, the pivotal plot of a fairy tale that could be identified with one from the stock of traditional tales. Shirley Grob mentions "The Golden Goose" as the typical example of the primitive form of fairy tale that Dickens uses with pointed irony. However, with regard to Satis House and its inhabitants, "Sleeping Beauty," as Harry Stone suggests, is the fundamental text for the story of *Great Expectations*. Because of some fatal incident that occurred long ago Satis House set itself outside the flow of time and, making barriers to protect itself from the intrusion of outside forces, has slumbered in a timeless world. As Pip noticed when he first visited this strange place, the house "had a great many iron bars to it"; windows were walled up or rustily barred, and even the courtyard was barred (84-85). There in the darkness Miss Havisham lives in the wedding dress she has worn since the fatal wedding day, stopping all the clocks at twenty minutes to nine, forever living in that moment when her heart was broken, but also perhaps sleeping forever in full outfit to receive the bridegroom who will never come. Time, with cruel disregard for her determination, has ravaged her body and dress but the decayed Sleeping Beauty is now replaced by a budding new one, Estella, whose coldness and remoteness suggest to Pip that she also is in a state of slumber, from which he as her knight hopes one day to arouse her. Pip imagines himself to be the hero of this romance of expectations—a significant departure from the apprentice stories. George Barnwell and Dick Whittington were roles Pip was made to play; their stories were grounded in a void that was to bring about their own undoing. In the fairy tale, however, Pip feels comfortably at home because the tale not only offers salvation from alien stories but also promises to fill the void engendered in Satis House, to satisfy the want, the horrible sense of deprivation he experienced at Estella's taunts. It is a story that he constructs for himself, building his groundless dreams about Miss Havisham and Estella. Circumstances, full of "attractive mystery," have eloquently contributed to this false construction. But even in this fairy tale world, can Pip actually be the hero? Is his construction of this story wholly independent of those outside forces that have kept him, "bound" him in the written text from the start?

The author of a story, the author in the sense we have been using it, is someone who maintains definitive authority over his creation, who determines and directs the course of action or plot of the story. The author of the fairy tale "Sleeping Beauty" can be identified with a character who, though no hero or heroine, is in complete possession of the destinies of heroes and heroines: the witch or fairy godmother. The fairy godmother is decisively important in the construction of the hero's or heroine's story, as is evident in "Sleeping Beauty." She is a prophetess, a visionary who foresees and determines the future. The hero or heroine, perfectly under her control, has virtually no freedom in choosing his course of action in the story. Despite all the precautions taken to keep her away from any spindle, the princess wounds herself on one, falling into a sleep of a hundred years and her sleep, however long and profound it may be, is instantly broken by a kiss from the prince. In Pip's version of "Sleeping Beauty," Miss Havisham, the fairy godmother, has decided and prescribed the destiny of the hero Pip in a way that is absolute and unchangeable. Neither wealth nor beauty is in Pip's power to achieve; they are things given, bestowed by the fairy god-mother whose will functions as the inevitable logic in the fairy tale structure. Thus Pip is deluded; since he has no power to create his life story, he can never be its real hero, the hero as author. Although he believes that in this dream world he has finally found a place congenial to his needs, he is still caught in a text written by a hand other than his. Pip remains a reader of texts. Max Byrd identifies "reading" as the crucial, pervading theme in the novel and points out that Pip, through his unreasonable, incorrect reading of texts, creates a fiction that tends to enclose him, "to transform him into a monomaniac: he begins to believe the fiction to be truth, indeed, the whole truth."[16] The story of *Great Expectations* is the most inclusive of those fictions Pip has built by reading others' texts and in which he finds himself enclosed.

However, this fiction proves to be fictional in a double sense: it is, as we know, a fiction that Pip constructs with the aid of a heavy reliance on circumstances rather than on concrete evidence, and it is a fiction whose author turns out to be the wrong one. The abnormality, timelessness and madness associated with Miss Havisham has made Pip believe that the fairy godmother cannot possibly be any other person in his book of fairies. Yet Mr Jaggers's initial announcement to him that the name of his "liberal benefactor remains a profound secret, until the person chooses to reveal it" (165), indicates that the "expectations" of this unfinished story are pointed expressly toward the future revelation of authorship. In the awaited denouement the fairy godmother reveals herself to be not Miss Havisham, not even a female, but the convict Abel Magwitch, who declares himself to be Pip's "second father" (337). The unmasking of the author/father instantly undoes the fairy tale, destroys its mirage, and transforms it into a hollowness, an absence: "Miss Havisham's intentions towards me, all a mere dream; Estella not designed for me; I only suffered in Satis House as a convenience, a sting for the greedy relations, a model with a mechanical heart to practice on when no other practice was at hand" (341). After the destruction of his dream Pip cannot attain wealth and gentleman's status with Magwitch's money, though it has been honestly earned by the transported convict, because the book Magwitch has written is utterly incompatible with his inner needs and desires, and also, because in the world of sober realities Pip regains his natural goodness of heart.

V

When the novel's central axis breaks down and the pivotal story of *Great Expectations* becomes absent, what are we left with? Is it only "the impression of a life that has outlived plot, renounced plot, been cured of it"[17] that we have here? But neither plot nor stories have yet been exhausted. Before arriving at the sense of a life "that is left over" we have to consider the moral framework in which Pip seems to remain even after the breakdown of the central story.

If the final meaning of the novel, the sum total of all its processes and plot workings, is the moral theme and the wisdom gained by the hero in his life story, *Great Expectations* manifests the moral orientation of the "great tradition" rather starkly, as a simple moral of the sort appended to fables and "moral tales." For the novel might be taken to be, as Edgar Rosenberg suggests, "a cautionary tale about an engaging, slightly contaminated young man whose head has been turned by his unwarranted expectations, who, confronted by the actualities of his situation, experiences a change of heart, and in the end gets more or less what he deserves."[18] Rosenberg's summary seems an exact description of the kind of moral tale the novel is, an amalgamation of the dual story of Hogarth's apprentices. Pip discards the simple life of apprenticeship because of his infatuation with a foolish dream and, becoming morally degenerate as a result, finally loses everything. Bewitched by a worthless woman, he throws away his true friend Joe and his sweetheart Biddy, and incurs just punishment. When he goes back to Joe's forge to propose to Biddy, having finally recognized his own folly after the deaths of Miss Havisham and Magwitch, he finds that Joe has just married her. Thus Pip, the penitent Idle Apprentice, exiles himself from

England to work as an industrious clerk at Clarriker and Co. for eleven years.

If we were to take this moral fable, the cautionary tale, as it is, Pip's return to the forge and his marriage to Biddy would be his return to and recovery of the story in which he can truly be the hero, the story to be reinstated after the breakdown of all the other, false, stories. Surely the moral framework of the novel seems to call for this as the norm from which Pip has deviated. Accepting the moral theme unreservedly, Forster and Bernard Shaw, and many critics following their lead, have voiced objections to the altered ending of the novel.[19] The hero who has gone astray from the path of honesty should be justly punished, whereas the happy (if equally sad) ending allows him to be united with Estella, the evil and worthless *femme fatale*. The critics claim that the revision is a falsification of the moral meaning of the story that does less than justice to the total moral framework that has been so carefully and expertly constructed. But is the cautionary tale really Pip's true story if he withdraws from it with a feeling not of despair but of relief and gratitude? Upon recovering from the first shock of the news of Biddy's marriage to Joe, Pip feels "great thankfulness that" he has "never breathed this last baffled hope to Joe." Thanking his good fortune in not disclosing his intention, thanking Joe and Biddy for all they have done for him and all he has "so ill repaid," asking forgiveness of both, he leaves them to go abroad (487-88). Why is the feeling of relief and gratitude predominant in the final crisis of Pip's life? It may be explained, as Milton Millhauser suggests, in terms of the insurmountable disparity between the state of the village blacksmith and that of the urban gentleman Pip has now become; for Pip, it is both impossible and actually impracticable to return again to Joe's class after his experiences in the upper sphere.[20] However, his feeling of relief and gratitude may also be explained in terms of the fundamental structure of the novel we have been discussing, the structure of stories constructed and destroyed, of presence made into absence. Pip feels relief because, the place of hero being justly occupied by Joe, he does not have to go back again to a story that is not his own. The story of Pip the Apprentice is alien to him, written by a hand other than his; it is quite unnatural for him to return to it. Or to put it otherwise, it is only too natural for an apprentice gone astray to go back with a penitent heart, after wandering and hardship, to the place where he naturally belongs. This would be to follow the moral pattern too neatly, to conform to the logical sequence of artificial moral fables. Instead, the final moral meaning that the novel offers suggests its own hollowness and falsity by being too neat and logical a construction. Moreover, according to the other forces at work in the novel, it is quite likely to be destroyed by its own artificiality. Why is this so? Why are natural outcome and logical sequence denied here? When even the moral fable that seemed to be the ultimate story present in *Great Expectations* is undone by the hero's withdrawal from it at the last moment, we are directed to the novel's deepest stratum.

VI

If Pip had been a character who acts and behaves according to the dictates of reason, the ending neatly and logically ordered would have been naturally his. But it is precisely at this point that logic fails because if he had been such a character, he would not have deviated from the path of the Industrious Apprentice in the first place; it would have been simply impossible for him to err so flagrantly in his choices. Actually Pip has always been a character motivated and compelled by a force to which reason, logic and morality are utter strangers. Because of this, the logical and moral outcome finally eludes him; the teleological drive in the text rejects him at the last moment. The character who symbolizes this demonic impulse in Pip is Estella. It is a strange neglect among the criticism and commentary on the novel that Estella has not received the critical attention she deserves as a character who controls Pip's life in a more profound way than even Miss Havisham or Magwitch. It is true that Estella is the novel's least realized character;

her frigidity and remoteness throughout give an impression of unreality and when her heart melts at the last meeting with Pip, it is unconvincing. She appears infrequently, providing the reader with few chances of penetrating into her inner self even to find the void there. However, Estella's influence on Pip is inordinately great compared with the scarcity of her characterization. As I indicated earlier, Estella transforms Pip's natural state of existence into a story alienated from him. Because of her strong sexual attraction a "poor dream," the desire of becoming a gentleman, is engendered in him. If apprenticeship is the norm, the moral standard, to which Pip should finally return, Estella must be regarded as the character of decisive importance because she first disrupts that standard.

While the critical censure of Pip's infatuation with Estella is valid, before making judgments too facile to be worth making, we must notice that Pip himself has been quite aware of the madness and foolishness of his passion for Estella from the start. He has already passed a forcible verdict on his own conduct when, as a young boy, he confesses to Biddy his desperate passion for another girl. Biddy asks him who it was that told him he was coarse and common and Pip, compelled by uncontrollable impulse, replies:

> 'The beautiful young lady at Miss Havisham's, and she's more beautiful than anybody ever was, and I admire her dreadfully, and I want to be a gentleman on her account.' Having made this lunatic confession, I began to throw my torn-up grass into the river, as if I had some thoughts of following it.
>
> 'Do you want to be a gentleman, to spite her or to gain her over?' Biddy quietly asked me, after a pause.
>
> 'I don't know,' I moodily answered.
>
> 'Because, if it is to spite her,' Biddy pursued, 'I should think—but you know best—that might be better and more independently done by caring nothing for her words. And if it is to gain her over, I should think—but you know best—she was not worth gaining over.'

Exactly what I myself had thought, many times. Exactly what was perfectly manifest to me at the moment. But how could I, a poor dazed village lad, avoid that wonderful inconsistency into which the best and wisest of men fall every day?

'It may be all quite true,' said I to Biddy, 'but I admire her dreadfully.'

In short, I turned over on my face when I came to that, and got a good grasp on the hair on each side of my head, and wrenched it well. All the while knowing the madness of my heart to be so very mad and misplaced, that I was quite conscious it would have served my face right, if I had lifted it up by my hair, and knocked it against the pebbles as a punishment for belonging to such an idiot. (156)

Here Biddy's is the voice of the moral guide, the teacher she has always been to Pip, the voice of reason and common sense. Her judgment of Estella is absolutely and impeccably right. Pip cannot by any means contradict her since he himself has seen the truth already. But what we hear as the truth transcending the truth of reason and common sense is Pip's, or rather the narrator's voice remembering that hopeless passion which seized the boy, "that wonderful inconsistency into which the best and wisest of men fall every day." What reason and common sense tell him "may be all quite true," it is "exactly what was perfectly manifest" to him at the moment; yet, all these manifest truths notwithstanding, he loves her "dreadfully." Moreover, in the desolation of his heart, Pip is quite aware of his folly, of how "mad and misplaced" his passion for Estella is. Yet he loves her simply because he "found her irresistible." He knew he "loved her against reason, against promise, against peace, against hope, against happiness, against all discouragement that could be" even when he was misled into believing that Miss Havisham had reserved Estella for him (253-54). In spite of the voice of reason, which is also his inner voice, in spite of Estella's warnings to him, in spite of Herbert's friendly admonition, he goes on loving her. His passion has already gone beyond the pale of rationality; Biddy admits, while teaching him, that Pip has "got beyond her" and her lesson is "of no use now" (157). When passion has taken such complete hold, it is no longer possible for either outside or inside voices to have any influence, since the passion has already become a part of the essential being. Pip's mad passion is his life: "it was impossible for me to separate her, in the past or in the present, from the innermost life of my life" (257). He declares to her, not in a high-flown romantic confession of love but in a painful farewell: "You are part of my existence, part of myself. . . . Estella, to the last hour of my life, you cannot choose but remain part of my character, part of the little good in me, part of the evil" (378). For better or worse, Estella has been, in a sense, Pip himself. Thus the rational outcome, the logical ending of the moral fable, eludes him simply because of its rationality, naturalness and morality. The system of the fable as a completed whole entailing ordered chronology and an overriding logos or reason is alien to Pip because his true identity lies where such systems or stories are disrupted by impulses springing from the innermost depth of his psyche. After the destruction of all the stories, Pip's unquenchable passion remains impermeable to that dissociating force at work in the novel.

Pip fails, however, to write his own story, the one faithfully following his irrational love for Estella. He fails because Pip and Estella have been enclosed in the texts and stories written by others. Pip has been a subject to be written by Pumblechook, Magwitch and others, Estella a subject in Miss Havisham's writing of the story of revenge upon men in general. Or to advance our argument a step further, they have been enclosed in the text of *Great Expectations*, in Dickens's novels, which are enclosed again in the context of the nineteenth-century English novel. It was imperative for Dickens's novels to conform to the traditional framework, a plot structure dependent on moral teleology and the closed system of the novel. The disturbing, irrational depths of human beings had to be tamed and explained away in the unfolding of the moral plot so that the reading public and the dominant social order would not be offended. Yet the self-destroying structure of *Great Expectations* finally reveals the centrality of Pip's irrational passion for

Estella, an instance of the irrationality, of the nonconformity to any systematizing, persistently felt in Dickens's novels. Dickens often presented irrational passion, madness and violence capable of breaking through the closure of the novel system, beginning with some of the interpolated tales in *The Pickwick Papers* and pursued in the murderous impulses of Sykes and Jonas Chuzzlewit in *Oliver Twist* and *Martin Chuzzlewit*, in the perverted sensuality of Quilp in *The Old Curiosity Shop*, in the lunacy and wild violence of *Barnaby Rudge* and *The Tale of Two Cities*. Though these passions are treated always in the melodramatic mode, they often go beyond the merely sensational as is evident in the mob violence in the two historical novels and in the psychological agony of Bill Sykes that was Dickens's own nemesis. This irrationality is profoundly dangerous as it tends to destroy the traditional story on which Dickens's plot is always modeled and, at the same time, puts the concepts of fiction and its closure into doubt. Writing can be a dangerous act when it is influenced by this subversive force. The writing of *Great Expectations* accomplishes just that dangerous act, an act of unwriting in which the stories present at all levels in the novel are continuously vacated by the very act of writing.

Thus Dickens's novels are fundamentally different from other multiplot novels of the Victorian era. In Dickens the multiplicity of plots may be replaced by multiplicity of stories, yet this multi-storied structure is always threatened with disintegration. The formula of the polyphonic novel, which Mikhail Bakhtin presents as the fundamental principle in Dostoevsky's poetics, can be applied with little modification to describe the basic structure of Dickens's novels. A Dostoevsky novel is "dialogic," "constructed not as the whole of a single consciousness, absorbing other consciousnesses as objects into itself, but as a whole formed by the interaction of several consciousnesses, none of which entirely becomes an object for the other."[21] This dialogical principle is at work in Dickens's novels: the stories of the Idle Apprentice and the Industrious Apprentice are vying with each other to dominate the novel, each failing to absorb the other to create a single unified consciousness or story. Yet submerged under this dialogue is another dialogue that is not the dialogue between two stories, between two different kinds of logic (*dialogos*), but the more radical struggle between story as logical and moral system and the suppressed yet primordial force of subversion. This force, which continually undermines the system of the novel, should be identified with Bakhtin's carnival. During carnival the "laws, prohibitions, and restrictions that determine the structure and order of ordinary, that is noncarnival, life are suspended. . . . what is suspended first of all is hierarchical structure and all the forms of terror, reverence, piety, and etiquette connected with it."[22] Carnivalistic life is "life drawn out of its *usual* rut, it is to some extent 'life turned inside out,' 'the reverse side of the world.'"[23] Dickens's early novels are brimming with carnivalistic life linked essentially with the irrational, the comic and the non-serious. *Pickwick*, *Nickleby* and *The Old Curiosity Shop* are typical carnival literature full of animal vitality and disorder where the most fundamental rite of carnival, of decrowning (of Mr. Pickwick, Squeers and Quilp, who are all to some extent Lords of Misrule), is repeatedly staged. But Dickens, being a novelist, had to curb his wild imagination to bring his work to a more or less orderly conclusion. Because carnivalistic life is essentially incompatible with closure (the public square is the center of carnival), it has to be suppressed in a final working-out of the plot; otherwise it would be simply impossible to complete a novel. As Dickens "matured" into a prestigious novelist this repression of carnival is more and more successfully undertaken in his writing. But in his most "serious" and "mature" novel the system of stories is shattered and now the absent, subversive force of carnival finally succeeds in making its irrepressible presence felt. The ending of the novel is actually the beginning of the absent story, the beginning of the greater dialogue between logos and passion, between story and carnival.

Though Pip has failed to write the true story of his life, failed to live his madness, his irrational passion, rooted in the core of his nature, asserts itself even in the final hour of the story's ordered chronology.

Right after his declaration to Biddy that his poor dream "has all gone by" he visits the site of the old Satis House, the ruins of texts and stories, to meet Estella, a being whose potential for a passion as warm as Pip's has failed to be actualized. Dickens has been very careful in suggesting this potential: when her identity is revealed Estella is found to be the daughter of a woman who "had some gipsy blood in her" (405). This woman had not only acted according to the traditional ideas of gipsy women in literature by murdering another for jealousy, but proves to be a descendant of the fiery witch of Colchis, Medea, who killed her own child by Jason in revenge for his betrayal; Estella's mother "was under strong suspicion of having, at about the time of the murder, frantically destroyed her child by this man—some three years old—to revenge herself upon him" (406). When we are faced with the essential similarity between Pip and Magwitch—they are orphans manipulated by authoritarian figures—it is hard not to see that the story of Magwitch and Molly might easily have been one in which Pip and Estella figure as hero and heroine. Yet this story of two passionate human beings capable of ignoring morality and hierarchy or any interdiction society might impose upon them is absent in *Great Expectations*.[24] Pip's story as written by others has already come to an end; the system of the novel has closed itself. Yet Dickens had to write again the ending that is really a beginning; Pip and Estella, the two with more fundamental characteristics in common than they are aware of, must meet again to begin to write the story of their love just as Pip and Magwitch had encountered each other at the beginning to begin their entirely different love story. In a final paradox, however, this absent story has already been written. If the ultimate message of the novel may be seen as the disclosure and destruction of alienating stories and the revelation of irrationality that transcends textuality, the story Pip will write cannot be anything other than the text that has been *Great Expectations*.

From *English Literary History* 53, no. 3 (1986): 593-614. Copyright © 1986 by The Johns Hopkins University Press. Reprinted with permission of The Johns Hopkins University Press.

Notes

1. Wayne C. Booth, *The Rhetoric of Fiction* (Chicago: Univ. of Chicago Press, 1961), 71-73. See also Seymour Chatman, *Story and Discourse: Narrative Structure in Fiction and Film* (Ithaca, NY: Cornell Univ. Press, 1978), 148-49.

2. For the discussion of various meanings of author and authority, see Edward Said's influential book, *Beginnings: Intention and Method* (New York: Basic Books, 1975). The problem of the father figure in *Great Expectations* has been given attention by many critics; the fullest consideration so far is Lawrence Jay Dessner, "*Great Expectations*: 'the Ghost of a Man's Own Father,'" *PMLA* 91 (1976): 436-49. See also Dianne F. Sadoff, "Storytelling and the Figure of the Father in *Little Dorrit*," *PMLA* 95 (1980): 234-45.

3. The problem of writing in *Great Expectations* has been discussed recently by Robert Tracy and Murray Baumgarten. Tracy is concerned with the tension between writing and speaking in the novel, the former, according to him, being constantly put into doubt; and Baumgarten's focus is on calligraphy as "writing that bridges hieroglyphic and phonetic systems." See Robert Tracy, "Reading Dickens's Writing," and Murray Baumgarten, "Calligraphy and Code: Writing in *Great Expectations*," *Dickens Studies Annual* 11 (1983): 37-72.

4. David Lodge, *Working with Structuralism: Essays and Reviews on Nineteenth- and Twentieth-Century Literature* (London: Routledge, 1981), 20. This, I find, is the fullest and most succinct definition of *fabula* and *sjuzet* of the Russian Formalists. See also Tzvetan Todorov, *The Poetics of Prose*, trans. Richard Howard (Ithaca, NY: Cornell Univ. Press, 1977), 45-46.

5. See, for example, Dorothy Van Ghent, *The English Novel: Form and Function* (New York: Harper, 1967), 154-70; John H. Hagan Jr., "Structural Patterns in Dickens's *Great Expectations*," *ELH* 21 (1954): 54-66; and E. Pearlman, "Inversion in *Great Expectations*," *Dickens Studies Annual* 7 (1978): 190-202.

6. Peter Brooks, "Repetition, Repression, and Return: The Plotting of *Great Expectations*," in *Reading for the Plot: Design and Intention in Narrative* (Oxford: Clarendon Press, 1984), 113-42. Brooks' essay was originally published as "Repetition, Repression, and Return: *Great Expectations* and the Study of Plot," *New Literary History* 11 (1980): 503-26.

7. All references are to *Great Expectations*, ed. Angus Calder (Harmondsworth: Penguin Books, 1965) and will be included in the text hereafter.

8. See Brooks, 131-32. Brooks asserts that "all texts eventually speak of Pip himself as an unjustified presence, a presence demanding interpretations." Yet the point of this scene is that interpretation is always a priori, already completed when Wopsle and Pumblechook trap Pip in an established story which does not allow any further designing or plotting.

9. Some critics have followed suit, notably Van Ghent. See 168.

10. See Ronald Paulson, *Emblem and Expression: Meaning in English Art of the Eighteenth Century* (Cambridge: Harvard Univ. Press, 1975), 58-78, for a detailed discussion of Hogarth's work. Paul B. Davis points out that perhaps Dickens "had the series in mind as he wrote *Great Expectations*; the account of Pip's apprenticeship seems

to be one point where Dickens's general indebtedness to Hogarth becomes specific." "Dickens, Hogarth, and the Illustrated *Great Expectations*," *The Dickensian* 80 (1984): 131-43.

11. See *The London Merchant*, ed. William H. McBurney (London: Edward Arnold, 1965), xv.

12. See *Dombey and Son*, ed. Peter Fairclough (Harmondsworth: Penguin Books, 1970), 98-99; and *Barnaby Rudge*, ed. Gordon Spence (Harmondsworth: Penguin Books, 1973), 302.

13. See *Barnaby Rudge*, 80.

14. "The Hero's Guilt: the Case of *Great Expectations*," *Essays in Criticism* 10 (1960): 69-70.

15. Shirley Grob, "Dickens and Some Motifs of the Fairy Tale," *Texas Studies in Literature and Language*, 5 (1964): 567-79; Harry Stone, "*Great Expectations*: The Fairy-Tale Transformation," *Dickens and the Invisible World: Fairy Tales, Fantasy, and Novel-Making* (London: Macmillan, 1980), 298-339.

16. Max Byrd, "'Reading' in *Great Expectations*," *PMLA* 91 (1976): 259-65.

17. Brooks, 138.

18. Edgar Rosenberg, "A Preface to *Great Expectations*," *Dickens Studies Annual* 2 (1972): 333. Rosenberg borrowed the term "cautionary tale" from the German scholar Ludwig Borinski.

19. John Forster, *The Life of Charles Dickens*, ed. A. J. Hoppe (London: Dent, 1966), 2: 289; George Bernard Shaw, "Foreword to the Edinburgh limited edition of *Great Expectations* 1937," rpt. in Stephen Wall, ed., *Charles Dickens: A Critical Anthology* (Harmondsworth: Penguin Books, 1970), 294. For the problem of the novel's ending see, among numerous others: Marshall W. Gregory, "Values and Meaning in *Great Expectations*: The Two Endings Revisited," *Essays in Criticism* 19 (1969): 402-9; Martin Meisel, "The Ending of *Great Expectations*," *Essays in Criticism* 15 (1965): 326-31; Milton Millhauser, "*Great Expectations*: The Three Endings," *Dickens Studies Annual* 2 (1972): 267-77; Edgar Rosenberg, "Last Words on *Great Expectations*: A Textual Brief on the Six Endings," *Dickens Studies Annual* 9 (1981): 87-115.

20. Millhauser, 271.

21. Mikhail Bakhtin, *Problems of Dostoevsky's Poetics*, trans. Caryl Emerson (Minneapolis: Univ. of Minnesota Press, 1984), 18. Dickens's influence on Dostoevsky has been studied by Donald Fanger, *Dostoevsky and Romantic Realism: A Study of Dostoevsky in Relation to Balzac, Dickens, and Gogol* (Chicago: Univ. of Chicago Press, 1967); N. M. Lary, *Dostoevsky and Dickens: A Study of Literary Influence* (London: Routledge, 1973); and Loralee MacPike, *Dostoevsky's Dickens: A Study of Literary Influence* (London: George Prior, 1981).

Peter K. Garrett has found it feasible to consider the multiplot baggy monsters of the Victorian age from the new point of view offered by Bakhtin. *The Victorian Multiplot Novel: Studies in Dialogical Form* (New Haven, CT: Yale Univ. Press, 1980), 8.

22. Bakhtin, 122-23.

23. Bakhtin, 122. Ronald Paulson in his study of eighteenth-century subculture revealed the ambiguities involved in Hogarth's *Industry and Idleness*. Ronald Paulson,

Popular and Polite Art in the Age of Hogarth and Fielding (Notre Dame: Univ. of Notre Dame Press, 1979), 21-22.

24. The absence may be explained also in terms of the paramount interdiction imposed upon their relationship. As Magwitch is Estella's real father and also Pip's "second father," their love could not be anything but incestuous. The possible perversity in Pip's love for Estella was pointed out by A. L. French, "Beating and Cringing: *Great Expectations*," *Essays in Criticism* 24 (1974): 151-58. See also Pearlman (note 5), 201; and Brooks, 128, for similar points.

Repetition, Repression, and Return:
Great Expectations and the Study of Plot_____

Peter Brooks

What follows is intended primarily as a discourse on plot, a concept which has mostly gone unhonored in modern criticism, no doubt because it appears to belong to the popular, even the commercial side of literature. "Reading for the plot," we were taught, is a low form of activity. Long caught in valuations set by a criticism conceived for the lyric, the study of narrative has more recently found its way back to a quasi-Aristotelian view of the logical priority of plot in narrative forms. In the wake of Russian Formalism, French "narratology" has made us sensitive to the functional logic of actions, to the workings of sequence and transformation in the constitution of recognizable narrative units, to the presence of codes of narration that demand decoding in consecutive, irreversible order.[1] Plot as I understand it, however, suggests a focus somewhat more specific than the questions of structure, discourse, and narrativity addressed by most narratology. We may want to conceive of plot less as a structure than as a structuring operation, used, or made necessary, by those meanings that develop only through sequence and succession: an interpretative operation specific to narrative signification. The word plot, any dictionary tells us, covers a range of meanings, from the bounded piece of land, through the ground plan of a building, the chart or map, the outline of a literary work, to the sense (separately derived from the French complot) of the scheme or secret machination, to the accomplishment of some purpose, usually illegal. All these meanings, I think, usefully cohere in our common sense of plot: it is not only the outline of a narrative, demarcating its boundaries, it also suggests its intention of meaning, the direction of its scheme or machination for accomplishing a purpose. Plots have not only design, but intentionality as well.

Some narratives clearly give us a sense of "plottedness" in higher degree than others. Our identification of this sense of plottedness may

---

provide a more concrete and analyzable way into the question of plots than an abstract definition of the subject, and a way that necessarily finds its focus in the readership of plot, in the reader's recognition of the need for structuring interpretative operations. The motive for plotting, the need for a sense of plot, may ultimately lie in the desire to recuperate pure successivity, passing time: a search, not so much for redemption *from* time, but redemption of time as the possible medium of significance. This may already suggest the predominant importance of the end as that moment which illuminates, and casts retrospective meaning on the middle, and indeed defines the beginning as a certain desire tending toward the end. If the promised end may once have offered an arrest of time in the timeless, in a secularized world the resonance of the end has increasingly become the anticipated echo of the individual human death. Thus Walter Benjamin can claim that "death is the sanction of everything the storyteller has to tell," because only at the moment of death does life acquire authoritative meaning and become transmissible. The problem for "man in the middest," to use Frank Kermode's term, is how to find that end and beginning that will give a significant closure, the closure on which depends meaning: that knowledge of death, Benjamin maintains, which is denied to us in terms of our own lives, and which precisely we seek in the fictions of others.[2] How do we find significant plots for our lives; how do we make them *narratable*? This is the problem to which I want to make an approach, and I will in a moment call upon Freud's speculations about how we understand our transit from birth to death, in *Beyond the Pleasure Principle*, as a source of illumination which may suggest the value of a psychoanalytically informed textual criticism.

The problems of closure, authority, and narratability show up in particularly acute form in any autobiographical narration. As Sartre succinctly puts it in *Les Mots*, to narrate himself to himself, he had to become "my own obituary." Whatever of an autobiographical account can be enclosed between beginning and end must have margins outside, margins of leftover "life" which allow the narrating I to objectify and look at the narrated I, and to see the plotted middle as shaped by its provisional start and finish. In the fictional pseudo-autobiography that is *Great Expectations*—my text of reference here, one that gives in the highest degree the sense of plottedness and the impression that its central meanings depend on the working-out of the plot—Dickens adopts the strategy of taking a "life" and creating the demarcations of a "plot" within it. The novel will indeed be concerned with finding a plot and losing it, with the precipitation of the sense of plottedness around its hero, and his eventual "cure" from plot. The novel images in its structure the kind of structuring operation of reading that plot is.

I

Great Expectations is exemplary for a discourse on plot in many respects, not least of all for its beginning. For what the novel chooses to present at its outset is precisely the search for a beginning. As in so many nineteenth-century novels, the hero is an orphan, thus undetermined by any visible inheritance, apparently unauthored. While there may be sociological and sentimental reasons to account for the high incidence of orphans in the nineteenth-century novel, clearly they present an author with the greatest possible opportunity to create all the determinants of plot within his text, to profit from what Gide called the "lawlessness" of the novel by starting with an undefined, rule-free character and then bringing the law to bear upon him—creating the rules—as the text proceeds. With Pip, Dickens begins as it were with a life which is for the moment precedent to plot, and indeed necessarily in search of plot. Pip when we first see him is in search of the "authority"— the word stands in the second paragraph of the novel—that would define and justify—authorize—the plot of his ensuing life.

The authority to which Pip refers here is that of the tombstone which bears the names of his parents, the names which have already been displaced, condensed, and superseded in the first paragraph, where Pip describes how his "infant tongue" (literally, a speechless tongue: a catachresis which points to a moment of emergence, of transition into language) could only make of the name, Philip Pirrip, left to him by the dead parents, the monosyllabic Pip. "So, I called myself Pip, and came to be called Pip."[3] This originating moment of Pip's narration and his narrative is a self-naming which already subverts whatever authority could be found in the text of the tombstones. The process of reading that text is described by Pip the narrator as "unreasonable," in that it interprets the appearance of the lost father and mother from the shape of the letters of their names. The tracing of the name—which he has already distorted in its application to self—involves a misguided attempt to remotivate the graphic symbol, to make it directly mimetic, mimetic specifically of origin. Loss of origin, misreading, and the problematic of identity are bound up here in a manner that will need further investigation later on. The question of reading and writing—of learning to decipher and to compose texts—is persistently thematized in the novel.[4]

The decipherment of the tombstone text as confirmation of loss of origin—as unauthorization—is here at the start of the novel the prelude to Pip's cogito, the moment in which his consciousness seizes his existence as other, alien, forlorn:

> My first most vivid and broad impression of the identity of things, seems to me to have been gained on a memorable raw afternoon towards evening. At such a time I found out for certain, that this bleak place overgrown with nettles was the churchyard; and that Philip Pirrip, late of this parish, and also Georgiana wife of the above, were dead and buried; and that Alexander, Bartholomew, Abraham, Tobias, and Roger, infant children of the aforesaid, were also dead and buried; and that the dark flat wilderness beyond the churchyard, intersected with dykes and mounds and gates, with scattered cattle feeding on it, was the marshes; and that the low leaden line beyond was the river; and that the distant savage lair from which the wind was rushing, was the sea; and that the small bundle of shivers growing afraid of it all and beginning to cry, was Pip.
>
> "Hold your noise!" cried a terrible voice. . . . [p. 2]

The repeated verbs of existence—"was" and "were"—perform an elementary phenomenology of Pip's world, locating its irreducible objects, and leading finally to the individual subject as other, as aware of its existence through the emotion of fear, fear which then appears as the origin of voice, or articulated sound, as Pip begins to cry: a cry which is immediately censored by the command of the convict Magwitch, the father-to-be, the fearful intrusive figure of future authorship who will demand of Pip: "Give us your name."

The scenario is richly suggestive of the problem of identity, self-consciousness, naming, and language which will accompany Pip throughout the novel, and points to the original decentering of the subject in regard to itself. For purposes of our study of plot, it is important to note how this beginning establishes Pip as an existence without a plot at the very moment of occurrence of that event which will prove to be decisive for the plotting of his existence, as he will discover only two-thirds of the way through the novel. Alien, unauthorized, self-named, at the point of entry into the language code and the social systems it implies, Pip will in the first part of the novel be in search of a plot, and the novel will recount the gradual precipitation of a sense of plot around him, the establishment of portents of intentionality.

Schematically, we can identify four lines of plot that begin to crystallize around the young Pip, the Pip of Part 1, before the arrival of his "Expectations":

(1) Communion with the convict/criminal deviance.
(2) Naterally wicious/bringing up by hand.
(3) The dream of Satis House/the fairy tale.
(4) The nightmare of Satis House/the witch tale.

These plots, we will see in a moment, are paired as follows: 2/1 = 3/4. That is, there is in each case an "official" and censoring plot standing over a "repressed" plot. In terms of Pip's own choices, we could re-write the formula: 3/4//2/1. When the Expectations are announced by

Jaggers at the end of Part One, they will apparently coincide with Pip's choices ("My dream was out; my wild fancy was surpassed by sober reality" [chap. 18, p. 139]), and will thus appear to take care of the problem of plot. But this will be so only on the level of official plots; the Expectations will in fact only mask further the true problem, the status of the repressed plots.

I choose the term *communion* for the first plot because its character-istic symbolic gesture is Pip's pity for the convict as he swallows the food Pip has brought him, a moment of sympathetic identification which focuses a series of suggestive sympathies and identifications with the outlaw: the bread and butter which Pip puts down his leg, which makes him walk like the chained convict; Mrs. Joe's belief that he is on his way to the Hulks; Pip's flight from the Christmas dinner ta-ble into the arms of a soldier holding out handcuffs, to give a few ex-amples. Pip is concerned to assure "his" convict that he is not responsi-ble for his recapture, a point he conveys in a mute exchange of glances which the convict understands, and which leads him to make a public statement in exoneration of Pip, taking responsibility for stealing the food. This in turn provokes an overt statement of community with the outlaw, which comes from Joe: "We don't know what you have done, but we wouldn't have you starved to death for it, poor miserable fellow creatur.—Would us, Pip?" (chap. 5, p. 39).

The fellowship with the convict here stated by Joe will remain with Pip, but in a state of repression, as what he will later call "that spell of my childhood" (chap. 16, p. 122)—an unavowable memory. It finds its official, adult, repressive version in the conviction—shared by all the adults in Pip's life, with the exception of the childlike Joe—that chil-dren are naturally depraved and need to be corrected, kept in line with the Tickler, brought up by hand lest their natural willfulness assert it-self in plots that are deviant, transgressive. Pumblechook and the Hub-bles, in their Christmas dinner dialogue, give the theme a choric state-ment:

"Especially," said Mr. Pumblechook, "be grateful, boy, to them which brought you up by hand."

Mrs. Hubble shook her head, and contemplating me with a mournful presentiment that I should come to no good, asked, "Why is it that the young are never grateful?" This moral mystery seemed too much for the company until Mr. Hubble tersely solved it by saying, "Naterally wicious." Everybody then murmured "True!" and looked at me in a particularly unpleasant and personal manner. [Chap. 4, p. 24]

The nateral wiciousness of children legitimates communion with the outlaw, but legitimates it as that which must be repressed, forced into other plots—including, as we shall see, "binding" Pip as an apprentice.

The dream of Satis House is properly a daydream, in which "His Majesty, the Ego" pleasures himself with the fantasy of social ascension and gentility. Miss Havisham is made to play the role of Fairy Godmother, her crutch become a magic wand, explicitly evoked twice near the close of Part 1.[5] This plot has adult sanction, its first expression comes from Pumblechook and Mrs. Joe when they surmise that Miss Havisham intends to "do something" for Pip, and Pip comes to believe in it, so that when the "Expectations" arrive he accepts them as the logical fulfillment of the daydream, of his "longings." Yet to identify Satis House with the daydream is to perform a repression of all else that Satis House suggests and represents—all that clusters around the central emblem of the rotting bride cake and its crawling things. The craziness and morbidity of Satis House repose on desire fixated and become sadistic, on a deviated eroticism which has literally shut out the light, stopped the clocks, and made the forward movement of plot impossible. Satis House, as the circular journeys of the wheelchair to the rhythm of "Old Clem" may best suggest, constitutes repetition without variation, a collapsed metonymy where cause and effect have become identical, the same-as-same. It is significant that when Pip returns from his first visit to Satis House, he responds to the interrogations of Pumblechook and Mrs. Joe with an elaborate lie—the story of the coach,

the flags, the dogs fighting for "weal" cutlets from a silver basket—
a fantasy which we can read as his response to what he calls a "smart
without a name, that needed counteraction" (chap. 8, p. 62). All the attempts to read Satis House as a text speaking of gentility and social ascension may be subverted from the outset, in the passage which describes Pip's first impression of Miss Havisham, which reads in part:

> It was not in the first few moments that I saw all these things, though I saw
> more of them in the first moments than might be supposed. But, I saw that
> everything within my view which ought to be white, had been white long
> ago, and had lost its lustre, and was faded and yellow. I saw that the bride
> within the bridal dress had withered like the dress, and like the flowers, and
> had no brightness left but the brightness of her sunken eyes. I saw that
> the dress. . . . Once, I had been taken to see some ghastly waxwork at the
> Fair. . . . Once, I had been taken to one of our old marsh churches to see a
> skeleton. . . . Now, waxwork and skeleton seemed to have dark eyes that
> moved and looked at me. I should have cried out, if I could. [Chap. 8, p. 57]

The passage records the formation of a memory trace from a moment
of unmastered horror, itself formed in repetition of moments of past visual impression, a trace which forces its way through the mind without
being grasped by consciousness, and which is refused outlet in a cry.
Much later in the novel, Pip—and also Miss Havisham herself—will
have to deal with the return of this repressed memory.

We have, then, a quadripartite scheme of plots, organized into two
pairs, each with an official plot, or interpretation of plot, standing over
a repressed plot. The scheme may lead us in the first instance to reflect
on the place of repression as one of the large "orders" of the novel. Repression plays a dominant role in the theme of education which is so
important to the novel, from Mrs. Joe's bringing up by hand, through
Mrs. Wopsle's aunt's schoolroom, to Mr. Pocket's career as a "grinder"
of dull blades (while his own children meanwhile are "tumbling up").
Bringing up by hand in turn suggests Jaggers's hands, representation of

accusation and the Law, which in turn suggest all the instances of censorship in the name of high authorities evoked from the first scene of the novel onward: censorship is repression in the name of the Law.[6] Jaggers's sinister hand-washings point to the omnipresent taint of Newgate, which echoes the earlier presence of the Hulks, to which Mrs. Joe verbally assigns Pip. Then there is the moment when Pip is "bound" as apprentice blacksmith before the magistrates, in a scene of such repressive appearance that a well-meaning philanthropist is moved to hand Pip a tract entitled, *To Be Read in My Cell*. There is a constant association of education, repression, criminality, the fear of deviance. We might note in passing Dickens's capacity to literalize the metaphors of education—"bringing up by hand," "grinding"—in a manner that subverts the order that ought to assure their figural validity. The particularly sinister version of the *Bildungsroman* presented by *Great Expectations* derives in some measure from the literalization of metaphors pertaining to education and upbringing. Societal repression and censorship are of course reinforced by Pip's own, his internalization of the Law and the denial of what he calls the "old taint" of his association with the criminal. The whole theme of gentility, as represented by the Finches of the Grove, for instance, or the punishment of Trabb's boy, consistently suggests an aggressivity based on denial. One could reflect here on the splendid name of Pip's superfluous valet: the Avenger.

The way in which the Expectations are instituted, in seeming realization of the Satis House dream, comprehends "bringing up by hand" (the other official plot) in that it includes the disciplines necessary to gentility: grinding with Mr. Pocket, lessons in manners from Herbert, learning to spend one's time and money in appropriate gentlemanly pursuits. There is in this manner a blurring of plot lines, useful to the processes of wish fulfillment in that education and indeed repression itself can be interpreted as agencies necessary to the pursuit of the dream. Realization of the dream permits acceptance of society's interpretations, and in fact requires the abandonment of any effort at personal interpretation: Pip is now enjoined from seeking to know more about the intentions of his donor, disallowed the role of detective which so much animates him in Part III of the novel—when the Expectations have proved false—and is already incipiently present in Part I.

Taking our terminology from the scene where Pip is bound as apprentice, we may consider that education and repression operate in the novel as one form of "binding": official ways of channeling and tying up the mobile energies of life. It is notable that after he has become apprenticed to Joe, Pip goes through a stage of purely iterative existence—presented in chapter 14—where the direction and movement of plot appear to be finished, where all life's "interest and romance" appear shut out as by a "thick curtain," time reduced to a repetitive durance. Conversely, when the Expectations have arrived, and Miss Havisham is apparently identified as the fairy-tale donor, and the Satis House plot appears securely bound, Pip need only wait for the next stage of the plot to become manifest. Yet it is clear that for the reader, neither binding as an apprentice (first accomplishment of an upbringing by hand) nor the tying up of Satis House as a fairy-tale plot constitutes valid and adequate means of dealing with and disposing of the communion with the convict and the nightmare of Satis House. The energy released in the text by its liminary "primal scene"—in the graveyard—and by the early visits to Satis House, creating that "smart without a name," simply are not and cannot be bound by the bindings of the official, repressive plots. As readers we know that there has been created in the text an intensive level of energy that cannot be discharged through these official plots.

In fact, the text has been working simultaneously to bind these disavowed energies in other ways, ways over which Pip's ego, and the societal superego, have no control, and of which they have no knowledge, through repetitions which, for the reader, prepare an inevitable return of the repressed. Most striking are the periodic fragmentary returns of the convict-communion material: the leg iron used to bludgeon Mrs. Joe, guns firing from the Hulks to signal further escapes, and especially the reappearance of Joe's file, the dramatic stage property

---

used by Magwitch's emissary in a "proceeding in dumb show . . . pointedly addressed at me." His stirring and tasting his rum and water "pointedly at" Pip suggests the establishment of an aim (Pip calls his proceeding "a shot"), a direction, an intention in Pip's life: the first covert announcement of another plot which will come to govern Pip's life, but of course misinterpreted as to its true aim. With the nightmare energies of Satis House, binding is at work in those repetitive journeys around the rotting bride cake, suggestive of the reproduction or working through of the traumatic neurotic whose affects remain fixed on the past, on the traumatic moment which never can be mastered. These energies can never be plotted to effective discharge. The compulsive repetition that characterizes every detail of Satis House allows us to perceive how the returns of the convict-communion suggest a more significant repetitive working through of an unmastered past. In both cases—but ultimately with different results—the progressive, educative plots, the plots of advancement, are threatened by a repetitive process obscurely going on underneath and beyond them. We sense that forward progress will have to recover markings from the beginning.

II

In my references to repetition and return as a process of "binding," I have had in mind a model of the text suggested by the model of the mental apparatus speculatively elaborated by Freud in *Beyond the Pleasure Principle*.[7] Freud's essay takes its departure from the compulsion to repeat that can be noticed in children's games, in literature (the literature of "the uncanny"), in the dreams of traumatic neurotics, which return again and again to the moment of trauma, to relive its pain, in apparent contradiction to the wish-fulfillment theory of dreams. Freud is led to postulate that the repetition compulsion constitutes an effort to "bind" mobile energy, to master the flood of stimuli that have breached the shield of the psychic apparatus at the moment of trauma, in order to produce the quiescent cathexis that allows the pleasure principle to assert its dominance in the psychic economy, and to lead energy to orderly and efficient discharge. Repetition as binding is hence a primary act, prior to the operations of the pleasure principle and more "primitive": it works to put affect into serviceable, controllable form. In analytic work, the repetition compulsion becomes particularly sensible in the transference, where patients display the need to reenact, reproduce, and work through repressed material as if it were present, rather than simply recollecting it as belonging to the past. Past history, lost to conscious memory, reproduces itself as an unmastered force in the present. To patients, the compulsion to repeat, to bind the unmastered past, speaks of a daemonic power, which for Freud (as in the literature of the uncanny) indicates the presence of the instinctual. Since for Freud the nature of the instinctual is radically conservative—an inherent urge to restore a prior state of affairs, which means essentially a return to the quiescence of the inorganic—repetition eventually speaks of the death instinct, of the fact that "the aim of all life is death." Yet the drive to return to death must conform itself to that divergence from an immediate return to quiescence which has been programmed into the organism as its response to outside stimuli: the death aimed at must be the right, the proper death, achieved through the complication of a detour, avoiding short circuit. The conflict of the death instincts and the self-preservative life instincts—Eros—provides a self-regulating economy where each set of instincts is dependent on the other, where the organism lives in order to die, but to die its proper death, which means that it follows a detour and a vacillating rhythm, with new beginnings in resistance to the impending end, in its movement to the end.

Of the complex intentions presiding over the composition of *Beyond the Pleasure Principle*, one appears to be a desire to consider how life is narratable, that is, how and why it has beginning and end, and how these are related in a pattern of extension with closure, which seems to be the requisite of talking about the shape or meaning of a life, about the plot of life. Freud's essay may offer a model suggestive of how narrative both seeks and delays its end. In particular, his concept of repetition seems fully pertinent, since repetition of all sorts is the very stuff of literary meanings, the basis of our creative perception of relation and interconnection, the means by which we compare and combine in significant patterns and sequences, and thus overcome the meaninglessness of pure contiguity. In the narrative text, repetition constitutes a *return*, a calling-back, or a turning-back, which enables us to perceive similarity in difference, consequence in contiguity, metaphor in metonymy. Since they are both calling-back and turning-back, repetitions may be seen as both returns to and returns of: for instance, returns to origins and returns of the repressed. The study of repetition as return can lead us to think about how the text speaks of its drive toward its end, and how the accomplishment of this drive must proceed through detour and vacillation, the textual middle, thereby enabling us to understand the end in relation to the beginning. Repetition, while speaking of the end, does so in such a manner—through its shuttlings back and forth—as to delay the end and to confer shape on the detour of the middle.

Freud's model seems in general pertinent to what I have been saying about the repetition and binding of Pip's official and repressed plots: their energy is being bound, overtly or covertly according to the case, and thus put into serviceable form within the textual economy. In particular, it may offer some illumination of the novel's middle—that place of mysterious necessity, which must be of a certain length in order to accomplish its processes—which is most notably characterized by the *return*. Literally, it is Pip's return from London to his hometown which appears as the organizing device of the whole of the London period, the time of the Expectations and their aftermath. Pip's returns are always ostensibly undertaken to make reparation to the neglected Joe, an intention never realized, and always implicitly an attempt to discover the intentions of the putative donor in Satis House, to bring her plot to completion. Yet the returns also always bring his regression, in Satis House, to the status of the "coarse and common boy" (chap. 29, p. 237) whose social ascension is hallucinatorily denied, his return to the nightmare of unprogressive repetition, and, too, a revival of the repressed convict association, the return of the childhood spell. Each return suggests that Pip's official plots, which seem to speak of progress, ascent, and the satisfaction of desire, are in fact subject to a process of repetition of the yet unmastered past, the true determinant of his life's direction.

The pattern of the return is established in Pip's first journey back from London in chapter 28. The decision to visit Joe is quickly thrown into the shade by the presence on the stagecoach of two convicts, one of whom Pip recognizes as the man of the file and the rum and water, Magwitch's emissary. There is a renewed juxtaposition of official, genteel judgment on the convicts, voiced by Herbert Pocket, "What a vile and degraded spectacle"—and Pip's inward avowal that he feels sympathy for their alienation. On the roof of the coach, seated in front of the convicts, Pip dozes off while pondering whether he ought to restore the two one-pound notes which the convict of the file had passed him so many years before. Upon regaining consciousness, the first two words he hears, continuing his dream thoughts, are: "Two one-pound notes." There follows the convict's account of his embassy from "Pip's convict" to the boy who had saved him. Although Pip is certain that the convict cannot recognize him, so changed in age, circumstance, and even name (since Herbert Pocket calls him "Handel"), the dreamlike experience forces a kind of recognition of a forgotten self, refound in fear and pain: "I could not have said what I was afraid of, for my fear was altogether undefined and vague, but there was great fear upon me. As I walked on to the hotel, I felt that a dread, much exceeding the mere apprehension of a painful or disagreeable recognition, made me tremble. I am confident that it took no distinctness of shape, and that it was the revival for a few minutes of the terror of childhood" (chap. 28, p. 232). The return to origins has led to the return of the repressed, and vice versa. Repetition as return becomes a reproduction and reenactment of infantile experience: not simply a recall of the primal moment, but a reliving of its pain and terror, suggesting the impossibility of escape from the originating scenarios of childhood, the condemnation forever to replay them.

This first example may stand for the other returns of the novel's middle, which all follow the same pattern, which all double return to with return of, and which show Pip's ostensible progress in the world to be subverted by the irradicable presence of the convict-communion and the Satis House nightmare. It is notable that toward the end of the middle—as the novel's denouement approaches—there is an acceleration in the rhythm of these returns, as if to affirm that all the clues to Pip's future, the forward movement of his plot, in fact lie in the past. Repetition as return speaks as a textual version of the death instinct, plotting the text, beyond the seeming dominance of the pleasure principle, toward its proper end, imaging this end as necessarily a time before the beginning. Even Pip's attempted escape with Magwitch, his voyage out to another land and another life, will lead him back, in the Thames estuary, to marsh country like his own, to the horizontal perspectives and muddy tidal flats that are so much a part of our perception of him during childhood.

We must come back in a moment to return, repetition, and the death instinct. First a word should be said about the novel's recognition scene, the moment at which the latent becomes manifest, the repressed convict plot is forcibly brought to consciousness, a scene which decisively enacts both a return of the repressed and a return to the primal moment in childhood. The recognition scene of chapter 39 is preceded by two curious paragraphs at the end of chapter 38 in which Pip the narrator suggests that the chapter he has just written, concerning his frustrated pursuit of Estella, constitutes, on the plane of narration itself, a last binding of that plot in its overt version, as a plot of romance, and that now he must move on to a deeper level of plot—reaching further back—which subsumes as it subverts all the other plots of the novel: "All the work, near and afar, that tended to the end had been accomplished." That this long-range plot is presented as analogous to "the Eastern story" in which a heavy slab of stone is carved out and fitted into the roof in order that it may fall on "the bed of state in the flush of conquest" seems in coded fashion to suggest punishment for erotic transgression, which we may want to read as return of the nightmare plot of Satis House, forcing its way through the fairy tale, speaking of the perverse, sadistic eroticism which Pip has covered over with his erotic object-choice—Estella, who in fact represents the wrong choice of plot and the danger of short circuit. To anticipate later revelations, we might note that Estella will turn out to be approximately Pip's sister—natural daughter of Magwitch as he is Magwitch's adoptive son—which lends force to the idea that she, like so many Romantic maidens, is marked by the interdict, as well as the seduction, of incest, which, as the perfect androgynous coupling, is precisely the short circuit of desire.[8]

The scene of Magwitch's return operates for Pip as a painful forcing through of layers of repression, an analogue of analytic work, compelling Pip to recognize that what he calls "that chance encounter of long ago" is no chance and cannot be assigned to the buried past, but must be repeated, reenacted, worked through in the present. The scene replays numerous details of their earlier encounter, and the central moment of recognition comes as a reproduction or reenactment of the novel's primal scene, played in dumb show, a mute text which the more effectively stages recognition as a process of return to the inescapable past:

> Even yet I could not recall a single feature, but I knew him! If the wind and the rain had driven away the intervening years, had scattered all the intervening objects, had swept us to the churchyard where we first stood face to face on such different levels, I could not have known my convict more distinctly than I knew him now, as he sat in the chair before the fire. No need to take a file from his pocket and show it to me; no need to take the handkerchief from his neck and twist it round his head; no need to hug himself

Critical Insights

with both his arms, and take a shivering turn across the room, looking back at me for recognition. I knew him before he gave me one of those aids, though, a moment before, I had not been conscious of remotely suspecting his identity. [Chap. 39, pp. 320-21]

The praeterition on which the passage is constructed—"no need . . . no need"—marks the gradual retrieval of the buried past as its involuntary present repetition. The passage offers the most striking example of the fact, already encountered in Pip's "returns," that key moments of Pip's life bring back the past not simply as recollection, but as reproduction: as a living-through of the past as if it were present. This corresponds to Freud's discovery—recorded in the essay, "Remembering, Repeating and Working-Through"—that repetition and working through of material from the past as if it were an active force in the present come into play when recollection properly speaking is blocked by resistance.[9] It becomes clear that the necessity for Pip to repeat and work through everything associated with his original communion with Magwitch is a factor of his "forgetting" this communion: a forgetting which is merely conscious. The reader has undergone a similar process through textual repetition and return, one which has had the function of not permitting him to forget.

The scene of Magwitch's return is an important one for any study of plot since it so well demonstrates how such a novelist as Dickens can make plotting the central vehicle and armature of meaning in the narrative text. All the issues raised in the novel—social, ethical, interpretative—are here simultaneously brought to climax through the peripety of the plot. Exposure of the "true" plot of Pip's life brings with it instantaneous consequences for all the other "codes" of the novel, as he recognizes with the statement, "All the truth of my position came *flashing* on me; and its disappointments, dangers, disgraces, consequences of all kinds" (chap. 39, p. 323—my italics). The return of the repressed—the repressed as knowledge of the self's other story, the true history of its misapprehended desire—forces a total revision of the subject's relation to the orders within which it constitutes meaning.

As Magwitch's unanswerable questions to Pip—on the origins of his property, the means of his social ascent—force home to him, Pip has covered over a radical lack of original authority. Like Oedipus, he does not know where he stands. The result has been the intrusion of an aberrant, contingent authorship—Magwitch's—in the story of the self. That it should be the criminally deviant, transgressive plot that is shown to have priority over all the others stands within the logic of the model derived from *Beyond the Pleasure Principle*, since it is precisely this plot that most markedly constitutes the detour from inorganic quiescence: the arabesque of the narratable. One could almost derive a narratological law here: the true plot will be the most deviant. We might be tempted to see this deviant arabesque as gratuitous, the figure of pure narration. Yet we are also allowed to remotivate it, for the return of the repressed shows that the story Pip would tell about himself has all along been subverted by the more complex history of unconscious desire, unavailable to the conscious subject but at work in the text. Pip has in fact misread the plot of his life.

III

This misreading of plots and the question of authority may serve to return us to the question of reading with which the novel began. Pip's initial attempt to decipher his parents' appearance and character from the letters traced on their tombstones has been characterized as "childish" and "unreasonable." Pip's decipherment in fact appears as an attempt to motivate the arbitrary sign, to interpret signs as if they were mimetic and thus naturally tied to the object for which they stand. Deriving from the shape of the letters on the tombstones that his father "was a square, stout, dark man, with curly hair," and that his mother was "freckled and sickly," for all its literal fidelity to the graphic trace, constitutes a dangerously figural reading, a metaphorical process unaware of itself, the making of a fiction unaware of its status as fiction-making. Pip is here claiming natural authority for what is in fact conventional, arbitrary, dependent on interpretation.

The question of texts, reading, and interpretation is, as we earlier noted, consistently thematized in the novel: in Pip's learning to read (using that meager text, Mrs. Wopsle's aunt's catalogue of prices), and his attempts to transmit the art of writing to Joe; the expressive dumb shows between Pip and Joe; messages written on the slate, by Pip to Joe, and then (in minimum symbolic form) by the aphasic Mrs. Joe; the uncanny text of Estella's visage, always reminding Pip of a repetition of something else which he cannot identify; Molly's wrists, cross-hatched with scratches, a text for the judge, and eventually for Pip as detective, to decipher; Mr. Wopsle's declamations of *George Barnwell* and *Richard III*. The characters appear to be ever on the watch for ways in which to textualize the world so that they can give their readings of it: a situation thematized early in the novel, at the Christmas dinner table, as Pumblechook and Wopsle criticize the sermon of the day and propose other "subjects":

Mr. Pumblechook added, after a short interval of reflection, "Look at Pork alone. There's a subject! If you want a subject, look at Pork!"

"True, sir. Many a moral for the young," returned Mr. Wopsle; and I knew he was going to lug me in, before he said it, "might be deduced from that text."

("You listen to this," said my sister to me, in a severe parenthesis.)

Joe gave me some more gravy.

"Swine," pursued Mr. Wopsle, in his deepest voice, and pointing his fork at my blushes, as if he were mentioning my christian name; "Swine were the companions of the prodigal. The gluttony of Swine is put before us, as an example to the young." (I thought this pretty well in him who had been praising up the pork for being so plump and juicy.) "What is detestable in a pig, is more detestable in a boy."

"Or girl," suggested Mr. Hubble.

"Of course, or girl, Mr. Hubble," assented Mr. Wopsle, rather irritably, "but there is no girl present."

"Besides," said Mr. Pumblechook, turning sharp on me, "think what you've got to be grateful for. If you'd been born a Squeaker—"

"He *was*, if ever a child was," said my sister, most emphatically.

Joe gave me some more gravy.

"Well, but I mean a four-footed Squeaker," said Mr. Pumblechook. "If you had been born such, would you have been here now? Not you—"

"Unless in that form," said Mr. Wopsle, nodding towards the dish. [Chap. 4, pp. 25-26]

The scene suggests a mad proliferation of textuality, where literal and figural switch places, where any referent can serve as an interpretant, become the sign of another message, in a wild process of semiosis which seems to be anchored only insofar as all texts eventually speak of Pip himself as an unjustified presence, a presence demanding interpretation.

We are constantly warned that texts may have no unambiguous referent and no transcendent signified. Of the many examples one might choose in illustration of the status of texts and their interpretation in the novel, perhaps the most telling is the case of Mr. Wopsle. Mr. Wopsle, the church clerk, is a frustrated preacher, ever intimating that if the Church were to be "thrown open," he would really "give it out." This hypothetical case never coming to realization, Mr. Wopsle is obliged to content himself with the declamation of a number of secular texts, from Shakespeare to Collins's Ode. The Church indeed remains resolutely closed (we never in fact hear the word of the preacher in the novel, only Mr. Wopsle's critique of it), and Mr. Wopsle "has a fall": into playacting. He undertakes the repetition of fictional texts which lack the authority of that divine word he would like to "give out." We next see him playing *Hamlet*, which is of course the text par excellence about usurpation, parricide, lost regal authority, and wrong relations of transmission from generation to generation. Something of the problematic status of textual authority is suggested in Mr. Wopsle's rendition of the classic soliloquy: "Whenever that undecided Prince had to ask a question or state a doubt, the public helped him out with it. As for example; on the question whether 'twas nobler in the mind to suffer, some roared yes, and some no, and some inclining to both opinions said 'toss up for it'; and quite a Debating Society arose" (chap. 31, p. 257). From this uncertainty, Mr. Wopsle has a further fall, into playing what was known as "nautical melodrama," an anonymously authored theater played to a vulgar public in the Surreyside houses. When Pip attends this performance, there occurs a curious mirroring and reversal of the spectacle, when Mr. Wopsle himself becomes the spectator, fascinated by the vision, in the audience, of what he calls a "ghost" from the past—the face of the novel's hidden arch-plotter, Compeyson. The vision leads to a reconstruction of the chase and capture of the convicts from the early chapters of the novel, a kind of analytic dialogue in the replay of the past, where Mr. Wopsle repeatedly questions: "You remember?" and Pip replies: "I remember it very well. . . . I see it all before me." The replay evokes an intense visual, hallucinatory reliving of a charged moment from the past:

> "And you remember that we came up with the two in a ditch, and that there was a scuffle between them, and that one of them had been severely handled and much mauled about the face, by the other?"
>
> "I see it all before me."
>
> "And that the soldiers lighted torches, and put the two in the centre, and that we went on to see the last of them, over the black marshes, with the torchlight shining on their faces—I am particular about that; with the torchlight shining on their faces, when there was an outer ring of dark night all about us?" [Chap. 47, pp. 390-91]

By an apparently gratuitous free association, from Mr. Wopsle's play-acting, as from behind a screen memory, emerges a drama on that "other stage": the stage of dream, replaying a past moment which the characters have never exorcised, that moment of the buried yet living past which insists on repeating itself in the present.

Mr. Wopsle's career as a whole may be seen to be exemplary of a general movement in the novel toward recognition of the lack of authorship and authority in texts: textures of codes without ultimate referent or hierarchy, signs cut loose from their apparent motivation, capable of wandering toward multiple associations and of evoking messages that are entirely other, and that all speak eventually of determinative histories from the past. The original nostalgia for a founding divine word leads to a generalized scene of writing, as if the plotting self could never discover a decisive plot, but merely its own arbitrary role as plot-maker. Yet the arbitrary is itself subject to an unconscious determinant, the reproductive insistence of the past history.

Mr. Wopsle's career may stand as a figure for Pip's. Whereas the model of the *Bildungsroman* seems to imply progress, a leading forth, developmental change, Pip's story—and this may be true of other nineteenth-century educative plots as well—becomes more and more as it nears its end the working through of past history, an attempted return to the origin as the motivation of all the rest, the clue to what must else appear, as Pip puts it to Miss Havisham, a "blind and thankless life" (chap. 49, p. 403). The past needs to be incorporated *as past* within the present, mastered through the play of repetition in order for there to be an escape from repetition: in order for there to be difference, change, progress. In the failure ever to recover his own origin, Pip comes to concern himself with the question of Estella's origin, searching for her patronymics where knowledge of his own is ever foreclosed. Estella's story in fact eventually links all the plots of the novel: Satis House, the aspiration to gentility, the convict identity, "naterally wicious" (the status from which Jaggers attempted to rescue her), bringing up by hand, the Law. Pip's investigation of her origins as substitute for knowledge of his own has a certain validity in that, we discover, he appeared originally to Magwitch as a substitute for the lost Estella, his great expectations a compensation for the impossibility of hers: a chiasmus of the true situation. Yet when Pip has proved himself to be the successful detective in this quest, has uncovered the convergence of lines of plot that previously appeared distinct, indeed has proved more penetrating even than Jaggers, he discovers the knowledge he has gained to be radically unusable. When he has imparted his knowledge to Jaggers and Wemmick, he arrives at a kind of standoff, between what he has called his "poor dreams" and the deep plot he has now exposed. As Jaggers puts it to him, there is no gain to be had from knowledge. We are in the heart of darkness, and the articulation of its meaning must simply be repressed. In this novel full of mysteries and occult connections, detective work turns out to be both necessary and useless. It can offer no comfort and no true illumination to the detective himself. Like deciphering the letters on the tombstone, it produces no authority for the plot of life.

The novel in fact toward its end records a generalized breakdown of plots: none of the schemes machinated by the characters appears to accomplish its aims. The proof *a contrario* may be the "oversuccessful" result of Miss Havisham's plot, which has turned Estella into so heartless a creature that she cannot even experience emotional recognition of her benefactress. Her plotting has been a mechanical success but an intentional failure. This appears to be articulated in her final words, in her delirium following the fire:

> Towards midnight she began to wander in her speech, and after that it gradually set in that she said innumerable times in a low solemn voice, "What have I done!" And then, "When she first came I meant to save her from misery like mine." And then, "Take the pencil and write under my name, 'I forgive her!'" She never changed the order of these three sentences, but she sometimes left out a word in one or other of them; never putting in another word, but always leaving a blank and going on to the next word. [Chap. 49, pp. 408-9]

The cycle of three statements suggests a metonymy in search of arrest, a plot that can never find satisfactory resolution, that unresolved must play over its insistent repetitions, until silenced by death.

We confront the paradox that in this most highly plotted of novels—where Dickens performs all his thematic demonstrations through the manipulation of plot—we witness an evident subversion and futilization of the very concept of plot. If the chosen plots turn out to be erroneous, unauthorized, self-delusive, the deep plots when brought to light turn out to be unusable—criminally tainted, deviant. Plot as direction and intention in existence appears ultimately to be as evanescent as Magwitch's money, the product of immense labor, deprivation, planning, which is in the end forfeit to the Crown. Like money in its role as universal modern (capitalist) signifier as described by Roland Barthes, tied to no referent (such as land), defined only by its exchange-value, capable of unlimited metonymic circulation, the Expectations of fortune, as both plot and its aim or intention, as vehicle and object of representation, circulate through inflation to devaluation.[10]

The ultimate situation of plot in the novel may suggest an approach to the vexed question of Dickens's two endings to the novel: the one he originally wrote, and the revision substituted (at Bulwer-Lytton's suggestion) that was in fact printed. As modern readers we may tend to prefer the original ending, with its flat tone and refusal of romantic expectation, and find that the revision, with its tentative promise of reunion between Pip and Estella, "unbinds" energies that we thought had been thoroughly bound and indeed discharged from the text. We may also feel that choice between the two endings is somewhat arbitrary and unimportant in that the decisive moment has already occurred before either of these finales begins. The real ending may take place with Pip's recognition and acceptance of Magwitch after his recapture—this is certainly the ethical denouement—and his acceptance of a continuing existence without plot, as celibate clerk for Clarriker's. The pages that follow may simply be *obiter dicta*.

If we acknowledge Pip's experience of and with Magwitch to be the central energy of the text, it is significant that the climax of this experience, the moment of crisis and reversal in the attempted escape from England, bears traces of a hallucinatory repetition of the childhood spell—indeed, of that first recapture of Magwitch already repeated in Mr. Wopsle's theatrical vision:

> In the same moment, I saw the steersman of the galley lay his hand on his prisoner's shoulder, and saw that both boats were swinging round with the force of the tide, and saw that all hands on board the steamer were running forward quite frantically. Still in the same moment, I saw the prisoner start up, lean across his captor, and pull the cloak from the neck of the shrinking sitter in the galley. Still in the same moment, I saw the face disclosed was the face of the other convict of long ago. Still in the same moment, I saw the face tilt backward with a white terror on it that I shall never forget, and heard a great cry on board the steamer and a loud splash in the water, and felt the boat sink from under me. [Chap. 54, p. 451]

If this scene marks the beginning of a resolution—which it does in that it brings the death of the arch-villain Compeyson and the death sentence for Magwitch, hence the disappearance from the novel of its most energetic plotters—it is resolution in the register of repetition and working through, the final effort to master painful material from the insistent past. Pip emerges from this scene with an acceptance of the determinative past as both determinative and as past, which prepares us for the final escape from plot. It is interesting to note that where the "dream" plot of Estella is concerned, Pip's stated resolution has none of the compulsive energetic force of the passage just quoted, but is rather a conventional romantic fairy-tale ending, a conscious fiction designed, of course, to console the dying Magwitch, but possibly also a last effort at self-delusion: "'You had a child once, whom you loved and lost. . . . She lived and found powerful friends. She is living now. She is a lady and very beautiful. And I love her!'" (chap. 56, p. 467). If taken as anything other than a conscious fiction—if taken as part of the "truth" discovered by Pip's detections—this version of Pip's experience leads straight to what is worst in Dickens's revised version of the ending: the suggestion of an unbinding of what has already been bound up and disposed of, an unbinding which is indeed sensible in the rather embarrassed prose with which the revision begins: "Nevertheless, I knew while I said these words, that I secretly intended to revisit the site of the old house that evening, alone, for her sake. Yes, even so. For Estella's sake" (chap. 59, p. 490). The original end has the advantage of denying to Pip's text the possibility of any new infusion of energy, any new aspirations, the undoing of anything already done, the unbinding of energy that has been bound and led to discharge.

As at the start of the novel we had the impression of a life not yet subject to plot—a life in search of the sense of plot that would only gradually begin to precipitate around it—so at the end we have the impression of a life that has outlived plot, renounced plot, been cured of it: life that is left over. What follows the recognition of Magwitch is leftover, and any renewal of expectation and plotting—such as a revived romance with Estella—would have to belong to another story. It is with the image of a life bereft of plot—bereft of movement and desire—that the novel most appropriately leaves us. Indeed, we have at the end what could appropriately be called a "cure" from plot, in Pip's recognition of the general forfeiture of plotting, his renunciation of any attempt to direct his life. Plot comes to resemble a diseased, fevered state of the organism caught in the machinery of a desire which must eventually be renounced. Plot, we come to understand, was a state of abnormality or deviance, suggested thematically by its uneasy position between Newgate and Old Bailey, between criminality and the Law. The nineteenth-century novel in general—and especially that highly symptomatic development, the detective story—regularly conceives plot as a condition of deviance and abnormality, the product of cities and social depths, of a world where *récit* is *complot*, where all stories are the result of plotting, and plotting is very much machination. Deviance is the very condition for life to be narratable: the state of normality is devoid of interest, energy, and the possibility for narration. In between a beginning prior to plot and an end beyond plot, the middle—the plotted text—has been in a state of *error:* wandering and misinterpretation.

IV

That plot should prove to be deviance and error is fully consonant with Freud's model in *Beyond the Pleasure Principle*, where the narratable life of the organism is seen as detour, a deviance from the quiescence of the inorganic which has been maintained through the dynamic interaction of Eros (desire, intention, the urge toward combination and meaning) and the death instinct (the drive toward the end). What Pip at one point has called his "ill-regulated aspirations" (chap. 39, p. 238) is the figure of plot as desire: Eros as the force that binds integers together in ever-larger wholes, totalizing, metaphoric, the desire for the integration of meaning. Whereas, concomitantly, repetition and return have spoken of the death instinct, the drive to return to the quiescence of the inorganic, of the nontextual. Yet the repetitions, which have served to bind the various plots, both prolonging the detour and more effectively preparing the final discharge, have created that delay necessary to incorporate the past within the present and to let us understand end in relation to beginning. Through the erotics of the text, we have inexorably been led to its end, which is precisely quiescence: to a "time after" which is an image of the "time before," to the nonnarratable. If we take a further step suggested by adducing the argument of "Remembering, Repeating, and Working Through" to that of *Beyond the Pleasure Principle* and say that repetition is a kind of remembering, and thus a way of reorganizing a story whose connective links have been obscured and lost, and if repetition speaks of the death instinct, the finding of the right end, then what is being played out in repetition is necessarily the proper vector of the drive toward the end. That is, once you've determined the right plot, plot is over. Plot itself is working-through.

Great Expectations is exemplary in demonstrating both the need for plot and its status as deviance, both the need for narration and the necessity to be cured from it. The deviance and error of plot may be necessary factors of the historicity of desire and the insistence on, and of, narrative meanings; the desire to wrest beginnings and ends from the uninterrupted flow of middles, from temporality itself; the search for that significant closure that would illuminate the sense of an existence, the meaning of life. The desire for meaning is ultimately the reader's, who must mime Pip's acts of reading, but do them better. Both using and subverting the systems of meaning discovered or postulated by its hero, *Great Expectations* exposes for its reader the very reading process itself: the way the reader goes about finding meaning in the narrative text, and the limits of that meaning as the limits of narrative.

In terms of the problematic of reading which the novel thematizes from its opening page, we could say that Pip, continuously returning toward origins in order to know the plot whose authority would lead him to the right end, never recovering origins and never finding the authoritative plot, never succeeds in going behind his self-naming to a reading of the missing patronymic. He is ever returned to a rereading of the unauthorized text of his self-given name, Pip. "Pip" sounded like a beginning, a seed. But of course when you reach the end of the name "Pip," you can return backwards, and it is just the same: a repetitive text without variation or point of fixity, a return which leads to an unarrested shuttling back and forth. The name is in fact a palindrome. In the rereading of the palindrome the novel may offer its final comment on its expectative plot.

What, finally, do we make of the fact that Dickens, master-plotter in the history of the novel, in this most tightly and consistently plotted of his novels seems to expose plot as a kind of necessary error? Dickens's most telling comment on the question may come at the moment of Magwitch's sentencing. The judge gives a legalistic and moralistic version of Magwitch's life story, his violence, his crimes, the passions that made him a "scourge to society" and led him to escape from deportation, thus calling upon his head the death sentence. The passage continues:

> The sun was striking in at the great windows of the court, through the glittering drops of rain upon the glass, and it made a broad shaft of light between the two-and-thirty [prisoners at the bar] and the judge, linking both together, and perhaps reminding some among the audience, how both were passing on, with absolute equality, to the greater judgment that knoweth all things and cannot err. Rising for a moment, a distinct speck of face in this way of light, the prisoner [Magwitch] said, "My Lord, I have received my sentence of Death from the Almighty, but I bow to yours," and sat down again. There was some hushing, and the judge went on with what he had to say to the rest. [Chap. 56, p. 465]

The passage is sentimental but also, I think, effective. What it does is juxtapose human plots—including those of the Law—to eternal orders which render human attempts to plot and to interpret plot not only futile, but ethically unacceptable. The greater judgment makes human plots mere shadows. There is another end that recuperates passing human time and its petty chronologies to the timeless. Yet this other end is not visible; the other orders are not available. As Mr. Wopsle's case suggested, the divine word is barred in the world of the novel (it is suggestive that Christmas dinner is interrupted by the command to repair handcuffs). If there is a divine master-plot for human existence, it is radically unknowable.

In the absence or silence of divine master-plots, the organization and interpretation of human plots remains as necessary as it is problematic. Reading the signs of intention in life's actions is the central act of existence, which in turn legitimates the enterprise of reading for the reader of *Great Expectations*—or perhaps, vice versa, since the reading of plot within the text and as the text are perfectly analogous, mirrors of one another. If there is by the end of the narrative an abandonment of the attempt to read plot, this simply mirrors the fact that the process of narration has come to a close—or, again, vice versa. But that there should be a cure from the reading of plot within the text—before its very end—and the creation of a leftover, suggests a critique of reading itself, which is possibly like the judge's sentence: human interpretation in ignorance of the true vectors of the true text. So it may indeed be. But if the master-text is not available, we are condemned to the reading of erroneous plots, granted insight only insofar as we can gain disillusion from them. We are condemned to repetition, rereading, in the knowledge that what we discover will always be that there was nothing to be discovered. Yet the process remains necessary if we are not to be caught perpetually in the "blind and thankless" existence, in the illusory middle. Like Oedipus, like Pip, we are condemned to reinterpretation of our names. But it is rare that the name coincide so perfectly with a fullness and a negation of identity as in the case of Oedipus. In a post-tragic universe, our situation is more likely to be that of Pip, compelled to reinterpret the meaning of the name he assigned to himself with his infant tongue: the history of an infinitely repeatable palindrome.

From *New Literary History* 11, no. 3 (1980): 503-523. Copyright © 1980 by The Johns Hopkins University Press. Reprinted with permission of The Johns Hopkins University Press.

Notes

1. Most useful to me has been the work of Tzvetan Todorov, esp. *Poétique de la prose* (Paris, 1971), in English, *The Poetics of Prose*, tr. Richard Howard (Ithaca, N.Y., 1977); Roland Barthes, esp. *S/Z* (Paris, 1970), in English, *S/Z*, tr. Richard Miller (New York, 1975); and Gérard Genette, esp. "Discours du récit," in *Figures III* (Paris, 1972).

2. Walter Benjamin, "The Storyteller," in *Illuminations*, tr. Harry Zohn (New York, 1969), pp. 94, 101. See also Frank Kermode, *The Sense of an Ending* (New York, 1967).

3. Charles Dickens, *Great Expectations* (New York, 1963), p. 1. My references are all to this Holt, Rinehart and Winston edition, and will henceforth be given within parentheses in the text. I will include chapter numbers to facilitate reference to other editions.

4. On the theme of reading in the novel, see Max Byrd, "'Reading' in *Great Expectations*," *PMLA*, 9, No. 2 (1976), 259-65.

5. See chap. 19, pp. 159, 160. Miss Havisham is thus seemingly cast in the role of the "Donor" (who provides the hero with a magical agent), one of the seven dramatis personae of the fairy tale identified by Vladimir Propp in *The Morphology of the Folktale*.

6. On the role of the law as one of the formal orders of the novel, see Moshe Ron, "Autobiographical Narration and Formal Closure in *Great Expectations*," *University of Hartford Studies in Literature*, 5, No. 1 (1977), 37-66. The importance of criminality in Dickens has of course been noted by many critics, including Edmund Wilson in his seminal essay, "Dickens: The Two Scrooges," in *The Wound and the Bow* (Boston, 1941).

7. A fuller exposition of this model will be found in my essay, "Freud's Masterplot," *Yale French Studies*, No. 55-56 (1977-78), 280-300. *Beyond the Pleasure Principle* is found in *The Complete Psychological Works of Sigmund Freud*, ed. James Strachey (London, 1953), XVIII, 1-64.

8. The pattern of the incestuous couple, where the implication of the brother-sister relation serves as both attraction and prohibition, has been noted by several critics. See esp. Harry Stone, "The Love Pattern in Dickens' Novels," in *Dickens the Craftsman*, ed. Robert B. Partlow, Jr. (Carbondale and Edwardsville, 1970), and Albert J. Guerard, *The Triumph of the Novel* (New York, 1976), p. 70. *Great Expectations* gives particular weight to the role of the Father as source of the Law: Magwitch, assuming in different registers the role of father both to Estella and to Pip, becomes, not a figure of authority, but a principle of pure interdiction.

9. "Remembering, Repeating and Working-Through" [*Erinnern, Wiederholen and Durcharbeiten*], *Works*, XII, 145-56.

10. See *S/Z*, tr. Richard Miller, pp. 39-40.

Realism as Self-Forgetfulness:
Gender, Ethics, and *Great Expectations*_____

Caroline Levine

In 1848, reviewer Edwin Percy Whipple asserted that *Jane Eyre* must have been partly penned by a man. His evidence was that it echoed the style of that decidedly masculine writer—the author of *Wuthering Heights*. Proved emphatically wrong by Charlotte Brontë's revelations of 1850, Whipple had learned his lesson by the time he came to review *Great Expectations* eleven years later. What he claimed to admire most in Dickens's new novel was the fact that the mystery had confounded him:

> In no other of his romances has the author succeeded so perfectly in at once stimulating and baffling the curiosity of his readers. He stirred the dullest minds to guess the secret of his mystery; but, so far as we have learned, the guesses of his most intelligent readers have been almost as wide of the mark as those of the least apprehensive. It has been all the more provoking to the former class, that each surprise was the result of art, and not of trick; for a rapid review of previous chapters has shown that the materials of a strictly logical development of the story were freely given.[1]

Whipple was not the only one to appreciate Dickens's skill in the art of plotting. The *Times* celebrated Dickens "as the greatest master of construction" of the era, the most expert at keeping "an exciting story within the bounds of probability." The *Athenaeum* praised him for his adroit sustaining of readerly interest: "Every week almost, as it came out, we were artfully stopped at some juncture which made Suspense count the days until the next number appeared." Even Margaret Oliphant, who dismissed *Great Expectations* as an absurd fantasy, understood that enthusiastic readers found the novel's incidents "strange, dangerous, and exciting."[2] Taken together, these nineteenth-century reviews suggest that suspense may have been the most alluring seduction of *Great Expectations* for the Victorian reader.

This chapter makes the case that Dickens not only thrilled his contemporaries by producing and sustaining a fascinating suspense plot, but he also articulated a clear ethical value for suspenseful plotting. Like *Jane Eyre*, *Great Expectations* brings together the exciting pleasures of suspense with its weighty significance. More surprisingly, perhaps, the novel suggests that in the context of Victorian culture, the gender of suspense was feminine. Dickens claims, as do Ruskin and Brontë, that we cannot unearth the hidden truths of the world without putting aside our most entrenched expectations; in order to know the world we must learn to suspend ourselves. And since Victorian culture insistently cast self-suspension as a quintessentially feminine virtue, women, it seemed, must be the most acute readers of the real. In this light, Biddy emerges as the epistemological ideal of *Great Expectations*.

Great Expectations also allows us to see how the skeptical epistemology of detective fiction moved beyond the literal inclusion of the detective. In order to make the claim that *Great Expectations* belongs in a tradition of detective fiction—quite as much as *Bleak House* or *The Mystery of Edwin Drood*—I start with a brief reading of Poe's "Purloined Letter," which, along with *The Moonstone*, is famous for having launched the genre. Poe shows us how central the suspension of the self is to the accumulation of hidden knowledge. If we read Poe alongside *Great Expectations*, we can see how the earliest detective fictions reveal a shared concern to disseminate a skeptical epistemology.

The Moonstone united the scientist and the detective, and Umberto Eco argues that such a combination is fitting, since they share a skeptical epistemology: they "suspect on principle that some elements, evident but not apparently important, may be evidence of something else that is not evident—and on this basis they elaborate a new hypothesis to be tested."[3] What science and detection have in common, in other words, is a thoroughgoing resistance to the assumption that the truths of the world are readily apparent. Dickens broadens the scope of this method to suggest that the scientist's paradigm of suspicion is necessary to solving all mysteries—from formal detection to ordinary reading, including the most commonplace interpretive puzzles of everyday life. Like Brontë, then, Dickens uses the novel to disseminate the critical suspension of judgment and the epistemological project of testing.

The Ethics of Suspense: Poe's "Purloined Letter"

Critics have often claimed that suspenseful plots comfort socially discomfited readers with neat, safe endings. Clive Bloom writes that Edgar Allan Poe's orderly plots are responses to the "decentered and *disordered* society he found himself in." Thus "Poe's art is an antidote to contemporary social displacement on a wide scale." Similarly, Leo Bersani writes that "Realistic fiction serves nineteenth-century society by providing it with strategies for containing (and repressing) its disorder within significantly structured stories about itself."[4] Nineteenth-century novelists supposedly forced the real world to conform, through artful plotting, to historically conditioned conceptual paradigms and ideological oversimplifications.[5]

But this is to miss the lessons of suspenseful narrative. Charlotte Brontë, in her crafty equivocations, taught us to mistrust convention and the workings of our own desire in unearthing the secrets of the world. Before turning to Dickens, we can see the demand for self-suspension as the very first lesson of detective fiction. In "The Purloined Letter," Poe teaches us to recognize the dangers of relying on entrenched assumptions and desires.[6] The crucial error made by the Prefect and his officers, according to Poe's wise Dupin, is that "They consider only their own ideas of ingenuity; and, in searching for anything hidden, advert only to the modes in which they would have hidden it" (12). Like Reynolds and Kant, Ruskin's pre-realist predecessors, the detectives retreat into their own minds in pursuit of the truth. What they refuse to perceive, therefore, is the potential *otherness* of the real. As Jacques Lacan puts it, "the detectives have so immutable a notion of the real that they fail to notice that their search tends to transform it into its object."[7]

Dupin concedes one point to the Prefect and his men: "They are right in this much, that their own ingenuity is a faithful representative of that of the mass; but when the cunning of an individual felon is diverse in character from their own, the felon foils them, of course" (12). Relying on their own preconceptions, which exemplify *general* rules and ideas, the detectives fail to consider what Ruskin would call the "infinite variety" of the real. And this has consequences for method. Unwilling or unable to recognize the world's likely resistance to convention, the detectives never question their habits of detection. "They have no variation of principle in their investigations; at best, when urged by some unusual emergency, by some extraordinary reward, they extend or exaggerate their old modes of practice without touching their principles" (12). To put this another way, they never experiment, obdurately refusing to transform the hypothesis—the principle—even when it does not correspond with the evidence. The result, of course, is that the detectives cannot solve the mystery. Nor can the naïve narrator, who is shocked at Dupin's willingness to overturn convention and exclaims: "You do not mean to set at naught the well-digested idea of centuries?" (13). Here, then, is realism in a nutshell: to know the world one must acknowledge its inaccessibility to traditional rules and conventions—and its basic, unyielding otherness.

It is this emphasis on alterity that leads me to argue that suspense not only offers a potentially subversive politics, as Brontë makes clear, but also disseminates an influential nineteenth-century ethics. Narrative mysteries in the Victorian period teach us to set aside self-interest and personal desire in order to attend to the surprising, unsettling world, a world that may well flout our prejudices and disappoint our expectations. From Poe to Dickens and beyond, the suspense of detective fiction unites ethics and epistemology in a skeptical method intended to teach us a new and more respectful relationship to the world.

Dickensian Suspense

Jaggers, in a perfect example of a plotted "snare," withholds a crucial piece of knowledge from Pip. "The name of the person who is your liberal benefactor remains a profound secret, until the person chooses to reveal it."[8] It is the checking of knowledge that leads directly to the production of Pip's mistaken expectations. And it is the failure to know the truth that gives rise to the desiring motors of the realist plot. We might even say that "great expectations" describes the experience of suspense so perfectly that Pip can only be a figure for the reader of the nineteenth-century novel.

But in fact, Pip and the reader have crucially different experiences of this particular mystery. For the reader, the withholding of the name of Pip's benefactor indicates quite unequivocally that a specific piece of knowledge is missing. By signaling the existence of a secret, Dickens forces us to recognize the fact of our ignorance and so piques a desire for further knowledge. Indeed, even if, as first-time readers, we suspect that it is Miss Havisham who is going to turn out to have been Pip's benefactor, the text offers us an inescapable sign that there is some reason for secrecy. We have to wait and wonder, to speculate and hypothesize, to know that there is something we do not know.

One of Pip's clearest failures in the novel is that he does not experience the moment of his inheritance as suspenseful: unlike the reader, he leaps to the conclusion that his benefactor is Miss Havisham, and he rushes to assume that this is all part of a plot to marry him to Estella. "[Miss Havisham] had adopted Estella, she had as good as adopted me, and *it could not fail to be her intention* to bring us together" (232; my emphasis). Pip, refusing to suspend judgment, sees the world as a reflection of his own hopes and expectations. The result is a drastic misreading. Harry Stone explains that Pip's "topsy-turvy vision" leads him to read the world in reverse.[9] And I would like to suggest that this topsy-turvy structure applies specifically to the text's realism. Pip exclaims: "My dream was out; my wild fancy was surpassed by sober reality; Miss Havisham was going to make my fortune on a grand scale"

(137). Inverting the realist experiment, Pip rushes to assume that "sober reality" coincides with his representations. Thus he is in for a rude shock. He will never solve the mysteries of the world if, like Poe's inflexible detectives, he does not put his own methods and assumptions on trial.[10]

The trial—the testing of hypotheses in order to arrive at knowledge. Dickens shows us clearly why we find so many trials, *both* legal and scientific, in the nineteenth-century novel. Trials, whether in the courtroom or the laboratory, demand the suspension of judgment. Both scientific experiments and courtroom narratives, by their very structure, insist on a delay between initial appearance and more certain knowledge.[11] Both are perfect vehicles for narrative suspense. And perhaps most importantly, both involve plot's ethical imperative: the arresting of arbitrary desires and prejudices in the face of tested knowledge. In *Great Expectations*, Jaggers, the great figure of the law, sounds almost like a broken record in his reiteration of the importance of not leaping to capricious conclusions. Directly before introducing the mystery of Pip's expectations, he offers a disquisition on the legal presumption of innocence to the crowd at the Three Jolly Bargemen. "Do you know, or do you not know, that the law of England supposes every man to be innocent, until he is proved—proved—to be guilty?" (133). The double utterance of the need for proof, here, underscores the fact that the static, unchanging Jaggers will simply repeat the same lesson to Pip, over and over again. "Never mind what you have always longed for, Mr. Pip," Jaggers says, "keep to the record" (138).

Jaggers's instruction to the crowd at the Jolly Bargemen focuses on their leap to assume the guilt of the convict without the rigorous tests of the fair trial. "Are you aware, or are you not aware," asks Jaggers of Mr. Wopsle, "that none of these witnesses have yet been cross-examined?" (133). If to examine is to suspend judgment, then to *cross-examine* is to return to questions already asked and answers already given, to inspect, to question, and often to undermine the evidence. In its exacting methods, legal cross-examination outstrips other models of skeptical interrogation and takes its place as the consummately fair paradigm of knowledge seeking.

But Pip's upbringing has not prepared him for fair trials. The first appearance of the unjust Mrs. Joe reads like a cruel parody of a court-room examination:

> "Who brought you up by hand?"
> "You did," said I.
> "And why did I do it, I should like to know!" exclaimed my sister.
> I whimpered, "I don't know."
> "*I* don't!" said my sister. "I'd never do it again. I know that." (9-10)

Assuming Pip's guilt and her own long-suffering goodness, Mrs. Joe's questions are hardly skeptical inquiries: she asks Pip to generate not knowledge but gratitude, not truths but justifications. This is capricious catechism rather than skeptical cross-examination.

In fact, Pip's childhood experience of the trial involves not only the presumption of his guilt and the willful disregarding of the facts, but the evil of questioning itself. "Drat that boy . . . what a questioner he is," Mrs. Joe says irritably, and adds: "Ask no questions, and you'll be told no lies" (14). Mrs. Joe claims to believe that questioning only invites falsehoods from the other. She therefore refuses to countenance inquiry altogether and considers questioning to represent a kind of guilt. "People are put in the Hullos because they murder, and because they rob, and forge, and do all sorts of bad; and they always begin by asking questions," she warns (14).[12] Pip seems to incorporate this lesson immediately, connecting his inquiry to his imminent crime: "I had begun by asking questions, and I was going to rob Mrs. Joe" (14).

On the one hand, Jaggers makes clear that the rigorous questioning of cross-examination is the sign of a fair trial; on the other hand, Mrs. Joe teaches Pip that to ask questions is to be guilty oneself. It is no mystery which of these two is in the right. Mrs. Joe does not even practice what she preaches: when Pip returns from Miss Havisham's, Dickens tells us pointedly that she asks "a number of questions" and shoves Pip's face against the wall for not answering the questions "at sufficient length" (66). She is rewarded with precisely the falsehoods she has claimed to expect when Pip invents a rich fantasy about the house he visits. Carried away with her own self-interest, she speculates greedily, enjoying her wonder about Pip's prospects. Criminalizing Pip's questions and violently insisting on answers to her own, however false, Mrs. Joe casts inquiry itself as a guilty, fruitless act, all the while enjoying it herself. Given this education in the failure of questions, is it any wonder, later, that Pip will not thoroughly interrogate his own "expectations"? He has not been educated in the fruitful patterns of plotted suspense, whether legal, or scientific, or novelistic. Dickens's readers will have the privilege of a different kind of education.

The Gender of Realism

If Jaggers in all his skeptical suspicion of the world is eminently, if impersonally, fair, while Pip's despotic sister criminalizes innocent inquiry, we can begin to draw a Dickensian link between skepticism and justice. Jaggers's presumption of innocence is a model of justice, and thus to be just one must begin by assuming that one does not know the truth, and in order to come to know the truth fairly one must conduct rigorous tests unprejudiced by personal preference and desire. Here is the quintessentially realist union of knowledge, ethics, and experimentation: the skeptical realist demands not so much the real itself, as a rigorously judicious relation to that real.

Yet, Jaggers is hardly the model of sympathetic humanity in *Great Expectations*. And despite his stated philosophy of presumed innocence, in the context of the courtroom Jaggers is not scrupulously fair but rather effectively partisan: it is a good thing when Jaggers is "for" one, no matter how guilty one is. Thus what he attempts to teach Pip is not his own practice but rather the impartial position of the law itself—the fairness of which demands the dual presumption of ignorance and skeptical inquiry. In theory, this ethical relationship to the world is all very well. But the impersonal logic of the law overlooks the force and experience of desire. However articulate a spokesman for abstract justice, the static Jaggers is missing the forward-looking pressures of aspiration and speculation, and so he is a poor model for Pip, whose desires make him all too susceptible to the joys of guesswork. Jaggers neglects the very impulses that motivate not only Pip but also the reader of suspenseful plots: the motors of keen preference and unfulfilled desire. It is easy enough to invoke the presumption of innocence; it is altogether another matter to quell conjecture, extinguish hope, and stifle inclination. The lawyer is not a good figure for the realist reader because, without desire, he does not have to work to set his desires aside; without prejudice, he does not have to labor to transform his prejudices into knowledge.

Unlike Jaggers, the realist text teaches us skepticism *in the face of* desire and prejudice. It is for this reason that realist experimentation is about self-denial, or as Pip calls it, "self-forgetfulness." The term "self-forgetfulness" actually appears in reference to Biddy, that consummate angel in the house, who repeatedly puts her own desires aside in order to attend to the needs of those around her.[13] At first, then, "self-forgetfulness" might seem a politically worrying description, attached as it is to the dangerously self-sacrificing model of Victorian womanhood. The familiar image of the self-denying woman would suggest that only one gender is required to "forget" its desires.[14] But to see Biddy as only an angel in the house is to miss her role as the text's most skillful reader, the novel's most expert interpreter of difficult and cryptic signs. In a text packed with misreadings, Biddy's interpretations of the world are sensitive, astute, and just. Quick to spot Pip's bad faith and Joe's pride, she is also adept at the technical skill of reading. Indeed, it is she who actually teaches both Pip and Joe to read in the first place, and it is she who remains Pip's literary equal even without the benefit of his formal education. Pip is perplexed by her superiority to him in this respect: "'How do you manage, Biddy,' said I, 'to learn everything that I learn, and always to keep up with me?'" (125). Biddy is intelligent, and above all, she is an intelligent *reader*.

I would like to suggest that one minor incident in the novel uncovers the ethical-epistemological structure that drives the text as a whole, and it puts Biddy's skill as an interpreter at its center. Mrs. Joe, after her beating, has been communicating by tracing cryptic signs on a slate, including "a character that looked like a curious T." Pip at first interprets it as an initial: "I had in vain tried everything producible that began with a T, from tar to toast and tub." This strategy fails to offer up the truth, and so, in good experimental fashion, he changes tactics, from reading the sign as arbitrary linguistic signifier to reading it as a pictorial referent. Now he is on the right track: "At length it had come into my head that the sign looked like a hammer," a hypothesis to which Pip's sister expresses "a qualified assent" (122-23). We have seen Pip read this way before—on the very first page of the novel he has read his parents' tombstones as if the letters were images. Cannily, then, he shifts reading practices when faced with a mystery and moves a step closer to solving it. This shift does not altogether solve the mystery, however, because Mrs. Joe is not interested in the hammer itself when Pip presents her with it. Pip is stumped. It is Biddy who comes to the rescue. More adept a reader than Pip, she changes reading practices yet again, focusing on the hammer's *associations*. Connecting the hammer with one who wields it in the forge, Biddy presents Mrs. Joe with Orlick. Pip's sister nods vigorously, and so the solution to the mystery is confirmed. The "T" is a metonymic signifier, as well as an ideographic one. The process of discovering this fact has entailed several radical shifts in hypothesis. Indeed, it has meant not only identifying an array of possible solutions to the mystery but also allowing variations in the practice of reading itself.

Consistently, Biddy emerges as the most skillful reader of the signs Mrs. Joe communicates, understanding her confusing signals "as though she had studied her from infancy" (122). It is this responsiveness that earns her a place as Mrs. Joe's caretaker. Thus what makes Biddy a sensitive reader is not only an experimental epistemology but also an ethical acuteness, which allows her to encounter the surprising alterity of the world on its own terms. Her quintessentially feminine labor as Mrs. Joe's nurse and interpreter involves both caring and knowing—both responding to the other and understanding that other. And unlike the abstractly fair Jaggers, Biddy's ethical-epistemological model is supple, *flexible:* she is not bound by written principles—the conventionalized letter of the law—but moves easily among paradigms of interpretation when confronted with the enigmas of the other.[15] Her letter can become metaphor or metonym, picture or arbitrary sign.[16] She can read the mysterious signs produced by Pip's sister because she can put aside her own presumptions to attend to the radical otherness of a mind unlike her own. This, then, is Biddy's "self-forgetfulness," just as it is the substance of experimental realism.[17]

If Biddy seems like a secondary character and her mysteries comparatively inconsequential, the text presents substantial evidence to suggest that her responses to the world should act as a model for both Pip and the reader. Pip, as we know, goes wrong when he does not follow Biddy's experimental example. When faced with the central mystery of his life, he does not test his hypotheses, and thus he imposes his mistaken guesses on the world. And it is Pip's self-absorption that makes him a poor reader: lacking humility, sure of his own judgment, he cannot put aside his own desires to ready himself for surprises. From the perspective of a scientific epistemology, Pip fails to know the hidden truth because he is incapable of what Tyndall calls "self-renunciation." Obviously consumed by self-interested desire, he reads into Jaggers's mystery just what he wants to understand—that Miss Havisham intends both her fortune and Estella for him—and therefore he misses the possibility that the world may not coincide with his expectations.

Biddy's skill at solving mysteries appears in the text directly—and suggestively—after Dickens has introduced a set of official detectives who fail to uncover Mrs. Joe's attacker. Much like Poe's Prefect, Dickens's detectives cannot solve the mystery because they rely entirely on their own ideas, refusing to discard hypotheses when these do not match the evidence. "They took up several obviously wrong people, and they ran their heads very hard against wrong ideas, and persisted in trying to fit the circumstances to the ideas, instead of trying to extract ideas from the circumstances" (121). Like Pip and Ruskin's Old Masters, they begin with the idea and assume that the important truths of the world will reflect the patterns of their minds. A better student of realism, Biddy solves her mysteries by knowing that she does not know, testing guess after guess against the evidence. Refusing rigid conventions and fixed principles, she comes both to know more and to act more compassionately than her novelistic counterparts.

And so, by uniting a sharp perceptiveness with a self-denying femininity, Dickens allows us to rethink the paradigm of the angel in the house. With Biddy as our model, it begins to look as though there might be a connection between Victorian femininity and Victorian science. Both demand a self-denying receptiveness to alterity. Both specifically call for the capacity to suspend desire and preconception in order to come to know the otherness of the world.[18] In this context, it is not surprising that Biddy is an unusually skilled reader in a world of perilously puzzling signs and willful misreadings—responding more skeptically and judiciously than any other character to the mysteries she encounters.[19] With "self-forgetfulness," Dickens is not simply offering us a limiting image of self-sacrificing femininity: Biddy, in responding to the otherness of the world on its own terms, is a model of reading for us readers. The thrusting, self-important hero would do well to learn the heroine's self-denying skepticism, both ethically and epistemologically. And if "self-forgetfulness" is both the foundation of realist knowledge and the ideal quality of Victorian womanhood, then the gender of realism is feminine.

The Lessons of Dickensian Suspense

Pip does finally recognize Biddy's wisdom as he sets off to marry her in the penultimate chapter of the novel, imagining that he will ask her to make him "a better man" (468). Indeed, though much has been made of the two endings of *Great Expectations*, we may say that there are really *three*. Before Pip encounters the lonely Estella in the last chapter, he deliberately and seriously plans to marry Biddy. We are treated to images of the happy home life with Biddy he forecasts for himself, "and of the change for the better that would come over my character when I had a guiding spirit at my side" (473). We are even given a verbatim account of the humble marriage proposal Pip has rehearsed, as if to underscore the earnestness of the plan. Then, the journey home is a suspenseful one: Dickens makes us wait as Pip gives full play to his expectations and finds them slowly disappointed, one by one. First his "hopeful notion of seeing [Biddy] busily engaged in her daily duties" is "defeated" (473); then "almost fearing," he finds the forge closed; and finally he discovers that he has arrived too late. Here, what Pip pointedly calls his "last baffled hope" (474) is not his marriage to Estella, but to Biddy.

Thus Pip fails to bring about the conventional end to the marriage plot—three tunes, and with two different women. Of the two candidates for marriage, Biddy is even a more credible companion for living happily ever after than Estella, as Dickens makes quite plain in Pip's rosy fantasies of their future together.[20] Furthermore, the suspense the novel builds up with Pip's "last babied hope" is in direct contrast to the flat unexpectedness of the final meeting with Estella, at least in the first ending. Eleven years after his failed attempt to marry Biddy, Pip tells her that his "poor dream . . . has all gone by" (477), and then he simply happens upon Estella, without anticipation, without particular plans or desires. In the first ending, there is no prospect of a marriage. In this version of the novel, Biddy is indeed Pip's last hope—the last of his great expectations, the final object of suspense. Indeed, Dickens called the final meeting with Estella "the extra end . . . after Biddy and Joe are done with."[21] At the advice of his friend Bulwer-Lytton, Dickens then added suspense into his second ending, allowing expectation to sneak back into the text.

Why must Pip endure the suspense and disappointed hope of marrying Biddy and then undergo suspense again with Estella in the second edition of the novel? Why are we still encountering "expectations" in the final paragraphs of the novel?[22] Peter Brooks argues that none of these endings matters terribly much because the plot is effectively over with "the decisive moment" that is the death of Magwitch.[23] But this conclusion overlooks the text's careful teaching of the lessons of skeptical realism. Doubt is not over because the larger mystery of the novel is solved. The fundamental premise of realism is that the otherness of the world is always mysterious—always demanding tests, doubts, and guesswork. Thus the text of experimental realism emphatically refuses to let us forget suspense, because it must carry over into our own lives. It does not want to let us rest easy, satisfied with neat answers and conventional closures. We must learn the alterity of the real from these fictional plots and then transfer the practice of skeptical, anti-conventional doubt to the mysteries of our lives.

If the Victorian novel suggests that suspense demands the rigors of self-denial and the pains of self-annihilation, its extraordinary power lies in the fact that it is also *pleasurable*. Dickens focuses our attention on the intriguing seductions of suspense toward the end of the novel. Magwitch has come to stay, and Pip wants desperately to keep his existence a secret. The most important task for him, therefore, is to hide the convict from his domestic servants. Perfectly in keeping with the lessons of "The Purloined Letter," Pip decides that the best way to screen Magwitch is not to try to keep him out of sight, but to display him as something other than what he is:

> The impossibility of keeping him concealed in the chambers was self-evident. It could not be done, and the attempt to do it would inevitably engender suspicion. True, I had no Avenger in my service now, but I was

looked after by an inflammatory old female, assisted by an animated rag-bag whom she called her niece, and to keep a room secret from them would be to invite curiosity and exaggeration. They both had weak eyes, which I had long attributed to their chronically looking in at keyholes, and they were always at hand when not wanted; indeed, that was their only reliable quality besides larceny. Not to get up a mystery with these people, I resolved to announce in the morning that my uncle had unexpectedly come from the country. (325)

To conceal is to "engender suspicion," and to keep a room secret is to "invite" curiosity. In other words, a mystery excites alert, skeptical attention. In this case, it is the attention of curious women that is "engendered," and perhaps it is no accident that the small male Avenger has been replaced by two daunting feminine investigators. Pip tries scornfully to divest these thieving domestics of their humanity—referring to them as an "inflammatory old female" and her "ragbag" niece—but one consequence of his scorn is that he narrows our knowledge of the servants to two basic facts: their femininity and their curiosity. Since Pip has markedly failed to indulge such curiosity himself, Dickens hints, once again, that the most canny readers are feminine readers, willing to acknowledge that the world may not match their expectations of it and enjoying the possibility that it might yield more than they know. If the elder servant and the person she "calls" her niece look through keyholes and try to grasp the hidden facts of the environment, Pip and the person he calls his uncle are their masculine others—the flip side of the epistemological coin, readers who fail to be interested in the mysteries around them, subjects of knowledge who do not enjoy the recognition that their desires may or may not match the world.

The female servants are strikingly like us, the readers of suspenseful fiction, and Pip, here, deliberately thwarts their excitement. Thus a knowing Dickens lays bare the structures of suspense: the excitement of interest in the not-self emerges from the knowledge that there is something we do not know. This withholding has a twofold effect: it compels the recognition that the world is other to us, and it acts as a spur to pleasurable, keen inquisitiveness. It is as if Pip, here, has not only learned the truth about his benefactor but also suddenly knows the truth about readerly desire: "to get up a mystery" is the surest way to stimulate the desire to solve that mystery, and, by contrast, to stifle the interest of cunning readers, one must know how to suppress and divert the enigmas of suspense. Pip masterfully disallows the pleasures of doubt—and thereby keeps himself safe from inquisitive reading.

By the time Pip comes to think of marrying either Biddy or Estella, he and the reader have, we hope, learned to doubt properly. We should have learned to enjoy our ignorance, not leaping to assume that our assumptions will be validated by events, not rushing to imagine that we know all of the answers. But just in case we have not learned our lesson, we are offered a coda of suspense, first with Biddy, later with Estella. We must not close the book thinking that there are no more questions, and so we are treated to a series of equally persuasive novelistic outcomes—all of which are plausible, and none quite realized. The conventional marriage plot is circumvented twice, only to reenter the text as an ambiguous, by no means certain, outcome in the second version.[24] If we are still reliant on conventional assumptions even after five hundred pages of suspense, then the multiple ending more or less inescapably leads us to doubt those assumptions. Willy-nilly, we must come to know that we do not know.

Competing endings are a fact of suspenseful plotting: for us readers to feel that there is interesting, unfinished business in the final pages of the novel, it must be plausible for Pip to marry or not to marry, to choose one woman or the other. By the end of *Great Expectations*, it may even be unclear whether it is Biddy or Estella who has all along been the most conventional mate for Pip, so plausible do both options appear. Dickens skillfully throws the conventional ending into question by explicitly including it while showing that it functions as only one alternative among several. Incorporating all manner of endings into the text proper, Dickens thus defamiliarizes suspense itself. We would not enjoy doubts about the narrative's course if it were not possible for it to end in a number of different ways.[25] Thus even conventional closure always takes its place among alternative outcomes, contending with less stable, less neat, less happy conclusions. The anxiety stirred up by suspense proves that we are not so sure that the happy ending is the necessary one. In fact, Dickens suggests that the ending hardly matters at all. Suspense is there to teach us to face the fact that time's unfolding might not offer us what we expect.

Notes

1. [Edwin Percy Whipple], unsigned review, *Atlantic Monthly* (September 1861); in P. Collins, *Dickens*, 428.

2. [E. S. Dallas], unsigned review, *Times* (17 October 1861), in P. Collins, *Dickens*, 432; [H. F. Chorley], unsigned review, *Athenaeum* (13 July 1861), in Dickens, *Great Expectations*, ed. Law and Pinnington, 54; [Margaret Oliphant], "Sensation Novels," *Blackwood's Magazine* (May 1862), in Collins, *Dickens*, 439.

3. Eco, "Overinterpreting Texts," 48-49. For a reading of the relationship between science and detection that focuses on their shared capacity to control and discipline, see Thomas, *Detective Fiction and the Rise of Forensic Science*.

4. Bloom, "Capitalising on Poe's Detective," 17; Bersani, *Future for Astyanax*, 63.

5. The list of critics who have faulted both suspense and realism for imposing too limiting a structure on the frightening disarray of the world is long. Gary Day, for example, sees "Realism, with its emphasis on order, coherence, and limitation" as the "dominant" Victorian mode. He writes: "Although the Victorians were troubled with uncertainty, they preferred to repress their doubts and cling instead to the view that ultimate truths did exist." In "Figuring Out the Signalman," 26.

6. "The Purloined Letter" has attracted a great deal of critical attention in the past few decades. My own brief look at Poe, here, is intentionally condensed and specific. For a rich range of other readings, see Muller and Richardson's *The Purloined Poe*, an excellent critical collection that includes Poe's story, Lacan's famous "Seminar on 'The Purloined Letter,'" Derrida's response to Lacan, and others. All references to the text are taken from this edition.

7. Ibid., 39.

8. Dickens, *Great Expectations*, ed. Margaret Caldwell, 137. All subsequent quotations refer to page numbers from this edition.

9. "He perceives the witch of his life as his godmother; just as that upside-down vision perceives the godfather of his life as his witch." Stone, *Dickens and the Invisible World*, 317.

10. As Graham Daldry puts it, "what [Pip] does not see" is that "the retrospect of the narrative does not necessarily include its anticipation." *Charles Dickens and the Form of the Novel*, 142.

11. Katherine Kearns suggests a similar conclusion, arguing that the alterity of the real gives rise to the novel's concern with legal trials: "The realistic novel's preoccupation with lawyers, court cases, and trials reflects the apprehension of a reality that must be pled into existence." *Nineteenth-Century Literary Realism*, 10.

12. Mrs. Joe is, of course, wrong about this, as we learn later, when Magwitch describes his own childhood, a childhood composed not of questions but of unfair accusations.

13. Biddy's working-class status and initially unkempt appearance might seem to disqualify her from the title of domestic angel, but the trajectory of her plot brings her to become an ideal wife and mother, and this ending is certainly fitting: she has always shown a willingness to sacrifice herself for others, an enthusiasm for education (particularly for literacy), and an industrious, respectable self-reliance. If she does not begin in the middle class, she certainly meets all of the requirements to join it.

14. Intriguingly, Gail Turley Houston argues that Estella too is "self-forgetful": "groomed to be the absent center of the Victorian male's affections." See her *Consuming Fictions*, 159.

15. Jaggers's "fair" system convicts Magwitch, who has indeed broken the law—but who is "innocent" of wrongdoing as far as the reader is concerned. Biddy's more flexible system of knowledge gathering suggests an alternative to the courtroom.

16. Martine Hennard Dutheil argues that Pip "evolv[es] from a naïve reading of signs to a much more skeptical view of language according to which there is more to words than necessarily meets the eye." I would suggest that this argument overlooks the fact that the "naïve" reading is helpful in the effort to make sense of Mrs. Joe's cryptic language, and also that it is reading *flexibility*, a willingness to pull from many competing paradigms of interpretation, that solves the mystery. In other words, the text does not advocate replacing the "naïve" with the sophisticated, but rather it advocates using all tools available for unearthing the secrets of the real. See "*Great Expectations* as Reading Lesson," 166.

17. Kathleen Sell claims that women in the novel repeatedly fail to live up to the model of "selfless" femininity, and Pip blames his own flaws on the failures of Mrs. Joe, Miss Havisham, and Estella. A look at Biddy, it seems to me, must shift Sell's conclusions. "Narrator's Shame," 222.

18. Sharon Aronofsky Weltman argues that Ruskin's science relied on a culturally feminine model rather than a masculine one: "The feminine type is Ruskin's model for scientists who perceive without piercing; who need no phallic swords or dissection tools or engines of war; and who open their hearts to receive the knowledge nature provides." "Myth and Gender in Ruskin's Science," 157.

19. In his impressive look at the theme of reading and interpretation in the novel, Peter Brooks overlooks Biddy altogether, suggesting that Pip learns to read thanks to Mr. Wopsle's aunt and mentioning Mrs. Joe's "aphasic" symbols without discussing who deciphers them. See his *Reading for the Plot*, 131.

20. Robert Garnett suggests that the logic of the text will not permit a marriage to Biddy, since only the emotionally "moderate" men in the novel—Joe, Herbert, and Wemmick—can be paired with moderate women. Pip's passions soften over the course of the narrative, but he never becomes a thoroughgoing moderate and so cannot be properly paired with Biddy. For Garnett, Estella is the more credible companion: "Estella plainly does not belong among the novel's temperate homebodies. . . . She is the very antithesis, for example, of Biddy's contented domesticity." "The Good and the Unruly in *Great Expectations*," 34.

21. From a letter to Wilkie Collins (23 June 1861), in Dickens, *Letters* 9: 428.

22. In this respect, *Great Expectations* is a clear exception to Robert Caserio's claim that "However much Dickensian plot cultivates diverse meanings and multiple directions . . . the ending, considered not as finale but as *telos*, organizes all that precedes, explains all suspenseful mysteries and indeterminacies, marshals every detail and contingency, every event and character, into a structure revealed at the last—as purposeful." *Plot, Story, and the Novel*, 169.

23. Brooks, *Reading for the Plot*, 136.

24. When he revised the text, Dickens changed the final phrase, "I saw the shadow of no parting from her," to the more ambiguous ending, "I saw no shadow of another parting from her" (480).

25. Thus suspense troubles Frank Kermode's conclusion that "plotting presupposes and requires that an end will bestow upon the whole duration and meaning." *Sense of an Ending*, 46.

From Magwitch to Miss Havisham:
Narrative Interaction and Mythic Structure in Charles Dickens's *Great Expectations*_____

Calum Kerr

Great Expectations was initially published, not in the novel form in which it is usually read today but as a serial story, two chapters at a time, starting in 1860 in *All the Year Round*, a weekly literary magazine founded and owned by Dickens himself. The result is a story that was crafted to create moments of suspense at the end of every other chapter, keeping the reader's interest and anticipation for the next installment. It was first published in book form in 1861 in three volumes. The result is a novel with a complex story and a dynamic structure, containing a mixture of genres (Allingham), which at the time formed a way-marker for the future of novel writing.

This complexity of story, structure, and genre emerges from the combination of Dickens's original story ideas and the action upon it of the serialization process. Dickens himself was aware of the problems that could arise from the tension between the desire to create a single piece of writing and the need to prolong it over an extended period. He discussed exactly these issues in two letters to his friend and biographer John Forster. In the first, dated September 1860, he discusses the conception of the idea that was to become *Great Expectations*:

> . . . such a very fine, new, and grotesque idea has opened upon me. . . . You shall judge as soon as I get it printed. But it opens out before *me* that I can see the whole of a serial revolving upon it, in a most singular and comic manner. . . . (Page 91)

At least part of the story had come to him as a single piece and he was already anticipating the form which the later parts of the story might take. However, in his second letter to Forster, dated April 1861, it can be seen that the propagation of this idea had come up against the realities of the publishing process, slowing and controlling Dickens's writing.

> . . . it is a pity that the third portion cannot be read all at once, because its purpose would be much more apparent; and the pity is the greater because the general turn and tone of the working out and winding up, will be away from all such things as they conventionally go. But what must be, must be. As to the planning out from week to week, nobody can imagine what the difficulty is, without trying. . . . (Page 91)

By this point, just a few months before the publication of the final installment, the frustrations of the serialization process are obviously showing, and the larger ideas within the story are pushing against the boundaries imposed by the requirements of the form and, it must be considered, the expectations of the audience. However, the comment that the "working out and winding up" will be unconventional shows that Dickens was not letting the constraints of the form stifle his creativity. It could even be argued that the fact of the serial form allowed Dickens to create a conclusion that would surprise his readers without fear that they could spoil it for themselves by turning to the end of the book.

This ending, which Dickens designed to be "away from all such things as they conventionally go," sees Pip and Estella meeting one last time with the revelation that she is remarried and happy, and, although Pip cannot in the end be with her, he is pleased with the change in her. This, it would seem, was so far from being the usual ending of such stories that, after protests—from his publisher and, in particular for Dickens, from fellow writer Edward Bulwer-Lytton—Dickens rewrote the ending to be more hopeful and to contain at least the prospect of the two of them having some kind of future together. Again Dickens wrote to Forster about this change:

You will be surprised to hear that I have changed the end of *Great Expecta-tions*. . . . I have put in as pretty a little piece of writing as I could, and I have no doubt that the story will be more acceptable through this alteration. (Forster 289)

The use of the word "acceptable" implies that Dickens felt con-strained—whether by public expectation or by the opinion of his peers—to change his ending to conform more closely to what was deemed conventional. However, as Forster comments in his biography of Dickens when discussing the change of the ending, "the first ending nevertheless seems to be more consistent with the drift, as well as natu-ral working out, of the tale" (Forster 289). This raises a contradiction. The original ending fits better with the general direction of the novel, and yet the audience who read this ending in the prepublication proofs required a more conventional "happy" ending. This contradiction, and the general form and complexity of the novel as a whole, can be better understood if the major narrative strands of the book are examined us-ing the kind of narrative models developed by Vladimir Propp or Jo-seph Campbell.

Classed as belonging to the movement known as structuralism, these theorists analyzed particular types of stories to find the underly-ing structures that informed them. By comparing similar texts, they found it was possible to discover tropes and motifs that continue from one story to another and can then be extrapolated to form a model for all such stories.

The structuralist movement itself emerged from the work of Ferdi-nand de Saussure in the field of linguistics but later expanded to take in literary theory and social sciences. The field of literary structuralism emerged at the beginning of the twentieth century from the Russian Formalist school, which consisted mainly of work undertaken by the Society for the Study of Poetic Language (OPOYAZ). This group tried to formulate a science of literature that would be independent, factual, and based on the internal history of development of formal structures within the literature, rather than on external material history (Sturrock 105-106). Vladimir Propp, a folklorist, is often associated with this school. His book *The Morphology of the Folk Tale*, published in Russian in 1928 and translated into English in the 1950's, uses this scientific approach to analyze the structure of Russian folktales and produce a list of functions from which all the analyzed tales could be derived. These functions—starting with such blocks of story as "The Initial Situation," "The Preparatory Section," and "Complications" (Propp 119-127)—are then gathered together based on their possible roles in various stories. They are shown, within their groups, to be interchangeable, creating different stories from the same structure in the same paradigmatic fashion as substituting words within a sentence structure.

A similar schematic approach to stories can be seen in Joseph Campbell's book *The Hero with a Thousand Faces*. Dealing with myths rather than folktales, Campbell undertakes a task similar to that of Propp, delineating the common elements in a variety of different myths from different cultures and times to create a single, encompassing ur-myth that he termed the "monomyth" (Campbell 3-46). This comes in the form of a series of steps through which any myth must go from "The Call to Adventure" and "Crossing the First Threshold" to "Crossing the Return Threshold" and "Freedom to Live." Campbell distills these various steps into a diagram that he calls "The Keys" (Campbell 245), which provides a simple way to explore the possible options within the mythical structure.

Campbell's concept of the monomyth has subsequently become the inspiration for many other works, most famously George Lucas's film *Star Wars IV: A New Hope* (Larsen and Larsen 541-543), and the underlying structure he identified has been seen to apply to many different types of nonmythic story. It is certainly a structure that can be seen within *Great Expectations*, and the "hero's journey," as Campbell terms it, is a useful way to analyze the underlying architecture of the novel to reveal both its complexity and the way in which it works as a story. It also allows us to understand the problem of the two endings.

At the opening of the book, Pip is inhabiting his ordinary life as an orphan living with his sister and her husband, Joe the blacksmith. There is the potential at this point, as Pip often reflects during the course of the book, for nothing at all extraordinary to happen to him. It is possible that he could become apprenticed to Joe and spend his life as a blacksmith. Although this is the most likely outcome in the real world, the fact that this is a story means that we require something more. Anny Sadrin comments in her essay on the narrative and generic forms of *Great Expectations* that "[Pip] is an ordinary hero placed . . . in a fairy tale setting" (188), and as such, extraordinary events need to occur to him.

In this way, we are already moving toward the first of the stages of the monomyth, the "Call to Adventure." This call arrives in the shape of a convict, the man later introduced as Abel Magwitch. He attacks and threatens Pip and bullies him into stealing food from home and a file from Joe's forge and bringing it back to him on the marshes. This is the start of Pip's adventure and leads directly to the bestowing of his "great expectations."

According to Campbell, the hero's next step is to attempt to refuse the adventure. This takes the form of Pip contemplating the terror instilled in him by Magwitch's threats. He desperately wishes to refuse the call but cannot because of his fears. He therefore carries out the promised thefts and returns to the marshes with the food and file. At this point Pip takes the next step of his journey. By undertaking Magwitch's instructions he crosses the threshold into adventure. Without this action he would not later be made into a gentleman or bestowed with his "great expectations." At this point we have crossed from ordinary life into the world of the adventure, and things to come fall within that scope. Thus, when we next see Magwitch, he has been captured by soldiers—a necessary action if he is to be transported to Australia so that he might make the fortune that he later bestows on Pip—and he is changed from the man who at first threatened to cut Pip's throat into a man who lies to protect the secret of Pip's theft. Pip is no longer the ordinary boy of the beginning of the story; he has become the fairy-tale hero around whom the action of the story molds itself.

What follows exposes the first complication within the story. We have crossed the first threshold into the adventure, but then nothing further seems to happen. Life returns to normal for Pip as he continues his routine of doing odd jobs and undertaking a small amount of education. The next significant event that occurs to Pip seems entirely unrelated to the adventure already commenced. He is called to go and play for Miss Havisham at her house. It is hard to see how this can relate to the story of Pip and Magwitch, so we must conclude that this is the start of a second adventure. Once more Pip is called from his ordinary life to cross a new and unexpected threshold. In this case it is the quite literal threshold into the house of Miss Havisham. Any desires on Pip's part to refuse the adventure are overridden by the people around him, particularly his sister and Uncle Pumblechook. In this way, they inhabit the role that Campbell names the "helper," who enables the hero's crossing of the threshold and serves to facilitate his journey at key points.

By examining this small section of the novel using Campbell's structure, it is already possible to see how such complexity arises in Dickens's novel as we have two separate adventures being undertaken by the same protagonist. The intricacy and effectiveness of the novel comes from the interaction of these two stories and the ways in which the audience is led to believe that various events—in particular the bestowal of the "great expectations"—belong to one story strand rather than the other.

This structure, whereby Pip's two journeys intertwine, can also be seen as serving the serial nature of writing and publication of the novel. By creating these two separate strands, Dickens creates increased tension and anticipation in his readership as they would not have known, from one week to the next, which strand of the story would be explored nor how they might relate to each other. The fact that this story was being published in Dickens's own magazine, *All the Year Round*, is also significant in the construction of such a narrative. As Forster revealed in his biography of Dickens, the concept of Pip and Magwitch was originally conceived for a different story, but because of the poor sales of the story—which was, at that time, being published in the magazine—Dickens decided to write *Great Expectations* as a serial publication. In re-visioning it, he created a second strand to run along the story of Pip and his "great expectations." This second strand is the story of Miss Havisham and Estella, which not only runs parallel to the story of Pip and his expectations but also at times connects to and influences it. It is the way in which these two separate journeys intersect that shows Dickens's mastery of his craft as a storyteller.

The first narrative strand, commencing with the meeting between Magwitch and Pip, is concerned with crime and punishment. As it unfolds, it moves from Magwitch to a second convict and then advances to London and to scenes of Newgate Prison, the courts, and the criminal lawyer Mr. Jaggers, all of which are ultimately bound up with Magwitch. An insight is given to the nature of the law, and there is much discussion of crime and punishment. It is the exploration of this topic and its eventual resolution in Pip's near-arrest and his relinquishing of his expectations that forms the first story.

In sharp contrast, the second narrative strand is essentially a love story. With the introduction of Estella in the second of the "calls to adventure," Pip starts on a separate journey that examines his unrequited love for Estella, the story of the failed wedding of Miss Havisham and the coldness of heart that Miss Havisham has inculcated in her adopted daughter. This story line also follows Estella's change from a bullying girl to an aloof and somewhat Machiavellian young woman, eventually leading to her marriage to Drummle. The story line resolves itself in the final chapter, the one that Dickens added to his original draft, in which Pip and Estella are reunited.

Campbell's scheme for his monomyth now proves a useful structure to help unpack the two narratives and also to show how similar characters and situations appear in different forms in the two narratives, creating a sense of "doubling" or "twinning" within the novel (Gillman and Patten 441-458). The next step in Campbell's structure calls for the hero to undergo a series of trials. He lists some of these with particular titles: "Brother-battle," "Dragon-battle," "Dismemberment," "Crucifixion," "Abduction," "Night-sea journey," "Wonder journey," "Whale's belly" (Campbell 245). This is not an exhaustive list, nor is it suggested that every hero must suffer through all of these things. However, it is possible to see echoes of many of these elements occurring during Pip's story.

First, following the story line concerned with Pip and Magwitch, we can see the concept of brotherhood and conflict appearing in a number of guises. Joe is Pip's brother by marriage, and although there is no literal battle between the two, it is easy to see their relationship in terms of Campbell's "Brother-battle." From the moment Pip embarks on his adventure, he becomes ashamed of Joe's lack of refinement. As he grows, he attempts to educate Joe and then later avoids visiting his brother-in-law or being seen in public with him. In effect Pip engages in a one-sided battle against his brother, seeking either to change or to eradicate him. However, this is a battle more concerned with Pip's snobbery and feelings of guilt than any real contention with Joe. Physical strife comes, instead, in the form of Dolge Orlick. He fulfils the role of another brother to Pip, perhaps even fulfilling the role of a double of Pip himself in that he is also apprenticed to Joe and later serves at Miss Havisham's house. However, if Orlick is a reflection of Pip, it is a shadowy reflection, and the contention between them is much greater than Pip's battles with Joe.

The first battle with Orlick comes when Joe allows Pip a half day's holiday to visit Miss Havisham. Orlick, more from jealousy than any real need, argues that he should also be allowed a half day's rest. This escalates into an argument that involves Pip's sister as well as Joe and Pip himself, leading directly to the sister's injury at Orlick's hands and ultimately to her death. The second battle comes when Pip discovers Orlick working as gatekeeper at Miss Havisham's house and has him dismissed from the post. Orlick's desire for revenge leads to the final battle between the two, in which Orlick captures Pip and ties him against a wall before attempting to kill him. Not only does this final battle contain elements of abduction and crucifixion; Pip's time in the old sluice house under Orlick's detention can also be seen as representative of passing down into the belly of a beast and emerging again.

Another "beast's belly" into which Pip descends, in the terms of his tale of crime and punishment, is London itself. In contrast to the marshes of his childhood, it is a place of prisons and courts and dark, dank places. It is in London that he undergoes his greatest "battle": his confrontation with Magwitch. As Campbell demonstrates, in the hero's journey, lesser trials will lead to the largest test of all, one that will allow the hero finally to redeem himself and gain the prize for which he has journeyed. In traditional myths, this is often a tangible article—fire, a golden fleece, a loved one snatched from the underworld—but can just as easily be something ephemeral, such as enlightenment, illumination, or transformation. Pip's relationship with Magwitch can be seen, as Pip himself finally identifies, as that of brothers, or of father and son. Yet, when Magwitch first arrives, Pip wishes nothing to do with him, and it is his attempts to rid himself of the convict that lead ultimately to Magwitch's capture, imprisonment, and death. It is during this period that Pip undergoes his greatest battle, which occurs mostly within himself. He begins to understand his debt to this criminal, his benefactor, an understanding that in turn illuminates his debt to Joe. Finally, with the death of the convict and his resulting illness, during which he is once more cared for by Joe, he gains enlightenment, realizing the proud and snobbish ways in which he has acted and seeing the atonement he needs to make to Joe, who as well as being literally his brother is also a figurative father. This is symbolized by Pip's leaving London for his old home in the marshes, as though emerging from the belly of the beast and back into the light. It also signifies the recrossing of the threshold back into the ordinary world, one where he is now free to take up his post with Clarriker and Co. and live a normal life free of the taint of crime and guilt that previously followed him. In this way, the first strand of Pip's journey comes to an end.

The second journey, commencing with Pip's call to visit Miss Havisham, contains its own series of trials, which also correspond to the steps of Campbell's hero's journey. Quite soon after his call to adventure, one of Pip's visits to Miss Havisham concludes in a quite literal "Brother-battle," when he is challenged to a fight by a pale youth who is later revealed to be Herbert Pocket. Upon their reacquaintance, the two young men become firm friends, and their slight separation in age and the strength of their bond emphasize the brotherly nature of their relationship. However, in this first meeting, Pip is called upon to fight this stranger and does so, knocking him down again and again before Herbert finally concedes. It is not revealed to Pip until later, but Herbert's presence in Miss Havisham's house at that time is as a direct challenge to Pip's love for Estella, and the fight is in fact secretly watched by the girl herself. In this way a fight that seems trivial at the time is actually much more significant in terms of Pip's journey to try to win the love of Estella.

Pip's trials in this strand continue through his relationship with Miss Havisham's family. After Pip is conferred with his "great expectations"—although it is later revealed that they do not come from Miss Havisham but instead from Magwitch—Miss Havisham uses the presumption of her being his benefactor to taunt and mock her cousins. This puts Pip in the difficult position, whenever he visits the house, of being a tool for Miss Havisham's malice. The weight of this is increased when Pip is sent to be tutored by Miss Havisham's estranged cousin, Matthew Pocket, Herbert's father. Pip sees how poorly the Pockets live in comparison with the life bestowed on him by, he thinks, Miss Havisham. Thus, he is once again engaged in a battle with his own guilt. This battle is finally resolved when he convinces Miss Havisham to reinstate Matthew and his family in her will, and later when she is persuaded to pay a sum of money to support Herbert's partnership in the Clarriker and Co. shipping company.

The most prominent trial that Pip faces in this second narrative strand, though arguably not the most important one, is his relationship with Estella. This commences with their initial meetings, in which she is cold and cruel to him. He, in contrast, has fallen immediately and deeply in love with her. The trial advances when she returns from France and has transformed into a great beauty whose coldness and cruelty have been honed rather than cured. On numerous occasions she tells Pip that she does not love him, and cannot love any man, for she does not have the ability. Later, when she moves to London, she keeps Pip close to her simply to taunt other men who would want to be likewise in her company. These men include the figure of Bentley Drummle. As fellow pupils of Mr. Pocket, Pip and Drummle take an instant dislike for one another, which leads to enmity and competition when Drummle starts to follow and woo Estella. These actions are almost exactly the same as those from Orlick toward Biddy, with Drummle acting as Orlick's double in this strand of the story by also providing a real physical threat to Pip. Finally, Estella's cruelty toward Pip and men in general reaches its peak when she marries Drummle. She explains that she does this not because she loves him but because it is the surest way to be cruel to all the better men who profess to love her. This part of the story is concluded in the final chapter, the one that Dickens added after receiving comments from readers of earlier drafts, which will be discussed in greater detail below.

Although the relationship with Estella is seen as crucial to the novel, it is not actually the center of this particular narrative strand. That is his relationship with Miss Havisham herself, and it is his interactions with her that form the greatest test of this second journey. Her treatment of Pip, especially with the knowledge that she is not responsible for the bestowal of his "great expectations," can be seen as an extended metaphorical crucifixion, whereby he his held up for a variety of tortures. The way in which he is set up by her as a gloating punishment for her cousins has already been discussed above, but she also holds him up, as though a man tied to a post, for Estella to practice her coldness and cruelty on. It is made clear quite early that Miss Havisham relishes the meanness with which the young Estella treats Pip, and when Estella returns as an educated woman, Miss Havisham maintains her instructions for both of the younger people to visit her together so that she can witness Pip's love for her adopted daughter and the ways in which it is ignored, rebuffed, and ridiculed. This is her way of seeking revenge on the man who abandoned her on her wedding day. The revelation of the true source of Pip's expectations exposes her machinations and leads to Pip's great battle in this narrative strand, where he informs Estella of his love, despite his knowledge that it will be scorned, and she informs him of her intention to marry Drummle. It is at this point that Miss Havisham's ability to torture Pip comes to an end, and the next time they meet, it is she who has gained enlightenment. She is a changed woman who is willing to give Pip the money he requests for Herbert's future and who seeks Pip's forgiveness for the way she has acted. It is telling that Estella has no part in this scene. Instead it is the culmination of a love story between Pip and Miss Havisham in which she finally realizes her errors and finds her love both for Pip and for Estella. This scene culminates in her immolation, which eventually leads to her death. Having finally given up her life of pain and cruelty, she is absolved by Pip and allowed to die in peace.

In Dickens's original version of the book, this would have been the grand ending of this strand of the story. There was, in this version, a final meeting between Pip and Estella, but it was only to reveal that Estella, having been ill-treated by Drummle, had separated from him and remarried to a doctor. The final conclusion was that her suffering in her marriage to Drummle had finally taught her the power of empathy. This seems a faint echo of the more powerful conversion of Miss Havisham. However, this ending did not satisfy those who read the proof copies of the novel, and Dickens was forced to change it. The reason for this can be seen through the progression of Campbell's scheme for the story, because ending this strand of the narrative in such a way did not allow for the expected "re-crossing of the threshold."

The formal structure that Campbell reveals is a common one to most storytelling, providing, as it does, a path that satisfies its audience by taking the protagonist on a journey from the ordinary world, through a series of increasingly hazardous and exacting trials, and ultimately to an apotheosis and a return to the ordinary world. Through his examination of myths, Campbell shows that this journey is fundamental to our expectations of story, and so any story that does not conform to this template leaves us unsatisfied. The original ending of *Great Expectations* did not resolve the narrative involving Estella. Redemption and return had been granted to Miss Havisham in that strand, but not to Pip. By changing the ending to provide Pip with the further expectation of spending his life with Estella, Dickens finally closes the circle of tribulation and compensation that the audience expects and returns Pip to an ordinary world in which Estella is not some extraordinary totem but instead a flesh-and-blood woman with whom he now may hope to spend the rest of his days. This ends both the second narrative strand and the book as a whole.

Of course, the simple fact of two separate narrative strands threading through the novel is not enough to generate all the complexities that occur in *Great Expectations*. They arise from the relationships between these two strands and the connections that Dickens creates. Although his work has often been criticized for the large number of coincidences that occur in his stories, these are the product of linkages between narrative strands: from Magwitch to the "expectations" to Miss Havisham, from Miss Havisham to Estella to Pip, from Pip to Mr. Jaggers to Magwitch, and so on.

Great Expectations is a complex and engaging novel. Analyzing the narrative structure through the lens of Campbell's monomyth shows how the book is formed from two separate strands, each with its own dynamic. Looking at each thread individually shows that there are peaks—moments of high excitement and adventure—and troughs—times where life seems to carry on as normal—in both narratives. However, because both strands are superimposed one upon the other, the story does not become boring during the troughs because Dickens was able to switch from one strand to another, constantly riding the peaks of the interlocking narratives. He could therefore generate the stimulation required by the readers of the original serial publication. The various links between the narratives, which become more numerous and more prominent over the course of the book, build on this and allow this narrative switching to operate smoothly as Dickens brings both stories to a satisfying conclusion at the end of what is still a well-respected and engrossing book.

Bibliography

Allingham, Philip V. "The Genres of Charles Dickens's *Great Expectations*— Positioning the Novel (1)." *The Victorian Web*, 22 September 2008. http://www.victorianweb.org/authors/dickens/ge/pva101.html.

Campbell, Joseph. *The Hero with a Thousand Faces*. London: Fontana Press, 1993.

Dickens, Charles. *Great Expectations*. Oxford: Oxford University Press, 1987.

Forster, John. *The Life of Charles Dickens in Two Volumes*. Vol. 2. London: Everyman's Library, 1969.

Gillman, Susan K., and Robert L. Patten. "Dickens: Doubles: Twain: Twins." *Nineteenth-Century Fiction* 39, no. 4 (March 1985): 441-458.

Jordan, John O. *The Cambridge Companion to Charles Dickens*. Cambridge: Cambridge University Press, 2001.

Larsen, Stephen, and Robin Larsen. *Joseph Campbell, A Fire in the Mind: The Authorized Biography*. Rochester, VT: Inner Traditions, 2002.

Page, Norman. *Hard Times, Great Expectations and Our Mutual Friend: A Casebook*. London: Macmillan, 1979.

Propp, Vladimir. *The Morphology of the Folk Tale*. Austin: University of Texas Press, 1998.

Rimmon-Kenan, Shlomith. *Narrative Fiction*. London: Routledge, 2001.

Sadrin, Anny. "*Great Expectations* as Romantic Irony." In *Great Expectations: Contemporary Critical Essays*. London: Macmillan, 1994. 187-202.

Sell, Roger D., ed. *Great Expectations: Contemporary Critical Essays*. London: Macmillan, 1994.

Sturrock, John. *Structuralism*. London: Fontana Press, 1993.

A Second Level of Symbolism in
*Great Expectations*_____

Elizabeth MacAndrew

Dickens sets up two levels of symbolism in *Great Expectations*. The "immediate" level, which informs the plot and may be said to *be* the novel, has been treated by others, in particular Joseph A. Hynes, in his comprehensive discussion of the subject.[1] I am concerned to show here that there is a second level on which abstract views of social institutions and spiritual states are symbolized. In the one case, the institutions are symbolized by their physical manifestations—church and prison buildings, for example. In the other, the weather—sunshine and rain, storm and calm—correspond, Romance fashion, to states of being. On the "immediate" level the symbols are woven into the plot. On the second level they stand out from it, "interpretable" much in the manner of allegory.

The principal theme of Pip's spiritual development is worked out on the immediate level. Hynes explores the over-riding irony of the work through a close examination of the imagery. This irony, symbolically expressed, is what makes the novel a *Bildungsroman*. Pip, writing with hindsight, reveals the mistaken values of which his great expectations are a sign. His growth to spiritual maturity lies in his gradual rejection of false values and adoption of true ones. The novel, however, contains a great deal of social comment, and Dickens's views require a special method to integrate the social with the personal. If he had simply blamed social conditions for his characters' spiritual poverty, the second level of symbolism would not be essential. But Dickens sees the solution to social evil in spiritual regeneration, and the faults of society as a reflection of the evil in individual men and women.

By using this dual system of symbolism, he presents his views of both the role of society as it impinges on the individual and the spiritual responsibility of the individual in relation to society, without distracting the reader's attention from his central theme. Pip's spiritual development is intimately connected with the social questions raised in the novel, and the second level of symbolism connects these two facets of the work. At the outset, church, gibbet, slaughterhouse, and beacon, symbolizing social institutions, stand in a spatial relationship to Pip and his world. Then, as Dickens develops his theme, weather symbolism representing spiritual states takes over, and we see that in Dickens's view, it is the spiritual which shapes the social.

The spatial relationship of these symbols to Pip's world shows us how to interpret them. When he is a child, the horizon is bounded by the river at the edge of the marshes. On that horizon stand, stark and black, the gibbet with its chains, which "once held a pirate," and the beacon "by which the sailors steered."[2] Low down on the water lie the hulks, the "wicked Noah's Ark" in which the convicts are imprisoned, and on the shore, the battery with its guns that boom in warning of a prisoner's escape. On the near side of the marshes stands the church with its graveyard. The church, a mile from the village, is not on the far horizon; it is on the edge of the world the child knows. The river leads to the sea, the source of wind and storm, beyond which is the sunny East. Gibbet, beacon, hulks, and church operate as symbols of the wider sphere of society within which the little world of the village lies. Beyond that larger society again lies a still more mysterious world, symbolized by the sea and the winds, the source of the weather symbolism which dominates the later sections of the novel.

The gallows and the beacon which guides men in from the sea are mysterious apparitions on the farthest horizon of Pip's life. The church just touches upon his existence, standing on the outskirts of the village. To it, Joe and Pip go in their "Sunday penitentials," and to it winds the funeral procession for Mrs. Joe, which Pip describes as a masquerade in which he recognizes under their black garb ordinary figures from the village. On Pip's first contact with the convict, Magwitch, the church displays its instability. It is first mentioned thus: "The man, after looking at me for a moment, turned me upside-down, and emptied my pockets. There was nothing in them but a piece of bread. When the church came to itself—for he was so sudden and strong that he made it go head over heels before me, and I saw the steeple under my feet—when the church came to itself, I say, I was seated on a high tombstone, trembling, while he ate the bread ravenously" (pp. 2-3). The repetition here of "when the church came to itself" attracts attention, and we see that this spiritual institution has failed to stand firm. In fact, in a sort of pun, Dickens shows us that it contains nothing that can prevent the child's life from being turned topsy-turvy in this moment of crisis. (This is why, later, the villagers are seen as masquerading when they attend it.) Magwitch keeps tilting the child backwards, terrifying him, and then, once more, "He gave me a tremendous dip and roll, so that the church jumped over its own weathercock" (p. 4).

In these opening pages of the novel, a further set of images, relating to butchery, is used to equate the society of the village, which thinks itself respectable, with the frightening convict. Magwitch threatens to eat Pip himself and then follows this up with the still more terrible threat of the "young man" who will tear out Pip's heart and liver, then roast and eat them, if Pip does not bring food and a file. We can compare these threats with Mr. Pumblechook's "dissertation" on pork at Christmas dinner, in which he suggests that Pip should be grateful not to have been born a "squeaker" to be sold to the butcher, who "would have shed your blood and had your life" (p. 28). It is hard to decide who is the more blood-thirsty, Pumblechook or Magwitch. Pumblechook's threats, after all, are gratuitous. This extraordinary recital, addressed to the only child present at this celebration of the birth of the Christ-child, is made to demonstrate to him "what you've got to be grateful for." It is followed by a "fearful catalogue" from Pip's sister of all the trouble he has been to her and "all the times she had wished me in my grave" (p. 28).

Thus, the most respectable members of the little society of which Pip is a part make the same threats and menaces against him as were made by the disreputable convict. These respectable adults spend the balance of their strangely celebrated Christmas hunting the wretched convict they despise. The symbolism places hunters and hunted on the same moral level.[3] It also establishes the real reason for Pip's guilt. The greatest authorities he knows think him fit for the graveyard or the butcher's knife. His stealing for Magwitch only confirms the ingratitude of which he has always been accused and thus turns the brief incident from his childhood into a permanent feeling of association with the convict, a "stain" of guilt which, he fancies, keeps reappearing.

When Pip lands in the middle of London, the center of the society of which the village is a part, the same symbols appear, but their positions in relation to each other and to Pip have changed. In case the significance of the move to the capital should be missed, Mr. Jaggers's office is placed in Little Britain.[4] With this setting Pip's story is intimately bound up. But it is when he goes out to escape its stuffy, funereal atmosphere that he finds himself in Smithfield, the site of London's slaughterhouses and meat market. He feels it is a "shameful place, being all asmear with filth and fat and blood and foam, [which] seemed to stick to me. So I rubbed it off with all possible speed by turning into a street" (p. 176).

Later, when he goes to meet Estella at the coach-station, he will similarly feel physically contaminated by Newgate and try to brush the stain of it off his clothes. It is when he flees from Smithfield that he finds himself in front of Newgate, with St. Paul's behind it. He turns the corner "into a street where I saw the great black dome of Saint Paul's bulging at me from behind a grim stone building which a bystander said was Newgate Prison" (p. 176).

This little excursion contributes nothing directly to the plot, but it again establishes the symbolic significance of these institutions and their spatial relationship to Pip's world. Now, in London, with his expectations seeming more definite, Pip has moved up slightly in society and, for the moment, is no longer threatened with direct physical violence. No longer does anyone threaten to butcher him. Smithfield is a more general symbol of butchery from which he can, or thinks he can, free himself.

When he does so, however, the church "bulging" at him over the prison is surely a renewed vision of its helplessness. And when Pip is shown the gallows in the prison yard—by a man wearing, he surmises, dead men's clothes—the symbol of butchery, Smithfield, no longer associated with Pip and Magwitch directly, is associated with Newgate as a symbol of prison as society's slaughterhouse. Pip describes the yard and the door where men are led out "to be killed in a row" (p. 176). Pip, having successfully "brushed off" the "shameful" atmosphere of Smithfield, is more immediately concerned with the prison and its gallows, and only remotely affected by the church. The relation of these institutions to his life has changed with their physical relation to each other. They are now at the center of the world, not on the horizon, and the prison has come to the foreground while the church has receded behind it.

While the plot draws significance from the symbolic setting on the immediate level, the second level of symbolism places the story in a wider context, which can be interpreted directly. Society's means of caging and butchering men were frightening matters just visible on Pip's mental horizon, as the signs of them stood on the physical horizon of his world. The church was more immediate, but faced with the consequence of society's inhumanity (Magwitch), it proved curiously unstable. Pip's childhood world was bounded by the river, and beyond that, out of sight, was the sea. That is, beyond society's institutions which affect Pip's immediate little world there is a huge and mysterious vastness, the "distant savage lair from which the wind was rushing" (p. 2). Then in London, when Pip has become more acutely aware of the institutions as such, of the prison as a human slaughterhouse, a shameful and contaminating place, and of the church as helpless behind it, he is deepest in his illusions and has lost sight altogether of the river with the ocean beyond it.

At the turning point of the novel, all this changes again. Throughout the whole reversal and recognition section, the weather and not the physical setting becomes supremely symbolic. The "lair of the winds," that vast and mysterious region that had previously lain beyond Pip's horizon, becomes of vital significance in his life, as if to say, symbolically, that to find his answer he must learn to look beyond the immediate and apparent causes in the social situation, to inexplicable forces that ultimately govern the events of this world.

The climax of the novel comes at the end of the second part, with a tremendous storm. The river has reappeared with Pip's move from Barnard's Inn to the more hopeful sounding Garden Court, in the Temple, on the bank of the Thames.[5] Light begins to break on his spiritual darkness, but this being a journey of the soul, he must first weather the storm and go through fire before reaching the full dawn. The great storm, in which Pip reaches the depths of despair, blots out the symbols of social institutions. Then, in the ordeal which follows it, the symbolism takes on biblical overtones which prepare us for the spiritual significance of the sunlight in which the last part of the novel is bathed.

The storm hurls rain violently against Pip's windows and blows out the lights in the court below and in the stairway. His room is like a "storm-beaten lighthouse" (p. 339), and to that beacon for ships, now the very center of his existence, comes Magwitch, returned from across the sea to the haven of Pip's protection. We remember here the beacon on the river, formerly on Pip's horizon, which guided men in from the sea.

Magwitch appears and, after a short interval, Pip recognizes him: "If the wind and the rain had driven away the intervening years, had scattered all the intervening objects, had swept up to the churchyard where we first stood face to face on such different levels, I could not have known my convict more distinctly than I knew him now" (p. 342). The storm, blowing aside the intervening period of "expectations," has placed him back at that point in his childhood at which his awareness of guilt began. The "stain" that had faded has come to the surface again. The awful personification of Pip's guilt turns out to be the source of his expectations, and rightly so, since his real guilt in pursuing them lies in his acceptance of the empty values of Pumblechook and his sister. This is why, as we shall see, he feels he has deserted Joe, whose values are the right ones. Still worse, Magwitch's life is in Pip's hands, and he could be "taken and hanged on my account" (p. 364). However Pip disguises him, he seems to look more like the convict than ever—that is, Pip can no longer refuse to face his guilt, although that guilt is still nameless, just as Pip is still ignorant of the nature of Magwitch's crime.

When the plot reaches its climax with the storm, the river and sea once again become important. Like the institutions before them, they have moved from the horizon to a central place in Pip's life. They are accompanied by an all-important but more vague symbol—light from the East. From beginning to end, the weather corresponds to Pip's mood and to his spiritual state, but in addition, the wind, the storm, and the light from the East are bigger, all-encompassing symbols, affecting not just him but the whole world of men. The storm is introduced by an allusion to an "Eastern story" in which the roof falls in—just as now, with the return of Magwitch, Pip says, "the roof of my stronghold dropped upon me" (p. 338). The weather is bad and "day after day, a vast heavy veil had been driving over London from the East, and it drove still, as if in the East there were an eternity of cloud and wind" (p. 339). Just as over the marshes the wind came rushing from a "distant savage lair" (the sea), so now "gloomy accounts had come in from the coast, of shipwreck and death. Violent blasts of rain had accompanied these rages of wind" (p. 339). To Pip, in his Temple rooms by the river, on the night of the big storm "the wind rushing up the river shook the house that night, like discharges of cannon or breakings of a sea" (p. 339). This description recalls that Christmas when the guns had boomed over the marshes to warn of the convict's escape.

Churches now are veiled and distant. At eleven o'clock, Pip hears "Saint Paul's, and all the many church-clocks in the City" strike the hour, the sound "curiously flawed by the wind" (p. 340). The association of disaster from the East and the flawed sounds of the church clocks comes at the point where it seems to Pip that destruction is rushing in upon him. Only when he has finally understood the true spiritual meaning of life does he find that salvation, too, lies in the East, just as what he has taken to be the source of his destruction, Magwitch, is in reality the source of salvation. But, for the moment, there is no sign of that salvation and no thought of it in Pip's mind.

When his astonishing visitor reveals himself, Pip describes his feelings in a way that suggests a man drowning in a heavy surf: "All the truth of my position came flashing on me; and its disappointments, dangers, disgraces, consequences of all kinds, rushed in in such a multitude that I was borne down by them and had to struggle for every breath I drew" (p. 345). Such is Pip's reaction to the revelation that he owes his advance in the world to the convict. His horror is expressed in the violent rejection of his benefactor: "The abhorrence in which I held the man, the dread I had of him, the repugnance with which I shrank from him, could not have been exceeded if he had been some terrible beast" (p. 346). Pip shudders at the thought that Magwitch's "hands might be stained with blood" (p. 348).

In the depths of his spiritual darkness, Pip is repelled by this apparition of his guilt. He subsequently endures much suffering and his very life is put in danger. In the course of this crisis, however, he learns the spiritual lesson which lies at the heart of the novel. In trying to protect Magwitch, and in risking his life for others, Pip transcends the selfish pursuit of worldly expectations. He learns, as we shall see, that he is indeed his brother's keeper, that salvation lies in brotherly love. At the same time, through the novel's symbolism, the reader learns that man's inhumanity to man is the cause, not the effect, of the corruption and evil of his social institutions. What for Pip is a personal lesson, is a general one for us.

With the arrival of Pip's ghostly visitor from the past, the "stain," the "taint of prison and crime," has appeared again, cutting him off utterly from Estella and all his hopes. Yet, it is neither his love nor his worldly position that preoccupies him. Rather, he is torn apart by a conflict of feelings. With Magwitch returned, he must accept or reject the idea that he is his brother's keeper. Magwitch's very presence makes an unbearable demand upon him: "The wretched man . . . had risked his life to come to me, and I held it there in my *keeping*! If I had loved him instead of abhorring him . . . it could have been no worse . . . for his preservation would then have naturally and tenderly addressed my heart" (p. 349; my italics). That is, Pip is aware that the convict's very presence amounts to a demand that he save him out of true Christian charity, not because he loves him in the ordinary sense of this world. At the same time, however, Pip sees this creature who has put his life in his hands as the very source of his, Pip's, own wrongdoing: "It was for the convict, guilty of I knew not what crimes, and liable to be taken out of those rooms where I sat thinking, and hanged at the Old Bailey door, that I had deserted Joe."

Pip does not yet realize the spiritual significance of his own thought here. He is not yet aware that he has lived his life in a graveyard of the spirit, represented in the imagery of the early part of the novel. The real graveyard in which the novel opens; the living tomb of Satis House; Mr. Jaggers's office, decorated with instruments of death and the death-masks of two hanged men and furnished with the lawyer's "own high-backed chair [which] was of deadly black horse-hair, with rows of brass nails round it, like a coffin" (p. 175); Pip's lodgings in Barnard's Inn, described as a "flat burying ground" (p. 184)—all these represent the dead world which he must learn to leave behind him. Having "contumaciously refused" to join his parents and his brothers in the real graveyard, Pip has been consigned to live in spiritual graveyards by a society which is spiritually dead.

Through the imagery, Dickens shows us that Pip has grown up among hard and greedy people who have lost sight of true values. In the little world of the village, on which, as we have seen, the larger society impinges peripherally, Pip's childhood guilt confuses his sense of values. The world of his sister and Pumblechook is inseparable from his idea of Joe. Consequently, Pip's sense of Joe's love, which he feels he has betrayed, is inextricably mixed with his feelings of guilt toward his sister, from whom he has stolen and who is, in fact, but with so little grace, her brother's keeper.[6]

For one so lost, the initial effect of escape, first into the center of society and then (in the move from Barnard's Inn to Garden Court) out of the spiritual graveyards, is a crisis, and this is represented by the storm, from which, after great pain, he emerges into the sunshine of renewed hope. The storm imagery at first dominates both the reader's thought and Pip's. Pip, when he thinks over Magwitch's dreadful revelation, says: "I began fully to know how wrecked I was, and how the ship in which I had sailed was gone to pieces" (p. 350).[7] After a short, disturbed sleep, he wakes to hear "the clocks of the *eastward* churches . . . striking five, the candles were wasted out, the fire was dead, and the wind and rain intensified the thick black darkness" (pp. 349-50; my italics). This dawn that is no dawn is an expression of Pip's despair now that he has come face to face with his guilt, rather than a description of a new day. It is not until he is able to accept Magwitch—indeed, is willing to sacrifice himself for him—that Pip can find reconciliation with Joe and, ultimately, spiritual peace.

In this black despair "the second stage of Pip's expectations" ends. The imagery he uses to describe it makes one think that he and Magwitch are at sea in a storm-tossed ship rather than in the center of London. Pip is afraid that "it might not be safe to be shut up there with [Magwitch] in the dead of the wild solitary night" (p. 351). The "wild wet morning" is followed by days and "long evenings and long nights, with the wind and the rain always rushing by" (p. 364).

When the storm imagery is ended and Pip sets out for Miss Havisham's, the weather still reflects his situation. He regards himself as obliged to refuse more money from Magwitch, and now, "the day came creeping on, halting and whimpering and shivering, and wrapped in patches of cloud and rags of mist, like a beggar" (p. 382).[8] The storm has passed but the land is still subjected to a drizzle. Before going to Miss Havisham's, Pip "washed the weather and the journey from my face" (p. 386), and yet he is greeted by her with: "And what wind . . .

blows you here Pip?" (p. 386). Leaving unhappier than when he entered, it seems to him that "the light of day" is of a "darker colour" (p. 393). After another frightening night of "gloom and death" (p. 395) during which he is afraid to go home, Pip learns that his friends have moved Magwitch to a house "by the riverside, down the Pool there between Limehouse and Greenwich." After an extraordinary journey through stranded and broken ships resting in ooze and slime, he comes to the house situated in "a fresh kind of place . . . where the wind from the river had room to turn itself round; and there were two or three trees" (p. 404). The signal by which Magwitch is to tell him that all is well is this: the "blind in that part of his window which gave upon the *east*" is to be pulled down (p. 409; my italics).

With the beginnings of hope, the weather becomes less stormy and Pip returns home by moonlight. Through several chapters of "revelations" and "recognitions" the weather plays no part. But, again, as soon as Pip's destiny is directly involved, it enters both figuratively and actually, along with further allusions to the East. Pip concludes the arrangements by which he is secretly to set Herbert up in life, and he refers to them as "the only good thing I had done . . . since I was first apprised of my great expectations" (p. 450).[9] Herbert is to manage a branch-house of a certain business in the *East*. This means Pip will be left alone in England, and he says, "now indeed I felt as if my last anchor were loosening its hold, and I should soon be driving with the winds and waves" (p. 450). This depressing state is alleviated by Herbert's "pictures of himself conducting Clara Barley to the land of the Arabian Nights" (p. 450).

Through Pip's attempt to save Magwitch and through his helping Herbert the idea of men's responsibility for one another has become clear. It is further established, as John Hagan, Jr., has shown, that through the intermeshing of the lines of the plot everyone is somehow connected with everyone else, even, for instance, Estella with Magwitch and Orlick with Miss Havisham.[10] Through Magwitch's Christian name, moreover, Dickens alludes directly to the biblical story of

Cain and Abel. In the account of Molly's trial, it is said of Magwitch that he "was only vaguely talked of as a certain man called Abel, out of whom the jealousy arose" (p. 440).[11] Pip has Magwitch's life in his hands, and in his initial feeling of horror over the situation, he in effect repeats Cain's cry, "Am I my brother's keeper?" Dickens believed that the answer was "Yes."

Orlick, in a sense, is used as a corollary of this point. He stands in a brother-like relationship to Pip.[12] Both have worked for Joe, and Orlick hates Pip because he does not have Joe's love, as Pip does. Orlick insists that Pip is responsible for Mrs. Joe's death: "It warn't Old Orlick as did it; it was you. You was favoured, and he was bullied and beat. . . . You done it; now you pays for it" (p. 461). Thus, Orlick's motive is not mere service to Compeyson, or the avenging of a past wrong, but Cain's sin itself: he would murder his "brother" out of a jealous longing for their "father's" love.[13] Pip, on the other hand, in going to meet Orlick, is following that commandment in Christ's last sermon to his apostles: "This is my commandment, That ye love one another, as I have loved you. Greater love hath no man than this; that a man lay down his life for his friends" (John 15:12-13). This is just what Pip risks doing for Magwitch.[14] With the reappearance of Magwitch, Pip has indeed become his brother's keeper.

Three times he is faced with an expiatory ordeal by fire: when he attempts to rescue Miss Havisham, when he goes to face Orlick in the sluice-house and risks the still more terrible fire of the lime-kiln, and finally, when he burns for days in a violent fever, from which he, in his turn, is saved by Joe's love and patience. Of these, the struggle with Orlick is the most significant, and it is surrounded by symbolic references to the weather.[15] Pip goes to meet Orlick in a night lighted by a "red large moon" (p. 456), but by the time he reaches the sluice-house, which he notes "would not be proof against the weather much longer," it is raining. However, when he and his rescuers leave after the defeat of Orlick there is again moonshine. This has been Pip's great trial, and after a night's sleep he awakes to the following scene:

Wednesday morning was dawning when I looked out of the window. The winking lights upon the bridges were already pale, the coming sun was like *a marsh of fire on the horizon. The river, still dark and mysterious,* was spanned by bridges that were turning coldly gray, with here and there a warm touch from the burning in the sky. As I looked along the clustered roofs, *with church towers and spires shooting into the unusually clear air, the sun rose up, and a veil seemed to be drawn from the river,* and millions of sparkles burst out upon its waters. *From me, too, a veil seemed to be drawn,* and I felt strong and well. (p. 469; my italics)

The passage recapitulates imagery and symbols from the entire novel in such a way as to show us Pip's redemption, now almost complete. The marshes have become a source of light on a new horizon; the churches stand tall; a veil (and we remember that the storm was described as a "vast heavy veil" over London) has been lifted, drawn from the dark and mysterious river.

The attempt to engineer Magwitch's escape on a ship going *east,* on a March day when it is "summer in the light, and winter in the shade" (p. 469), fails. Magwitch is finally sentenced to death, on a day with "drops of April rain" and "rays of April sun" (p. 494), which reflects Pip's new feelings for the convict. It is here that that oft-quoted passage occurs describing the shaft of light falling between the judge and the condemned prisoners, "reminding some among the audience, how both were passing on, with absolute equality, to the greater Judgment" (p. 495).[16] The symbolic significance of the weather is thus explicitly connected with God's judgment at this moment when Pip has fully accepted Magwitch.

Waiting for the day of execution, Pip now roams the "weary *western* streets of London" (p. 496; my italics), and Magwitch tells him he has been better to him "since I was under a dark cloud than when the sun shone" (p. 497). Pip has passed through a spiritual transformation, learning to love his fellow-man in Magwitch. From these transitional states of weather he finally emerges, toward the end of the novel, into the sunshine of June and finds the "country-side more beautiful and peaceful" than he has ever known it. He then leaves England to join Herbert and that vaguely-identified "Eastern Branch" of the company for which he works. There he finds peace, works hard, and pays all his debts.[17]

Dickens has raised many social issues, yet the core of the novel lies in Pip's learning that form of brotherly love which is Christian charity. By subjecting him to the storms and vicissitudes of life, however, until he finds peace in a spiritual haven, Dickens shows that social institutions are collective expressions only of man's inhumanity to man. Bad social institutions are symbols of the evil in men.

Dickens sets the symbols for these institutions at a physical distance that is in direct proportion to their impact on the events of the plot, then blots them out in the spiritual storm from which his hero emerges far beyond them, in a world where brotherly love is a reality. The fact that it is a remote world shows that Dickens had no illusions about the permanence of human evil. The helpless church, the prisons which are society's slaughterhouses, will remain. But for those who weather life's spiritual storms, there is the light of revelation in the East. By interpreting the second level of symbolism, we find that Dickens has included social criticism in his *Bildungsroman* because spiritual regeneration is meaningless except as a manifestation of brotherly love, and a society without such love is dead.

Newgate and the hulks are more than just prison and prison-ship. They stand for society's way of treating its outcasts. Church and cathedral stand for the helplessness of religion in a society that is indicated as unchristian in its victimization of the helpless. The beauty of the method lies in the use of literary symbols that are also symbolic in men's minds in real life. A church building *does* symbolize the religion celebrated in it. London is the center of English society. And Dickens makes the source of storms and light as mysterious and unspecific as the spiritual forces which, he says, ultimately direct men's lives.

Notes

1. Joseph A. Hynes, "Image and Symbol in *Great Expectations*," *ELH*, 30 (1963), 258-92.

2. Charles Dickens, *Great Expectations*, ed. Louis Crompton (Indianapolis, Indiana: Bobbs-Merrill, 1964), p. 5. All further references are to this edition and appear in parentheses in the text.

3. See Karl P. Wentersdorf, "Mirror-Images in *Great Expectations*," *Nineteenth-Century Fiction*, 21 (1966), 221. He sees the adults—Magwitch, Mrs. Joe, Pumblechook, the convict with his "invisible gun," and Miss Havisham—as "authority-figures who had seemed to threaten young Pip with death as a boy," and as all coalescing into Joe in Pip's mind. He does not mention images of butchery. See also Paul Pickrel, "*Great Expectations*," in *Dickens*, ed. Martin Price (Englewood Cliffs, N.J.: Prentice-Hall, 1967), p. 159, who states that Magwitch "is everything a weak and passive child fears in the adult world: its capacity for wickedness, the brutality of its emotions, its strength and violence and consummate egoism, the threat of being utterly outcast and utterly alone." He thus implies the parallel between Magwitch and the "respectable" adult world.

4. Dickens's creation of a world of his own, so often referred to, is so effective because it is still made up of real places. Here, his symbolic use of the real geography of London makes his symbolism especially powerful.

5. See Hynes, pp. 285-86, concerning the symbolic value of gardens.

6. See Hynes, p. 268, where he discusses the imagery which describes Satis House as a prison, and p. 267, where he views Pip's visit to Satis House as prompting Pip to "misvalue himself and many of the people about him as well." Later (p. 276), Hynes refers to Satis House as a "dream world."

7. See Hynes, p. 328, concerning the relation of this to the imagery of sailboats.

8. Hynes, p. 261, also notes this parallel.

9. Herbert has made a brother of Pip, even giving him a new name (significantly, Handel, for Pip is the handle to Herbert's success). Thus, as Pip sets Herbert up in the world—doing his charitable act in secret, as the Bible commands—it is an act of brotherly love.

10. "The Poor Labyrinth: The Theme of Social Injustice in *Great Expectations*," *Nineteenth-Century Fiction*, 9 (1954-55), 172. See also Hynes, p. 259, concerning the vengefulness which links Magwitch and Miss Havisham.

11. Hynes mentions the name, but only to suggest the ambiguity in the character which the "innocent 'Abel'" suggests (p. 259).

12. See also Karl P. Wentersdorf, "Mirror-Images," p. 203. He sees Orlick as Pip's double, the "dark side" of his character, as do Julian Moynahan, "The Hero's Guilt: The Case of *Great Expectations*," *Essays in Criticism*, 10 (1960), 70, and Harry Stone,

"Fire, Hand, and Gate: Dickens's *Great Expectations*," *Kenyon Review*, 24 (1962), 669-70. Stone also sees him as a satanic figure. Both are quoted by Wentersdorf.

13. Pip first mentions Orlick thus: "He pretended his Christian name was Dolge—a clear impossibility. . . . When he went . . . away at night, he would slouch out, like Cain or the Wandering Jew" (p. 119).

14. See Hynes, p. 268: "Such freedom or liberation as is humanly available, comes as the paradoxical result of giving one's self. The giver gains; he who would gain his life must lose it."

15. When he comes through this last ordeal he is a man spiritually reborn. Lest we should doubt it, Dickens makes him have dinner beforehand "in a little octagonal commonroom, like a font" (p. 454).

16. See, for example, J. Hillis Miller, "*Great Expectations*," *Charles Dickens: The World of His Novels* (Cambridge, Mass.: Harvard Univ. Press, 1958), p. 276.

17. The double meaning of "debts" in biblical language is applicable here. See also Hynes, who notes that "ironically, [Wemmick] pays the debts of Pip, who is bankrupt in more than one sense" (p. 272).

Christian Allusion, Comedic Structure, and the Metaphor of Baptism in *Great Expectations*_____

John Cunningham

Critics have demonstrated the richly symbolic structure of *Great Expectations* by displaying such recurrent figurative motifs as those of, among others, fairy tale, parable, dream, and allegory; but one characteristic relevant to interpreting the novel that critics have no more than mentioned is a pattern of Christian allusion that Dickens so introduces into the novel that metaphors of baptism and of the redemption adumbrated by this sacrament take their place among the other controlling symbolic structures of the book. The novel opens, as I take it, with a parody of the Christian sacrament of baptism, by which (according to Prayer Book notions) people are born into a new life free of original sin; in Dickens's use of the figure, however, persons—namely Pip and Magwitch—are "born" instead into guilt and death. Janet L. Larson has written that the Bible in Dickens's mature novels is becoming "a locus of hermeneutical instability"; she speaks of the scriptures as a "broken" or "fractured code" (3). I take it that by perverting the stereotype of regeneration Dickens dislocates it from cliché; then as the novel comes toward its conclusion when Magwitch, Compeyson, and Pip plunge into the Thames (Byrd 262; Robison 436), he transforms the corrupted figures of baptism into genuine ones, and comic regenerations open onto new lives.[1] He restores the fractured or unstable meanings into Christian significance. Comic structure, as is often the case, regenerates its images. Christian analogy and imagery suggest a providential order that works toward the comic conclusion that many critics have described in terms of regeneration and redemption. In this essay I offer a sustained account of Christian emblems and allusions in *Great Expectations* and indicate how they cohere to form a major pattern of meaning in the novel;[2] for Dickens uses analogies of Christian comic archetypes to effect the resolution of the moral problems posed as the book develops.

The matrix of baptismal imagery includes symbols drawn from Christian typology. This figurative way of reading the Bible sees imperfect types and shadows—anticipations—of Christ throughout the Old Testament. By the last decade of the eighteenth century, sermons, tracts, biblical commentaries, hymns, and stained-glass windows taught Christians of all stripes to read scripture in this figurative way (Landow, *Hunt* 12-13). Typological reading was so widespread in the nineteenth century that any person who could read, even an unbeliever, was likely to recognize allusions to Old Testament figures and to know that these worthies served as types of Christ; the antichrist was also prefigured in the Old Testament (Landow, *Victorian* ix, 22-34; *Hunt* 11-12). This figurative way of reading scripture will prove useful in discussing a novel that alludes to Abel and Noah (types of Christ) and to Cain (a type of the antichrist), for Dickens draws typological references into the metaphoric structure of his novel. Dickens's parody of Christian typology and of the baptismal rite manifests itself in figures of Noah and in several patterns of imagery: death-in-life, false resurrection, of the old man, of clothing, and of Christmas.

The type of Noah provides one example of Dickens's use of parody. From ancient times Christians have seen the ark—a means by which the righteous few were given a new beginning—as a type of baptism in which wickedness suffered death by water (see 1 Pet. 3.18-21). At the end of the first full day of the novel, Pip sees a "black Hulk," "cribbed and barred and moored by massive rusty chains," "like a wicked Noah's Ark" (71). Years later he recalls "the wicked Noah's ark lying out on the black water" (252). This typology of Noah and the ark appears in the Flood Prayer of the Prayer Book (1662) baptismal office that nineteenth-century Anglicans would have heard repeatedly in their parish churches.[3] In that rite the priest prays "that the old Adam in this child may be so buried that the new man [Christ, who is the second Adam]" may be "raised up in him."[4] But the ark Dickens described is "wicked," a prison ship lying on the "black waters," a parody of the new beginning, of the new life, and of the forgiveness suggested by the allusion to Noah.

The "birth" that Pip experiences at the opening of the book is not into new life but into metaphoric and moral death. In the churchyard on Christmas Eve, Pip's "birth" comes with his "first most vivid . . . impression of the identity of things" and of his own identity as "a small bundle of shivers," like a newborn babe (35-36); but Magwitch's actions associate Pip with death. The convict seats the boy directly on a tombstone, to which Pip clings. When he asks Pip where his mother is, the boy points to her grave as if death were his origin. Metaphors of death-in-life pervade the first two-thirds of the novel and carry forward the figurative birth-into-death introduced in the first pages; they parody both the new beginning suggested by the allusion to Noah and also the new life promised in baptism. Miss Havisham is "withered" and "shrunk," a skeleton, a "ghastly waxwork" like some "personage lying in state" (87). She is brokenhearted, emotionally, morally, and spiritually dead; and she has stolen the heart away from Estella and "put ice in its place" (88, 412). Estella's contempt is "infectious," and Pip catches it (90). In fact, Pip cannot separate Estella "from the innermost life of [his] life" (257); moral infection and death stand at the center of Pip. He visits Miss Havisham annually on his birthday, celebrating his introduction to Satis House, as it were, as a kind of anniversary of his birthday into moral death in the churchyard. Because of the convict, he chooses to steal; because of Miss Havisham and Estella, he chooses to lie. Metaphors of death follow Pip from the country to London. Jaggers's office with its domineering death masks is a "dismal" place, like the churchyard and like Satis House. Jaggers's chair with its deadly black and its rows of brass nails is like a "coffin" (188). Here the lawyer presides over Pip's twenty-first birthday in such a way as to remind the young man of "that old time when [he] had been put upon a tombstone" (305). Barnard's Inn, Pip's London residence, is in a "melancholy little square" that looks to Pip "like a flat burying ground" (196).

In the first scene of the novel, the presence of the burial ground beside a church should remind those alive, "the Church Militant on earth," of the unity of all "lively members of Christ's Church" with "the Church Triumphant" beyond the grave (Davies 20). This unity is achieved in baptism. But the churchyard at the beginning of *Great Expectations* is a parody of these themes; it is a place that speaks only of death, not of the expectant life mentioned in the baptismal office. The brambles there seem to the young Pip like "the hands of the dead people, stretching up cautiously out of their graves, to get a twist upon . . . [Magwitch's] ankle and pull him in" (38); and the graves of his five dead brothers suggest to Pip those who have given "up trying to get a living, exceedingly early in that universal struggle." Pip then repeats a phrase, twice saying that his parents and brothers are "dead and buried" (35); those as familiar as Dickens was with matins and evensong would easily recognize the phrase as coming from the Apostles' Creed,[5] the formula composed specifically for the rite of baptism (Shepherd 284). The creed goes on to add, but Pip does not, "and the third day he arose again from the dead." Paul links baptism with resurrection (Rom. 6.4); but Magwitch's starting "up from among the graves" (36) represents an ironic parody of resurrection. He is like "the pirate come to life [but going back to the gibbet] . . . to hook himself up again" (39). Likewise, Miss Havisham's appearance suggests a false resurrection and makes Pip think of "a skeleton in the ashes of a rich dress, that had been dug out of a vault under the church pavement" (87). Seeming to Pip as if she "might rise in those grave-clothes of hers" (122), she is a parody of Lazarus rising in his "grave-clothes" (John 11.44).

Moreover, on Christmas Eve, Pip is also born into a guilt like the first Adam's, into something like the Fall and not into the new innocence and forgiveness of those just baptized. His growing guilt accounts for the moral death that comes more and more to possess him. Pip says, "I think my sister must have had some general idea that I was a young offender whom an Accoucheur Policeman had taken up (on my birthday) and delivered over to her, to be dealt with according to the outraged majesty of the law" (54). Later, by his own choice, he does consent to the guilt into which he is born; the guilt which he embraces from his first awareness is fixed and compounded by his association with Miss Havisham and Estella. He begins to love Estella "against reason, against promise, against peace, against hope, against happiness" (253-54). Pip "made [his] own snares" and became a "self-swindler" (374, 247). He returns home from Satis House oppressed by the "ungracious condition of [his] mind" and by his "ungracious breast" (134, 136).

For Pip, the guilt that he has acquired at Satis House is symbolized by the unwanted bloody fight with Herbert. When Pip admits that "the young gentleman's blood was on [his] head" (121), he introduces words that point to a series of scriptural allusions. These references associate him with both the shedding of Abel's blood and also the crucifixion of Christ.[6] Moreover, a "sponge dipped in vinegar"[7] forms part of the ritual of the fight (119). Pip covers the traces of Herbert's blood "with garden mould from the eye of man" and fears arrest and vengeance as a result of his assault. He then tries "to wash out that evidence of [his] guilt" (122), but his guilt cannot be thus washed out. The assault on Herbert that Pip does not initiate is like the assault on Mrs. Joe that Pip does not initiate either; yet he unexpectedly, even mysteriously, shares in the attack on his sister by helping Magwitch to free himself from the manacle that Orlick uses to attack her. Pip thinks that he must somehow share responsibility for the attack, as in fact Orlick says he does: "'It was you as did for your . . . sister'" (437). Pip may not literally kill his brother Abel when he bloodies Herbert nor even literally kill his sister; and yet in the metaphorical structure of the novel he takes his place beside Cain.

In so doing, he participates in the state of death-in-life that all the unredeemed share. Both Paul (Rom. 6.6; Eph. 4.22; Col. 3.9) and the baptismal office define this extreme state (see Col. 2.12-13) and the condition of guilt inherent in it by the term "old man." The purpose of baptism is to give the old man, the mortal and fallen Adam, the death blow. The dominant figure of the old man in *Great Expectations* is "old Orlick,"[8] who is driven by the bitterness, wrath, anger, clamor, evil speaking, and malice that Paul attributes to the old man in Ephesians

4.31. Twice Pip reports his belief that Orlick has assumed "Dolge" as his "pretended Christian name" to affront people (139, 158); metaphorically, then, Orlick has no baptismal name, no name of a new man. Adam was a creature of earth, and Orlick is one who seems to have "started up . . . from the ooze," one who is "very muddy" (158, 146). Moreover, Orlick is, in Pip's words, "like Cain" (140), a son of fallen Adam; and he is the agent of death for Mrs. Joe and the would-be agent of death for Pip. He is, also in Pip's words, "like . . . the Wandering Jew" (190), who, according to legend, taunted and rejected the new Adam.

In confronting Orlick, Pip also confronts the old man, the figure of death and guilt; as such, he is Pip's doppelgänger. Orlick is like Cain; but Pip is like Cain in relation to Herbert. Orlick is also a figure of the old man, the doppelgänger never on this side of the grave completely drowned even in the baptized; hence he is associated with many of the characters who are violent and often labeled as old. Orlick is linked with Mrs. Joe by her violent rage and blind fury; he is linked with Bentley, "an old-looking . . . man" (213), by malice and a sulky and unforgiving disposition. He comes into the employ of Miss Havisham, who has her own wrath and anger. Orlick also comes into the employ of Compeyson; and he utters a parody of the baptismal pattern of union when he says of Compeyson and Bentley, "'I've took up with new companions and new masters'" (438).[9] By the epithet "old"[10] he is linked to Barley who roars and growls, full of anger, wrath, malice.

That the old man has died in baptism is symbolized by new white clothes; they represent the new life and innocence conferred in the rite. Paul wrote to Christians in Ephesians 4.22-24 and Colossians 3.9-10 that those buried in the baptismal waters must "put off," like a suit of clothes, the old man and "put on the new." The church early introduced into the ceremonial of baptism the putting off of old clothes and the putting on of new white ones. Pip's new clothes, however, are not like these new clothes; rather they are like the clothes that God gave Adam and Eve in their guilt. In pride Pip goes to put on his new clothes at

Pumblechook's, but they prove a disappointment as has "every new and eagerly expected garment ever put on since clothes came in" (183)—as they did, of course, with the Fall.

The baptismal imagery of clothing is inverted, then, in the first parts of *Great Expectations*, but so are other parts of Pip's world. No sooner does Pip come to his first impression of the identity of things than Magwitch places him upon a tombstone and literally turns him upside down. From almost the first, Pip's "interior landscape is inverted" (Van Ghent 135), as is the imagery of baptism, as is the presentation of Christmas in the opening chapters. The perversion of baptism enacted in the first pages of the novel takes place in the context of the perversion of Christmas, the birthday of the Last Adam. The book opens on a Christmas Eve as Pip experiences a kind of birth. Moreover, the names of his mother and his foster father are Georgiana Maria and Joseph. Christmas is important to baptismal themes because, according to the Prayer Book, the baptized is born into the second Adam (Christ). In fact, Christ's own baptism is observed in many calendars during the Christmas-Epiphany season.[11] Dickens carries the initial perversion of Christmas further by using imagery of darkness. The coming of light is part of the iconography of Christmas. The rite of a feast begins on its eve, and this novel begins on Christmas Eve; but darkness is the imagery of the opening pages as night comes on. And darkness closes Christmas day and the hunt for Magwitch; Pip says, "It had been almost dark before, but now it seemed quite dark, and soon afterwards very dark" (69). Light is put out as "the ends of the torches [are] flung hissing into the water . . . as if it were all over with [Magwitch]" (71). Dickens introduces the symbols of the gibbet and the beacon as Magwitch leaves Pip on Christmas Eve. Both are "ugly" and "black things" (39) because they are corruptions of Christian symbols—the gibbet suggesting the cross, and the beacon suggesting the "light [shining] in the darkness" of the gospel reading appointed in the Prayer Book for Christmas. The motif of light in darkness, in turn, suggests the story of the unbaptized Nicodemus, who came by night to Christ the light inquiring of salvation and learned that by water he must be born again; this lesson, from John 3, occurs in the Prayer Book rite of adult baptism and is the source of the ancient Christian iconography that associates light with baptism.

Pip in exile is like Nicodemus in the darkness; he is also like the fallen Adam in his clothes but, as will be seen, unlike Adam exiled from Eden. Pip alludes directly to the last lines of *Paradise Lost* as he sets out for London, saying, "The world lay spread before me" (186). After suffering and repenting and after having been given a vision of the new man, Adam in *Paradise Lost* is exiled but is given, like the baptized, a new beginning, and he journeys in hope of attaining the "paradise within," that is, the Kingdom of Heaven promised in the baptismal office. The night before he leaves for London, Pip suffers nightmares of failed journeys, of coaches going to wrong places. The allusion to *Paradise Lost* is followed by a description of London as "ugly, crooked, narrow, and dirty" (187)—hardly a paradise, more nearly exile.

Great Expectations attains a comic resolution as the perverted figures of baptism discussed hitherto are metamorphosed into true ones and as regenerations open onto new lives. Despite the almost pervasive presence of death in the novel, evidence of life nevertheless persists; but the life present in death must be freed, usually by the discipline of suffering that characterizes most comedy. Pip calls the night on which Magwitch comes to his London chambers "the turning point of my life" (318). That night is characterized both by figures of rain and flood (typologically associated with baptism) and by figures of destruction, of apocalypse (also typologically associated with baptism [Daniélou 75-85]). These images reach their symbolic completion in death-by-water when Magwitch, Compeyson, and Pip suffer shipwreck and descend into the Thames.[12] In the rhythm of the final chapters, the counter movements—one of death and one of life—come to their resolutions. Pip must come to see that his great expectations are not Estella and Miss Havisham's money but regeneration, which will offer him the paradise within that the allusion to Milton—"the world lay spread before me" (186)—finally invokes. Dickens renews the motifs of baptism that have had negative connotations throughout much of the novel and gives them positive meanings: the death of the old man makes possible the birth of the new man; unprofitable guilt gives way to fruitful contrition and humility; life comes out of living death through painful baptismal fire and through life-giving water, violence and malice metamorphose into forgiveness. Magwitch, Miss Havisham, and Mrs. Joe experience various aspects of regeneration that precede and anticipate Pip's rebirth. Light replaces darkness, and Dickens transforms the perverted Christmas of the opening chapters into genuine celebration at the end of the novel.

The drowning of Compeyson in the waters of the Thames is like the death of the old man in the baptismal office; he is everyone's secret companion, everyone's inner darkness. Like Magwitch he is a prisoner. Like Miss Havisham he is a failed marriage partner. Like Orlick he is a criminal. Like Pip he is a gentleman. He is ubiquitous; everyone may see his or her own likeness in him (Gilbert 98). Early in the novel we see Compeyson and Magwitch, linked like Cain and Abel, in a death-grip, splashing water and mud in the ditch; then we see them tied together to be taken to the hulks. They go overboard together; as in the scene in the ditch, they are fiercely locked in each other's arms. After "a struggle underwater," Magwitch disengages himself, finally, forever free of Compeyson, who goes to an "unshriven death" (Stone 687), "tumbling on the tides, dead" (Dickens 458). Like the newly baptized, Magwitch is given new clothes at the Ship. Simultaneously with the killing of Compeyson occurs the "death" of the old man in Magwitch, and Pip sees the new man "bearing towards [him] on the tide" (455), severely injured, the "old sound in his throat softened" (457).

The metaphors of resurrection associated with Magwitch at the beginning of the book are, as we have seen, perverted images; by the conclusion of the novel they have been metamorphosed into genuine figures of rebirth. Pip thinks that, as Provis, changes have already begun in Magwitch who has "softened—indefinably" (391); on the boat he sits, "smiling with that softened air upon him" (448). Magwitch knows full well that "'it's death'" to return to England (340). The cataclysmic shipwreck has sealed his transformation. He has begun his passage "beyond Gravesend," which Pip calls the "critical place" (429, 445, 449). Before his trial he shows "submission or resignation," knowing that he cannot "bend the past out of its *eternal* shape" (465; italics mine).

At his trial he can accept his "sentence of Death from the Almighty" and can bow to the sentence of death from the judge. Pip mentions at this juncture the "greater Judgment that knoweth all things and cannot err" (467); his words—"knoweth all things"—are quoted from the twentieth verse of 1 John 3, a chapter that speaks of the baptized as "sons of God" who will, when God appears, "be like him" (3.2) because in baptism they are "born of God" (3.9) and will pass "from death to life" (3.14). After the judgment Magwitch becomes more and more "placid" (468, 469) while Pip takes as "the first duty of life" to prepare Magwitch for death, "to say to him, and read to him, what I knew he ought to hear" (465). The collect for Ash Wednesday asks God to "create and make in us a new and contrite heart." Magwitch's heart, "humble and contrite" (466), has become the kind of sacrifice that, according to the psalm (51.17) appointed for Ash Wednesday, God will not despise. Abel can finally offer the acceptable sacrifice that makes him a type of Christ. "Mindful, then, of what [they] had read together," Pip can knowingly and deliberately apply to Magwitch specifically words applicable to all sinners generally and pray, "'O Lord, be merciful to him, a sinner!'" (470).

The rhythm of baptism by which the old dies and the new is born is also the pattern of comedy, in which life almost implausibly comes out of death and joy implausibly out of sorrow. In fact, in several cases in *Great Expectations*, literal death of the old is requisite for new life: old Barley must die in order that Clara may marry Herbert; Miss Havisham must die that Matthew and Herbert may be financially secure; Bentley must die that Estella may put her new heart into employ; Mrs. Joe and Mr. Wopsle's great-aunt must die that Biddy and Joe may wed; Compeyson must die for Magwitch to end well. As death has not in it the wherewithal of life nor sorrow the wherewithal of joy, Dickens's comedy implies the operation of a theistic providence that can use pain to effect joy.

John the Baptist announced that, while he baptized "with water unto repentance," one would succeed him who would painfully baptize "with fire" (Matt. 3.11). In the context of this passage, purification by water pertains to Magwitch, one of Pip's foster parents, and purification by fire concerns Miss Havisham, another of his foster parents. Pip holds the burning Miss Havisham down "with all [his] strength, like a prisoner," "struggling [with her as if they were] . . . desperate enemies" (414); the struggle is desperate because the old man in her wants to flee his painful baptismal death. Miss Havisham becomes "insensible," as in death, later to revive and speak "collectedly." The fire destroys the old in her, the "faded bridal dress," "every vestige of [which] was burnt" and "all the ugly things that sheltered" in the decay on the table. The fire also makes way for the new, for the "phantom air [about her] of something that had been and was changed"; it is a kind of baptism (414-15). Likewise, the white cotton-wool and the white sheet that replace the old clothes suggest the baptismal change of apparel. Miss Havisham's hope that she might die on her birthday and that she might then be laid out on the feast table comes to pass when her bed is laid there upon this day in which she is "changed" and established in a new moral life.

The cleansing flame actually seals a work that has already commenced because Pip has led her to recognize the evil that she has perpetrated. In the "'looking-glass'" (411) of Pip's suffering she sees what she once felt and, we may suppose, can now see herself as like Arthur and Compeyson, who betrayed her; and she begs Pip's forgiveness. In granting it, Pip, who himself "'want[s] forgiveness'" (410), enters the rhythm of the Lord's Prayer; and in forgiving her he becomes an analogue of Christ.[13] In showing a "new affection" (411) toward Pip and in asking to serve him as well as Herbert, Miss Havisham is ready for her baptism by fire.

In fact, the theme of forgiveness, which is also a theme of baptism, becomes particularly of great import as the novel moves toward its conclusion. In Mrs. Joe, too, who is "left . . . for dead" (437) after Orlick's blow, the old dies.[14] It dies that the new may indeed come to life. Early in her infirmity, "her temper [is] greatly improved" (150); as she emerges from one of her bad states, she wants to put her arms around Joe's neck, and she asks pardon (302). The announcement of her death comes to Pip in the words "[She has] departed this life" (297); this locution comes from the prayer for the church in the Holy Communion. In this instance, too (see above 38), anyone as familiar with the liturgy as Dickens was would recognize this allusion immediately; that prayer speaks of those who have "departed this life in [God's] faith and fear." Penance, asking forgiveness, amendment of life, requisites for adult baptism, precede the entry of Mrs. Joe, as well as Miss Havisham, into death, which the church sees as a second baptism (Daniélou 24). In Estella likewise suffering brings life out of death. At an early stage of their acquaintance, she tells Pip, "'I have no heart'" (259); somewhat later she says to him, "'You address nothing in my breast, you touch nothing there'" (376). Then, in the first, more austere ending, Bentley's death releases her from the "suffering [that] had been stronger than Miss Havisham's teaching, and [that] had given her a heart to understand what [Pip's] heart used to be" (496). One may assume that the new heart and its ability to love are put into employ in her marriage with the Shropshire doctor. The second ending is even more hopeful for Estella.

Like Miss Havisham, Mrs. Joe, and Estella, Pip, too, experiences suffering, repentance, and regeneration. He is baptized by fire and then by water, and it is to his moral regeneration that Dickens gives the most attention. Even before his boat is wrecked and he is immersed in the Thames, Pip introduces imagery of a ship at sea. When Herbert announces his intention to go to the East, Pip says, "I felt as if my last anchor were loosening its hold, and I should soon be driving with the winds and waves" (427-28). Pip must cast away, or have cast away for him, all his anchors—his great expectations of being a gentleman and his hopes regarding Estella, his companionship with Herbert, his illusory "last baffled hope" (487) of marrying Biddy, even his life in England—and he must become fully a castaway before he can become a "twice-born" hero (Westburg 115). Drowned with Magwitch, burned with Miss Havisham and by his own fever, brought to the point of death by Orlick, reduced to debt and almost to imprisonment, bereft even of Biddy, sent for eleven years' exile into the East, Pip is drawn into the pattern of baptism and of comedy.

Pip experiences baptismal death-by-fire, first by participating in Miss Havisham's fiery baptism and then by confronting Orlick. As he struggles on the floor with Miss Havisham, he suffers a state like death until his awareness revives: "[T]hat [the events described] occurred I knew through the results, but not through anything I felt, or thought or knew I did," Pip says, "I knew nothing . . ." (414). Pip's encounter with Orlick, described repeatedly with imagery of fire, is, typologically speaking, a battle against the old man. Against his doppelgänger Orlick Pip "struggle[s] with all the [previously unknown] force . . . within [him]." When "after a blank . . . [he] recover[s] consciousness" (440), he thinks that he has been lying in the sluice house "two days and nights" (441). By the "noose" (434) that Orlick uses to capture Pip and by the "perpendicular ladder" (435) to which Orlick binds him, Dickens associates Pip, as he has associated Miss Havisham, with that figure of death and resurrection, the gibbet (see above 41).[15] Like a catechumen preparing for baptism, Pip admits his "miserable errors," "humbly beseech[es] pardon . . . of Heaven" (437), and intends amendment of life. In both fiery encounters Pip loses consciousness, as if he were dead, and regains it, as if he had come to life again; he participates in a kind of comedic baptismal death and rebirth.

The same rhythm that obtains in Pip's encounters with Magwitch, Miss Havisham, and Orlick also obtains in his descent into both debt

and sickness and in his ascent out of them. Illness and the consequences of his debt come upon Pip simultaneously. In his sickness Pip
descends into the isolation and the hell of his soul, confronts and rejects what he finds there, and rises to a new kind of life. In his fever he
enters a "night . . . of great duration . . . which teem[s] with anxiety and
horror"; he frequently loses his hold on reality (470-71). After a fever-
ish delirium he "tries to settle" the details of his hallucination with
himself and "to get [them] into some order" (471). As his encounters
with Magwitch, Miss Havisham, and Orlick have the figurative shape
of death followed by rebirth, so, too, does his encounter with the fever.
In his sickness, Pip struggles with people whom he takes to be murder-
ers and then understands that they intend to do him good and "sink[s]
exhausted in their arms" (472). Apparently, however, all these "people" are Joe, to whom he is restored. As he gains strength he fancies
himself "little Pip again," like a "child in [Joe's] hands" (476). Pip's
metaphoric birth in the churchyard occurs in winter, a season metaphoric of death. Pip's recovery occurs during May and June; and his
first outing is on Sunday, the day commemorating the resurrection that
the "Sunday bells" celebrate (476). As a boy, Pip had looked at seeds
and bulbs jailed in Pumblechook's drawers and wondered if they
wanted "of a fine day to break out . . . and bloom" (83). But while Pip
has now lain "burning . . . on [his] bed," the little wild flowers that he
sees on his Sunday outing have been "forming" (476) and suggest the
new life of springtime to which his own pip has come.[16] Baptized when
he was given his "Christian name," Pip at seven falls into the world of
guilt and sorrow; brought to repentance by several purgatorial ordeals
of testing and trying, he asks forgiveness, recovers innocence, and regains a kind of paradise.

When the castings-off enforced upon Pip are complete—when he is
fully a castaway with "no home anywhere" (461), a clerk from some-
where in the East—Pip can approach the paradise within only by working and repaying his debts. He leaves England, carrying out Christ's
commandment to those who seek eternal life or the kingdom of

heaven: "I sold all I had" (489). But Pip cannot redeem "his [own] soul" (Wentersdorf 224)—either in terms of baptism or in terms of the comic structure of the novel; for an act of substitution must occur in each. Baptism is validated only by Christ's actual death and resurrection; and in the comic rhythm of the novel Joe must redeem Pip's debt of "'hundred and twenty-three pound, fifteen, six'" (471). Likewise, Pip suffers and Miss Havisham is redeemed; Joe and Pip suffer and Mrs. Joe is redeemed. In order that Magwitch may know redemption Pip goes beyond Jaggers's prudential advice that he abandon the returned felon. These acts of substitution (of suffering and forgiving) essential to the economy of the novel partake in a pattern of Christian analogy. They are acts of charity, of disinterested love.

Dickens describes such love by imagery of light. One of the corrupted figures of baptism that the comic rhythm of the novel renews is that of light, which was perverted at the beginning of the novel into darkness. Before the novel ends, light becomes a genuine emblem of divinity. Dickens establishes this value of the metaphor when he allows Estella to describe her ignorance of love by using an analogy of the absence of sunlight. Having been taught from the first that daylight is her enemy and destroyer, that it would blight her, and having been brought up wholly in the "dark confinement" of Satis House, Estella cannot be expected "to understand the daylight" (324). Love is like the sunlight or the daylight. Moreover, Pip analyzes Miss Havisham's history in terms of the same analogy. "In shutting out the light of day," she has "shut out *infinitely* more" (italics mine), a "thousand natural and healing influences." Consequently, her mind has "grown diseased, as all minds do and must and will that reverse the appointed order of their Maker" (411). Light is like love: and both are like the healing influences that the "Maker" orders as remedies.

Imagery of fire in *Great Expectations* is figurative of the painful cleansing necessary to metaphoric death; imagery of light is figurative of the fertility of that new life. It describes the regeneration of Magwitch—and also of Pip. Two baptismal emblems govern Pip's interpretation of Magwitch's trial: "drops of April rain" and "rays of April sun" (466). The trial takes place during both the natural season of rebirth and fertility and also the liturgical season of resurrection. The sun striking the great court windows links the prisoners in a "broad shaft of light" suggesting to Pip a "greater Judgment," the justice of one whom Magwitch calls "the Almighty" (467).

Dickens metamorphoses his perverted figures of baptism, and he ends the novel by returning to Christmas; the imagery of this feast is also transformed. Roberta Schwartz points out that Pip's return "upon an evening in December" (489) from eleven years in Egypt completes the Nativity cycle (65).[17] The novel has come full circle; it ends where it began—but with a major difference. Pip finds that a proper father has married a proper mother to provide a proper family and a proper home; they have produced a new Pip, in whom the old can vicariously find his second chance (Meisel 329). Joe and Biddy have "'giv' him the name of Pip'" (490); that name they would have given him during the rite of his baptism. His name is not that of a dead father. He has not been baptized into the exile into which Pip was "born." The young Pip is about seven. Pip replaces Magwitch as a kind of adoptive father: on a visit to the churchyard, he repeats Magwitch's gesture by setting the young child upon a tombstone, but not in such a way as to invert his world.

* * *

Scholarship has informed us of the widespread understanding of biblical typology among the English public of the nineteenth century. At the same time, as Larson has argued in the passage I cited at the outset, the Bible was becoming for Dickens and his audience "a locus of hermeneutical instability," a "broken" and "fractured code." Larson recognizes Dickens's many allusions to the Bible and *The Book of Common Prayer* and displays ambiguities that Dickens introduces into the allusions; however, she does not suggest the strategies by which the novelist restores the meaning and significance inherent in them. Nor does she discuss *Great Expectations*. I believe my analysis of this novel helps us see just how Dickens breaks the code and how he then restores it. What is true of *Great Expectations*, I presume, is true of Dickens's other mature novels.

Dennis Walder records the equivocal remarks that Dickens made in places other than his novels about baptism and goes on to add that Dickens's beliefs are rarely made explicit; rather they are implicit in the texture of his novels. One must study them as they are embodied in "significant moments," in images, themes, and structures. The novels are the only expression of the inner life of Dickens. In *Great Expectations*, Dickens relies "on the familiar underlying pattern of sin, repentance and regeneration" (Walder 200, 3, 14, 15, 209); this pattern is the rhythm of baptism and implies a providential order.[18] Dickens mentioned this order in a letter to Wilkie Collins. He said that the "business of art is to lay all [the] ground carefully . . . to show . . . what everything has been working to. . . . These are the ways of Providence, of which ways all art is but a little imitation" (125). We may say that Dickens's allusions define this shaping order as Christian.

Notes

I am grateful to Professors George Walton Williams, Clyde Ryals, Eric Trethewey, Brian Gillespie, Iain Crawford, and Nickolas Pappas, to the late Doctor John Kassman, and to Mr. Robert Whitaker for suggestions toward the improvement of this essay.

1. The Christian figure of the wedding feast and the sacrament of the eucharist of which it is an emblem also occur in *Great Expectations*. Like the metaphor of baptism, they appear first in a perverted form and then in a genuine one. I discuss the pattern of this other transformation in "The Figure of the Wedding Feast in *Great Expectations*."

2. I do not, however, find the pervasive "allegory" in *Great Expectations* that Jane Vogel does, nor do I find the profusion of Christian allusions that she sees (45-80).

3. That prayer addresses God, the one who did "save Noah and his family in the

ark from perishing by water . . . figuring thereby [his] holy baptism" and asks that the baptismal candidate may be "received into the ark of Christ's church," may "safely pass the waters of this troublesome world," and may be led to the "land of everlasting life." The office speaks of the baptized as "regenerate and born again," as "lively members of Christ's church," who by "mystical" and "heavenly washing" have experienced "remission of sin"; therefore, they may be "partakers of Christ's resurrection."

4. Behind the Prayer Book formularies stands Paul's discussion in Romans 6. There the apostle says that the faithful have been "baptized into Christ's death" and have been "buried with him by baptism into death" so that they may be "raised into likeness of his resurrection, . . . knowing that the old man is crucified in him."

5. Dennis Walder writes that Dickens demonstrates his intimate knowledge of the Bible and of *The Book of Common Prayer* (1662) "by frequent, accurate, and often surprisingly relevant allusion throughout his works" (290).

6. See Matt. 27.25; Luke 11.51; Acts 18.6.

7. See Matt. 27.48.

8. At the climax of his attempt to destroy Pip, Orlick calls himself "old" twelve times (437-39); five other times in the novel he uses this adjective to describe himself. Dickens's insistence on the old raises it to a metaphoric significance.

9. See the passage from the baptismal office in the Prayer Book where the priest gives thanks for receiving the "Child by adoption" and for incorporating him into God's "holy Church" and when he announces that the child has been "receive[d] into the congregation of Christ's flock." By the adoption, the child receives a new master and enters a new society.

10. Used eight times to describe Orlick in two pages (389-90).

11. As in the office lectionary of *The Book of Common Prayer.*

12. Landow shows that Christian writers since Augustine have used the voyage as an image of movement toward the second Eden; the traditional use of the figure of the voyage allows for such a cataclysmic event as shipwreck that may result either in a failure to reach the second Eden (as with Compeyson) or in testing and trying (as with Pip and Magwitch). See *Images* 16, 7, 20, 17, 91.

13. In so doing, Pip fulfills a role foreshadowed in his baptism, for in the metaphor of baptism he had already become an analogue of Christ when he received his "Christian name." Allusions to one's "Christian name," given at baptism, occur throughout the novel: 58, 105, 139, 202, 215, 362.

14. If a lime kiln had been nearby, Orlick says, "She shouldn't have come to life again" (437).

15. "I fancied that I saw Miss Havisham hanging to the beam" (413).

16. In this connection, Dorothy Van Ghent cites John 12.24: "Except a corn of wheat fall into the ground and die, it abideth alone: but if it die, it bringeth forth much fruit" (379).

17. See Matt. 2.19-21. See also Matt. 2.15: ". . . that it might be fulfilled which was spoken of the Lord by the prophet, saying, Out of Egypt have I called my son."

18. Walder concludes that Dickens "did not ever break entirely his connections with broadly Anglican faith and practice."

Works Cited

The Book of Common Prayer (1662). Crown copyright, various editions.

Byrd, Max. "Reading in *Great Expectations*." *PMLA* 91 (1976): 259-65.

Cunningham, John. "The Figure of the Wedding Feast in *Great Expectations*." *Dickens Quarterly* 10.2 (1993): 87-91.

Daniélou, Jean. *The Bible and the Liturgy*. South Bend, IN: U of Notre Dame P, 1956.

Davies, Horton. *From Watts and Wesley to Maurice, 1690-1850*. Vol. 3 of *Worship and Theology in England*. Princeton, NJ: Princeton UP, 1961. 5 vols. 1961-75.

Dickens, Charles. *Great Expectations*. Ed. Angus Calder. Harmondsworth, Middlesex: Penguin, 1965.

_____. *The Letters of Charles Dickens*. Vol. 3. Ed. Walter Dexter. Bloomsbury: Nonesuch, 1938. 3 vols.

Gilbert, Elliott L. "'In Primal Sympathy': *Great Expectations* and the Secret Life." *Dickens Studies Annual* 11 (1983): 89-113.

Landow, George. *Images of Crisis. Literary Iconology, 1750 to the Present*. Boston: Routledge, 1982.

_____. *Victorian Types, Victorian Shadows: Biblical Typology in Victorian Literature, Art, and Thought*. Boston: Routledge, 1980.

_____. *William Holman Hunt and Typological Symbolism*. New Haven, CT: Yale UP, 1979.

Larson, Janet L. *Dickens and the Broken Scripture*. Athens: U of Georgia P, 1985.

Meisel, Martin. "The Ending of *Great Expectations*." *Essays in Criticism* 15 (1965): 326-31.

Robison, Roselee. "Time, Death and the River in Dickens' Novels." *English Studies* 53 (1972): 436-54.

Schwartz, Roberta. "The Moral Fable of *Great Expectations*." *North Dakota Quarterly* 47 (1979): 55-66.

Shepherd, Massey Hamilton, Jr. *The Oxford American Prayer Book Commentary*. New York: Oxford, 1950.

Stone, Harry. "Fire, Hand, and Gate: Dickens' *Great Expectations*." *Kenyon Review* 24 (1962): 662-91.

Van Ghent, Dorothy. *The English Novel: Form and Function*. New York: Holt, 1953.

Vogel, Jane. *Allegory in Dickens*. Studies in the Humanities 17. University: U of Alabama P, 1977.

Walder, Dennis. *Dickens and Religion*. London: Allen, 1981.

Wentersdorf, Karl P. "Mirror-Images in *Great Expectations*." *Nineteenth-Century Fiction* 21 (1966): 203-24.

Westburg, Barry. *The Confessional Fiction of Charles Dickens*. De Kalb: Northern Illinois UP, 1977.

Memory and Confession in *Great Expectations*

Samuel Sipe

I

For most readers of *Great Expectations*, Dickens's success in creating a convincingly vulnerable and flawed central character—one who is both a victim of and an accomplice to crimes of ingratitude and manipulation—is matched by his success in resolving the problems which that character faces in a convincing, unsentimental fashion. Somehow the guilty and inadequate Pip of the early and middle sections of the novel, a character of manifestly uncertain identity who can ask his friend Herbert "what shall I say I am—to-day?,"[1] achieves, by the end of the novel, an authentic selfhood and exhibits a distinct "quality of moral resolution."[2] And as Pip undergoes this change, so the violent and selfish world of *Great Expectations* comes to appear as an unmistakably human world, one which affords ample scope for man's more generous impulses to be expressed.

How is it that these transformations come about? Readers can point to a whole series of chastening physical experiences which the young Pip undergoes during the final stages of his expectations: his trial by fire at Miss Havisham's, his brush with death at the limekiln, his immersion in the Thames, and his delirious illness that follows upon Magwitch's death. According to Marshall W. Gregory, it is this cumulative experience of "great suffering which purges [Pip's] character, mettle, passions, and values of all pretentiousness and vanity, thus rendering him capable of taking his place in the world as a whole man."[3] Certainly Pip suffers, but what or where is this "place" which Gregory speaks of? And if Pip has learned from his suffering, it must be acknowledged that when he arises from his sickbed he is still an incomplete individual who is prey to unrealistic expectations; his plan to make a place for himself by asking for Biddy's hand in marriage soon proves to be one "last baffled hope" (p. 454).

In Pip's case suffering may be seen as a necessary prelude to the creation of an authentic identity, but it does not in itself determine the essence of that identity. Given Dickens's repeated novelistic emphasis of the importance of certain human relationships (those existing between parent and child and man and wife, in particular), it seems more reasonable to identify Pip's emergence as a "whole man" with his formation of intimate interpersonal bonds at the end of the novel than with his purgation by fire, fear, water, and illness. Certainly Pip's new devotion to Magwitch, his surrogate father, represents an attempt to atone for his own guilt and indicates a change in the direction of his life. But Pip's bond with Magwitch can only be the dominant fact of that life as long as the convict himself lives: "when I took my place by Magwitch's side, I felt that that was my place *henceforth while he lived*" (p. 423; my italics). Once Magwitch dies, Pip has no clearly defined "place" in the world, unless the reader is to assume that his union with Estella which is foreshadowed at the end of the novel develops into an abiding and sustaining love.

The controversy over the two endings of the novel and the final nature of Pip's relationship with Estella has flared intermittently ever since Forster first published the original version in which Pip simply meets Estella on a London street and learns that she too has suffered. Although early critics—Forster, Gissing, and Shaw among them—objected to the revised ending on the grounds that it is unrealistic and sentimental, a number of recent critics argue that this ending, with its hint of a marriage to come, dispels any mists of uncertainty as to Pip's situation, replacing them with a discretely sober, neo-Miltonic glow.[4] But do we really think of Pip, the essential Pip, as being defined by a relationship which we the readers must imagine? The Estella of the final paragraphs of the novel is an insubstantial figure, and the life she will lead with Pip is altogether a matter of inference. Those who invoke the parallel between the endings of *Paradise Lost* and *Great Expectations* forget that there is nothing at the end of Dickens's novel which is comparable to the extensive orientation to the future which Adam is given in Books XI and XII of Milton's epic.

Great Expectations is a novel which remains enclosed in the world of the past, Pip's past.

Surely it is in this past that Pip, author of his life's history, discovers the origins of his identity, and just as surely it is in the sum of Pip's past experiences and his present attitudes towards them that the readers of *Great Expectations* discover Pip the whole man. The conception of identity which emerges from this novel is not the spatially oriented one of "place" (social position, economic role, familial relationship), but an essentially temporal conception. If there is any one single action which should be identified with Pip's emergence as an adequate self, it is the telling of his life's story whereby he enters into his own past and discovers himself as someone who has continuity in time, someone whose life has, from the perspective of the present, a coherent meaning. In the process of telling about himself, Pip completes himself and reveals himself as a mature and secure individual. His experiences of suffering and the human relationships which he enters into are important as part of the larger pattern of his life which he himself discovers through memory and validates by casting it in verbal form.

II

Most readers of *Great Expectations* have observed that the novel is more carefully structured than Dickens's other works and have pointed to the symmetrical division of the book into the three stages of Pip's expectations as a clear manifestation of a concern with narrative form.[5] A somewhat more complex aspect of formal ordering in the novel involves the extensive use of analogous actions and situations, specifically with respect to the themes of expectations and manipulation.[6] But these examples of spatial form should not be allowed to obscure the recognition of another and more fundamental principle of order at work within the book, the juxtaposition of the consciousness of Pip the character, caught up in a particularized world of people and things, caught, quite frequently, in successive instants of time, with the consciousness of Pip the narrator who has moved through that world and entered the realm of the storyteller's present.

This juxtaposition of consciousness is made apparent in at least four different ways. It is most obvious when the narrator calls attention to a transition from one level of awareness to another by alluding to the passing of time: "Since that time, which is far enough away now, I have often thought that few people know what secrecy there is in the young, under terror" (p. 12). The existence of two consciousnesses is also apparent when Pip the character engages in conversation and utters statements which are distinctly foreign to the sensibility of the narrator, as in the following passage where the narrator's perceptive, affectionate observations about Biddy are in sharp contrast to young Pip's blunt insensitivity:

> We talked a good deal as we walked, and all that Biddy said seemed right. Biddy was never insulting, or capricious, or Biddy to-day and somebody else to-morrow; she would have derived only pain, and no pleasure, from giving me pain; she would far rather have wounded her own breast than mine. How could it be, then, that I did not like her much the better of the two?
>
> "Biddy," said I, when we were walking homeward, "I wish you could put me right."
>
> "I wish I could!" said Biddy.
>
> "If I could only get myself to fall in love with you—you don't mind my speaking so openly to such an old acquaintance?"
>
> "Oh dear, not at all!" said Biddy. "Don't mind me."
>
> "If I could only get myself to do it, *that* would be the thing for me." (pp. 123-24)

Such juxtapositions of the voices of the younger Pip and Pip the narrator occur quite frequently, especially in the early chapters of the novel, but it is even more common for the reader of *Great Expectations* to be made aware of the presence of the two Pips by the narrator's ironic comments on the actions or opinions of his younger self. It is this extensive use of verbal irony which, more than any other aspect of technique, controls the reader's responses to the erring Pip as he moves towards the grand dramatic irony of the novel, the advent of Magwitch and the disastrous culmination of his expectations. The particular effectiveness of this technique in *Great Expectations* is that the narrator's irony is not so harsh as to create a sense of discontinuity between himself and the younger Pip; on the contrary, the justness of the narrator's ironic comments and the concern for his past self which they imply serve to underscore Pip's continuity, to suggest the process of *becoming* which informs the novel. For example, in the second paragraph of the narrative, Pip speaks with a mild, indeed a sympathetic, irony about his childish ignorance:

> As I never saw my father or my mother, and never saw any likeness of either of them (for their days were long before the days of photographs), my first fancies regarding what they were like, were unreasonably derived from their tombstones. The shape of the letters on my father's gave me an odd idea that he was a square, stout, dark man, with curly black hair. From the character and turn of the inscription "*Also Georgiana Wife of the Above*," I drew a childish conclusion that my mother was freckled and sickly. (p. 1)

Pip's compassion for the "unreasonable," "childish" self he once was is as unmistakable here as is the distinction between the two minds and their different degrees of awareness of the world. But when the younger Pip ceases to be a mere victim of his oppressive surroundings and begins to behave pretentiously or ungratefully, his older self is capable of placing his mistakes in perspective with a more biting remark:

> As I passed the church [of his rural parish], I felt . . . a sublime compassion for the poor creatures who were destined to go there, Sunday after Sunday, all their lives through, and to lie obscurely at last among the low green

mounds. I promised myself that I would do something for them one of these days, and formed a plan in outline for bestowing a dinner of roast-beef and plum-pudding, a pint of ale, and a gallon of condescension, upon everybody in the village. (p. 139)

The mature Pip exposes the vain, self-important attitudes of his younger self, but even as he does so, the humor of "sublime compassion" and "gallon of condescension" suggests that he remains in touch with the person he once was.[7]

The final manifestation of the juxtaposition of two consciousnesses in the narrative of *Great Expectations* is the explicit moral commentary which Pip the narrator applies to his younger self. These moral judgments sometimes incorporate the sort of ironic observations discussed above and are essentially similar in spirit, for while they are direct, they are neither dogmatic nor self-righteous. Speaking, for example, of his initial reluctance to confess the theft of the food and the file, Pip says, "in a word, I was too cowardly to do what I knew to be right, as I had been too cowardly to avoid doing what I knew to be wrong. I had had no intercourse with the world at that time, and I imitated none of its inhabitants who act in this manner. Quite an untaught genius, I made the discovery of the line of action for myself" (p. 37). Though he does not hesitate to identify himself as a coward, Pip manages, through the ironic phrase "untaught genius," to temper the severity of his judgment with a note of understanding. Throughout the book, the tone of his moral observations is one of intimate self-knowledge, a tone which avoids the extremes of unwarranted rigor and self-pity.

Although considerably more space could be devoted to an examination of the ways in which the consciousnesses of the two Pips interact to determine the texture of the narrative of *Great Expectations*, it should be apparent that the narrator controls this interaction and that the kinds of control he exercises suggest that he recognizes the continuity of his being, that he finds the origins of his present self in the past. This control does not involve a rigid imposition of temporal separation between the two Pips; in fact, on numerous occasions Pip the narrator allows his consciousness to merge with that of his past self in order to record more effectively those subjective perceptions and states of mind which are essential to both the drama and meaning of his life's story. His description of his initial encounter with Magwitch on the marshes and his account of the trip down the Thames near the end of the novel are just two instances of the narrator's willingness and ability to relive the past in vivid physical and psychological detail. At no point, however, does the mature Pip allow himself to be engulfed in his memories against his will.[8]

Granted that there is a careful temporal ordering in the narrative of *Great Expectations*, that Dickens, in Herman Daleski's words, "consistently succeeds in simultaneously evoking both the world of the young boy and that of the adult who is telling his story,"[9] what grounds exist for suggesting that Pip's narrative is the crucial vehicle of his self-realization? It may be possible to speak of Pip the narrator as someone who has an interest in his life's story, but is it not more reasonable to speak of him as a simple projection of Dickens the novelist, a convenient and conventional voice for telling a story which focuses on the activities of one individual? This assessment of Pip the narrator as a conventional first person spokesman for the author is implicit in many readings of the novel and is stated explicitly by Robert Garis:

> The narrative voice of Pip which we hear in *Great Expectations* is consistently that of an older, wiser man looking back on his youthful follies. But it is not the voice of a man who, in any specific way, shows the markings of having been through the particular experiences of Pip which form the body of the novel; it is not the voice of a man who has been shaped into a special and individual kind of maturity by special experiences. The voice of Pip is, in a word, the voice of a stock-character. It is a decidedly traditional impersonation of middle-age looking back on youth that Dickens is performing here.[10]

A partial refutation of Garis's statement already exists in the foregoing discussion of the quality of the narrator's ironic observations and moral judgments, but in order to demonstrate that Pip the narrator is the continuation and completion of his past self, it is necessary to examine those "special experiences" which reveal his reasons for telling his life's story.

III

The primary meaning of the verb "expect" is "to look forward to," and indeed the younger Pip of the first two sections of Dickens's novel is a character whose life is oriented towards the future. Though it is natural—in fact necessary—for youth to plan for the years ahead, Pip's commitment to the future tense is so extreme as to lead him to ignore both the past and the present, a sin of omission which ultimately causes him to experience feelings of guilt and inadequacy. When, for example, the lawyer Jaggers presents to Pip a seemingly meaningful future with the announcement of his expectations, Pip immediately becomes "lost in the mazes of [his] future fortunes, and [can] not retrace the by-paths [he and Joe have] trodden together" (p. 133). Here it appears that Pip's ingratitude to Joe, a primary source of his sense of guilt, has a distinctly temporal dimension. Similarly, when Pip takes up the life of an apprentice-gentleman in London, his commitment to an indefinite future renders him virtually incapable of performing any meaningful actions in the present.

The reappearance of Magwitch produces a sudden change in the temporal impetus of Pip's subjective life. In identifying the convict, Pip inadvertently but unavoidably travels back into his own past: "I knew him! Even yet I could not recall a single feature, but I knew him! If the wind and the rain had driven away the intervening years, had scattered all the intervening objects, had swept us to the churchyard where we first stood face to face on such different levels, I could not have known my convict more distinctly than I knew him now" (pp.

300-01). Pip's subsequent realization that he cannot disavow the man who has had such an extensive effect on his life entails the realization that he cannot disavow his past; thus the gradual development of the intimate bond between Pip and Magwitch is accompanied by Pip's growing awareness of his past misdeeds: "For now my repugnance to him had all melted away, and in the hunted wounded shackled creature who held my hand in his, I only saw a man who had meant to be my benefactor and who had felt affectionately, gratefully, and generously towards me with great constancy through a series of years. I only saw in him a much better man than I had been to Joe" (p. 423).

Once Magwitch dies, Pip continues to discover the importance of his past and those human relationships which he forsook for his expectations. The presence of Joe during his period of convalescence is a particularly powerful stimulus to his memory: "the tenderness of Joe was so beautifully proportioned to my need that I was like a child in his hands. He would sit and talk to me in the old confidence, and with the old simplicity, and in the old unassertive protecting way, so that I would half believe that all my life since the days of the old kitchen was one of the mental troubles of the fever and was gone" (p. 442).

But the most dramatically striking instance of Pip's new involvement in his past life is reserved for the penultimate scene of the novel. When, after eleven years abroad, Pip finally returns to visit the forge, it is almost as if he has returned into the past as a spectator of his own childhood:

> There, smoking his pipe in the old place by the kitchen firelight, as hale and as strong as ever, though a little grey, sat Joe; and there, fenced into the corner with Joe's leg, and sitting on my own little stool looking at the fire, was—I again!
>
> "We giv' him the name of Pip for your sake, dear old chap," said Joe, delighted when I took another stool by the child's side (but I did *not* rumple his hair), "and we hoped he might grow a little bit like you, and we think he do."

I thought so too, and I took him out for a walk next morning, and we talked immensely, understanding one another to perfection. And I took him down to the churchyard, and set him on a certain tombstone there, and he showed me from that elevation which stone was sacred to the memory of Phillip Pirrip, late of this Parish, and Also Georgiana Wife of the Above. (p. 457)

It would be an instance of over-reading, perhaps, to suggest that Pip's discovery of someone resembling his past self in his old boyhood environment and his re-enactment of a vital scene of his youth are the events which precipitate the writing of his book, but certainly this scene dramatizes Pip's awareness of the importance of his past, and it is this turning towards the past which culminates in the telling of his life's story. The assertion made by Pip the character in his final conversation with Biddy, shortly after he has met this new Pip, that "I have forgotten nothing in my life that ever had a foremost place there, and little that ever had any place there" (p. 457) sounds like one which the narrator might make. But only the telling of the story can validate this statement.

If Pip's discovery of the significance of the past and the power of memory reveals him to be the sort of individual who might wish to re-create his personal history, a more precise motivation for his decision to write his narrative is to be found in his lifelong preoccupation with the idea of confession. The origins of this theme are found in Pip's initial act of criminal complicity, stealing from the forge to aid Magwitch, which produces intense feelings of guilt in the young boy. Even after Magwitch has generously though falsely confessed the theft of the food, Pip feels uneasy:

I do not recall that I felt any tenderness of conscience in reference to Mrs. Joe, when the fear of being found out was lifted off me. But I loved Joe—perhaps for no better reason in those early days than because the dear fellow let me love him—and, as to him, my inner self was not so easily composed. It was much upon my mind (particularly when I first saw him looking about for his file) that I ought to tell Joe the whole truth. Yet I did not, and for the reason that I mistrusted that if I did, he would think me worse than I was. The fear of losing Joe's confidence, and of thenceforth sitting in the chimney-corner at night staring drearily at my for ever lost companion and friend, tied up my tongue. (p. 37)

The young Pip senses that confession is a possible antidote to his sense of guilt, but the very source of his guilt—his fear of the loss of Joe's affection—is what keeps him from risking the exposure of himself. Later, after the brutal attack on Mrs. Joe, an attack in which Pip is implicated through his unwitting provision of the leg-iron which is used as a weapon, the possibility of confession again suggests itself:

I suffered unspeakable trouble while I considered and reconsidered whether I should at last dissolve that spell of my childhood and tell Joe all the story. For months afterwards, I every day settled the question finally in the negative and reopened and reargued it next morning. The contention came, after all, to this;—the secret was such an old one now, had so grown into me and become a part of myself, that I could not tear it away. (p. 114)

Instead of dispersing in time, Pip's sense of guilt germinates in the dark recesses of his consciousness until it becomes an organic part of him, an odious but integral aspect of his being. Though he longs to confess, he is, at the same time, unwilling to destroy the self he has become and begin the world anew. This dilemma persists throughout his years in London; he lives "in a state of chronic uneasiness respecting [his] behavior to Joe" (p. 258), but he remains afraid to expose his inadequate self to the scrutiny of others by speaking out.

Just as the reappearance of Magwitch has the effect of making Pip conscious of his past, so it is the convict's return and the shattering effect it has upon Pip's life of spurious gentility which is the necessary precondition of his confession. But Pip's impulse to confess is not immediately fulfilled, for unlike the act of recalling one's past, which can be a wholly private one, the act of telling about one's past requires an appropriate audience and a propitious moment for speaking out. The Pip of the closing chapters of *Great Expectations* has the strongest reasons for opening himself up to others, for he feels "the dread of being misremembered after death" (p. 404), yet he finds no appropriate occasion for the comprehensive narrative which his confession would require. The acts of forgiving Magwitch and of asking forgiveness of Joe and Biddy are implicit admissions of wrong conduct, but they are clearly insufficient as means of dispelling years of deeply felt guilt.

It is only in writing his book that Pip completes, in a more eloquent and elaborate fashion, the expiation of his guilt which began with his acknowledgement and acceptance of his intimate ties with Magwitch. Clearly Pip the narrator wants to make himself intelligible to himself, but he also wants to explain himself to others, and it is this impulse which makes his narrative an unmistakable example of the confession, a prominent form of English fiction from its very outset.[11] Not only is the general tone of Pip's narrative one of candid self-revelation, but the specific language which he uses makes this confessional impulse explicit:[12]

> I confess that I expected to see my sister denounce [Orlick], and that I was disappointed by the different result. (pp. 116-17)

> Let me confess exactly, with what feelings I looked forward to Joe's coming [to visit Pip at his chambers in London].
> Not with pleasure, though I was bound to him by so many ties; no; with considerable disturbance, some mortification, and a keen sense of incongruity. If I could have kept him away by paying money, I certainly would have paid money. (p. 206)

> How best to check this growing change in Joe was a great perplexity to my remorseful thoughts. That I was ashamed to tell him exactly how I was placed, and what I had come down to, I do not seek to conceal; but I hope my reluctance was not quite an unworthy one. (p. 446)

Pip's narrative affords him a chance to recreate his behavior in all its detailed complexity, and he embraces this opportunity to disburden himself.

While Pip's desire to confess his complicity in the crimes of his world is a motivation for telling his story, that desire also appears as a source of the continuity of self which he is seeking in his past. To the extent that his story is a confession, it represents the fulfillment of Pip's youthful urge to tell Joe the truth about his relationship with the convict, an urge that was stifled by his timid nature and his fear of losing Joe's love. Now that the full consequences of that early failure to confess have become apparent, a more comprehensive confession is called for. Pip's early associations with the convict have grown organically into the story of his life; the confession which would originally have involved only the brief episode on the marshes now involves years of guilty experience and numerous related episodes, including the initial failure to confess.

IV

The suggestion that Pip's account of his life's story should be regarded as a consciously chosen, intentional act rather than as a conventional narrative device depends primarily upon the realization that the narrative of the mature Pip represents the culmination of his involvement in his own past and fulfills his lifelong urge to confess and atone for his guilty behavior. But while Pip's narrative is a logical outgrowth of his own individual experience, it also seems to be related to his observations of the experience of others with respect to matters of confession and memory. Although there is not space to consider this subject in detail, it can be demonstrated that Pip's subjective motivations for writing his life's story are reinforced and made objective by the behavior of some of the other major characters in the novel.

The significance of the attempt to explain oneself by telling one's life story is made vividly apparent to Pip by the autobiographical fragment which Magwitch relates shortly after announcing himself as Pip's benefactor. The importance of this oral narrative is that it suggests the softening, humanizing effect which the account of an individual's private history can have on his audience. Before Pip sits down to listen to the convict's tale, his feeling towards him is one of unmistakable "repugnance" (p. 322), but Magwitch's story of his miserable childhood and his subsequent victimization at the hands of Compeyson and established society makes Pip feel "great pity" (p. 333) for the persecuted man. If Magwitch can gain the sympathetic understanding of his fellows by recounting his life of oppression and crime, so, perhaps, can Pip, whose early career follows a similar pattern. Indeed it almost appears that in sitting down to write his life's story, Pip has consciously imitated one feature of Magwitch's tale, for both narrators begin by reverting to the crucial moment of dawning self-awareness in their respective lives. Pip's statement that "my first most vivid and broad impression of the identity of things, seems to me to have been gained on a memorable raw afternoon" (p. 1) appears as a more eloquent, perhaps more consciously literary version of Magwitch's description of the onset of self-consciousness: "'I first became aware of myself down in Essex, a thieving turnips for my living'" (p. 328).

As Magwitch gains Pip's compassion by telling the story of his life, so Miss Havisham seems to recognize the powerful effect which the narrative of one's private history can have on one's listeners: "'If you knew all my story,' she pleaded, 'you would have compassion for me, and a better understanding of me'" (p. 378). Pip does know parts of her story and they have inspired him with a measure of sympathy for her. To a certain extent, his narrative is a fulfillment of Miss Havisham's fervent last wish that Pip "Take the pencil and write under [her] name 'I forgive her!'" (p. 382). But while Pip commiserates with Miss Havisham, he cannot alter the facts of her life, for to do so would be to violate his own memory, "to bend the past out of its eternal shape" (p. 432).

Pip has, of course, learned the danger of abusing memory from his own experience, but the lesson is confirmed by his observations of others. Miss Havisham does not ignore the past, as the young Pip did, but she is obsessed by one particular memory which obscures all others. For Miss Havisham, time stopped on the day when Compeyson abandoned her, and she remains voluntarily imprisoned in her recollections of that day, just as she remains voluntarily imprisoned in Satis House, "secluded . . . from a thousand natural and healing influences" (pp. 377-78). Although she can ask forgiveness of Pip, Miss Havisham cannot forgive the man who wronged her and enter again the stream of time.[13]

An even more compelling illustration of the significance of memory, for Pip, is found in Estella's attitude towards her past. Like Miss Havisham, who has made her what she is, Estella does not completely disregard her past, but remains trapped in a certain segment of it. When Miss Havisham accuses her of forgetting her girlhood experiences at Satis House, Estella replies bitterly, "'No, not forgotten . . . Not forgotten, but treasured up in my memory. When have you found me false to your teaching? When have you found me unmindful of your lessons? When have you found me giving admission here,' she touched her bosom with her hand, 'to anything that you have excluded?'" (pp. 290-91). Estella's memory is dominated by the image of Miss Havisham's "strange and frighten[ing] face" (p. 290) and her no less frightening doctrines; she is incapable of recalling any warmer, more comforting aspects of her past. When Pip, frustrated by Estella's indifference to him, chides her for being unable to recall their first childhood encounter, she replies by saying "'that I have no heart—if that has anything to do with my memory'" (p. 224). The association of the words "heart" and "memory" is revealing. Estella's inability to remember may be one cause of her present heartlessness, and it also prevents her from discovering that she might once have had a heart. It would seem that the destruction of Estella's capacity for affection has been too thorough for her to learn to feel deeply for another human being. And yet it is precisely such a change of heart which the reader of *Great Expectations* must accept if he is to believe in Estella's final union with Pip.

Having heard Estella's testimony regarding her involuntary but unavoidable dissociation from her own past, the reader is confronted, in the final scene of the novel, with the evidence of a radical transformation:

> "I have often thought of you," said Estella.
>
> "Have you?"
>
> "Of late, very often. There was a long hard time when I kept far from me the remembrance of what I had thrown away when I was quite ignorant of its worth. But, since my duty has not been incompatible with the admission of that remembrance, I have given it a place in my heart." (p. 459)

On the surface, Estella's words seem thematically appropriate, for if she were to discover her heart, it would have to be through a recognition of the significance of previously forgotten episodes in her past. But how is the reader to know that the words which Estella speaks here are not simply hollow utterances, devoid of any experiential content? In order for the reader to accept Estella's transformation, he must see the softening effect of her memories on her inner life, and not simply hear her pay lip service to the process. Pip's narrative is evidence that such a change can take place and a dramatization of the way it happens, but it is precisely this element of dramatization which is lacking in Estella's case. The reader who believes Estella must recreate in his own imagination the drama of her inner life. Pip's own subjective life can be taken as a model for Estella's, but it is the very presence of his revealing narrative which gives rise to strict standards of credibility with respect to her change of heart.

V

Whether or not the reader is willing to make the imaginative contribution to Estella's story which would validate her transformation and, in turn, her union with Pip, that union can only be understood as an adjunct to the true resolution of the novel, which is Pip's emergence in his narrative as someone whose life has continuity and meaning. In the course of discovering his past and confessing his criminal complicity, Pip purges himself of guilt and demonstrates himself to be capable of, if not irrevocably committed to, standing alone in the world.

Though the act of writing is implicit in the existence of Pip's narrative, the reader of *Great Expectations* does not actually see the mature Pip living and acting in the present. Pip's appearance as a whole man is not a function of his adoption of a particular life style, but a function of the unmistakably self-sufficient and mature sensibility which manifests itself throughout his narrative. The controlled irony and the apposite moral observations of the mature Pip are aspects of this sensibility; so is Pip's unpretentious wisdom and unpretentious prose, a prose that is generally more subdued than the energetic and consciously rhetorical language of Dickens's third person narrators. The Pip who emerges as the convincing hero of *Great Expectations* is the one who, in speaking of his walk across the fields to his sister's funeral, reveals the necessity of compassion and understanding in a harsh world:

> It was fine summer weather again, and, as I walked along, the times when I was a little helpless creature, and my sister did not spare me, vividly returned. But they returned with a gentle tone upon them, that softened even the edge of Tickler. For now the very breath of the beans and clover whispered to my heart that the day must come when it would be well for my memory that others walking the sunshine should be softened as they thought of me. (p. 264)

This passage conveys something of the nature of the mature Pip's insights into his world; moreover, through a juxtaposition of the memories of Pip the character and Pip the narrator, it embodies a precise illustration of the way memory functions in the context of the novel as a whole. Not only is memory a way of discovering what one has been and become, it is also the vital power which can assure one's continued existence in other people's thoughts. Pip recognizes the double power of memory, and acts on this recognition; instead of leaving a cold and inarticulate gravestone as a monument to his memory, as his parents did, he leaves his life's story.

From *Essays in Literature 2*, no. 1 (Spring 1975), pp. 53-64. Copyright © 1975 by Western Illinois University. Reprinted by permission of Western Illinois University.

Notes

1. Charles Dickens, *Great Expectations* (London: Oxford Univ. Press, 1953), p. 234. Subsequent page references are placed in the text in parentheses.

2. Howard Mumford Jones, "On Rereading *Great Expectations*," *Southwest Review*, 39 (1954), 331.

3. Marshall W. Gregory, "Values and Meaning in *Great Expectations:* The Two Endings Revisited," *Essays in Criticism*, 19 (1969), 403.

4. For a brief discussion of the controversy over the two endings, see Robert A. Greenberg, "On Ending *Great Expectations*," *Papers on Language and Literature*, 6 (1970), 152-62. Critics who have discussed the Miltonic echoes in *Great Expectations* include: Edgar Johnson, *Charles Dickens: His Tragedy and Triumph* (New York: Simon and Schuster, 1952), II, 993-94; Monroe Engel, *The Maturity of Dickens* (Cambridge, Mass.: Harvard Univ. Press, 1959), p. 157; J. Hillis Miller, *Charles Dickens: The World of His Novels* (Bloomington: Indiana Univ. Press, 1958), p. 278; and Greenberg.

5. See John H. Hagan, "Structural Patterns in Dickens's *Great Expectations*," *ELH*, 21 (1954), 54-66. Hagan divides the three main stages of Pip's career into substages and suggests that Dickens "arranges his resolutions in the same sequence as that in which the problems were first presented" (p. 55).

6. See Herman Daleski, *Dickens and the Art of Analogy* (New York: Schocken, 1970), p. 239.

7. It should be noted that the carefully modulated irony of *Great Expectations* is one element which distinguishes its tone from that of Dickens's earlier autobiographical novel, *David Copperfield*. Whereas Pip's use of irony implies self-awareness and the temporal continuity of his being, the absence of this quality from David's narrative may be partially responsible for the discontinuity apparent in the second half of the novel between David the character and David the narrator.

8. For a contrasting interpretation of the narrative technique of *Great Expectations*, see Ann B. Dobie, "Early Stream-of-Consciousness Writing: *Great Expectations*," *Nineteenth-Century Fiction*, 25 (1971), 405-16. Dobie says that "Dickens does strive to maintain a degree of narrative coherence while depicting the images and asso-

ciations of Pip's mind, but the qualities of rambling thought, discontinuity, and private associations are strongly evident" (p. 410).

9. Daleski, p. 249.

10. Robert Garis, *The Dickens Theatre* (London: Oxford Univ. Press, 1965), pp. 195-96.

11. For a discussion of the confession as a basic form of fiction, see Northrop Frye, *Anatomy of Criticism* (New York: Atheneum, 1965), pp. 307 ff. Among early English novels, a number of Defoe's works, notably *Robinson Crusoe* and *Moll Flanders*, take the form of the confession.

12. Jones overlooks the confessional element in Pip's narrative, saying that the novel makes the reader believe in "an incredible assumption—the assumption that a sensitive man will be the willing chronicler of his own dishonors" (p. 331).

13. According to Alexander Welsh, "Dickens formulated a special doctrine of the function of memory in moral life. Its most deliberate articulation is the fifth Christmas book, *The Haunted Man.* . . . In the course of the story, Dickens's doctrine of memory is proved and demonstrated to the hero: memories of past wrongs and sorrows are not emotionally destructive but morally constructive; without such memories human beings will harden and become friendless, because they will have no continuing need to practice forgiveness." *The City of Dickens* (Oxford: Clarendon Press, 1970), p. 101.

Manual Conduct in *Great Expectations*_____

William A. Cohen

If one were writing the masturbator's guide to the English novel, certain correspondences would soon become evident. Like the novel, the discourse that constitutes masturbation (as a medical condition, a moral sin, a personal identity, a psychological stage) first arose early in the eighteenth century; like the novel, too, it achieved full cultural currency by the Victorian period and began its decline early in the present century.[1] By the middle of the nineteenth century, both masturbatory practice and novel-reading were firmly installed in popular imagination and culture. With the cultural designation of these practices as significant, anxieties about an unregulated, excessively productive imagination arose, impelling both anti-onanist doctrine and anti-novel invective.[2] Through famously repressive techniques, medical authorities sought to control the onanistic vice that, as we now suppose, they thereby invented; the novel, meanwhile, so perilously implicated in encouraging kindred forms of imaginative self-abuse, had to find ways of managing the erotic reveries it was accused of arousing in its readers.

Having been stigmatized for its association with fantasy, the novel eventually internalized and accommodated that charge. By the mid-nineteenth century, fictional narratives were seeking to exonerate themselves from incrimination in readers' imaginations. Even as the novel strove to redirect its readers *away* from masturbatory vice, however, this now-dominant form of imaginative literature could hardly cease its sexual provocations. The novel increasingly learned how to perform this simultaneously regulatory and arousing function while having (perhaps until Hardy) ever *less* to say about sex overtly. Through specifiable narrative techniques, the Victorian novel at once encrypted representations of sexuality and demonstrated a frantic need for managing and redeeming sexual practices.

In the masturbator's guide to the English novel, at least under the heading "men's bodies," Charles Dickens would doubtless merit a good deal of attention. Charley Bates, a character in *Oliver Twist* (1837-39), first alerts us to the valence of the term in Dickens's corpus. When, as sometimes happens, he is called "Master Bates," we are assured of not being able to lose sight of the pun; yet when, more usually, he is referred to as "Master Charles Bates," we are guaranteed to continue imagining it—like the onanist, always fantasizing about what isn't at hand in order to keep aroused what is. The volatility of Charley's name might in itself make us suspicious, for in the mouth of the narrator it constantly shifts toward and away from the little joke. When he first appears, for instance, he is described as "a very sprightly young friend . . . who was now formally introduced to [Oliver] as Charley Bates." Further down on the page, he is referred to as "Mr. Charles Bates." Finally, he delivers the gear for cleaning up whatever mess his name might imply: "'Wipes,' replied Master Bates; at the same time producing four pocket-handkerchiefs."[3]

The peculiar attention to the young scoundrel's name is dramatically amplified by the following exchange:

> [The Dodger] looked down on Oliver, with a thoughtful countenance, for a brief space; and then, raising his head, and heaving a gentle sigh, said, half in abstraction, and half to *Master Bates:*
> "What a pity it is he isn't a prig!"
> "Ah," said *Master Charles Bates*; "he don't know what's good for him."
> The Dodger sighed again, and resumed his pipe: as did *Charley Bates*. They both smoked, for some seconds, in silence.
> "I suppose you don't even know what a prig is?" said the Dodger mournfully.
> "I think I know that," replied Oliver, looking up. "It's a th—; you're one, are you not?" inquired Oliver, checking himself.
> "I am," replied the Dodger. "I'd scorn to be anything else." Mr. Dawkins gave his hat a ferocious cock, after delivering this sentiment, and looked at *Master Bates*, as if to denote that he would feel obliged by his saying anything to the contrary. (181; emphasis added)

Through this, one of the many scenes depicting Oliver's initiation into the secret community of male adolescence, the term "prig" floats with as much instability as that of "Master Bates." The gloss on "prig" that Oliver is incapable of uttering is presumably "thief," yet the persistence with which the term goes undenoted throws us deliberately back upon the signifier—where, with the alacrity of any English schoolboy, we might take the usual phonemic detour from a bilabial to a fricative and detect a "frig" (Victorian slang for manual stimulation of the genitals). If the revelation that Master Bates himself is a "prig" merely establishes a relation of synonymity, the Dodger nonetheless asserts superiority over the smaller boys with his "ferocious cock."

Dickens's linguistic attention to the male body and male eroticism compels all his *Bildungsromane* to trace not only their heroes' social, emotional, and intellectual development, but their sexual maturation as well. While *Oliver Twist* confines its fantasies about boys' budding bodies to closeted puns, *Great Expectations* (1860-61) refers those same sexual feelings back onto the bodies of its characters. In so doing, however, the later novel relegates sexual sensations to parts of the body different from those in which they are usually imagined to originate; *Great Expectations*, on this reading, manages to anatomize whole species of erotic dispositions without ever mentioning sex.

Let us look, for example, at a scene in *Great Expectations* thematically paralleling the one I have discussed in *Oliver Twist*, in which Dickens raises the issue of masturbation by referencing it in such a way as to announce the impossibility of articulating it as such. The scene that probably constitutes Dickens's most vivid account of the pleasures and anxieties of autoeroticism occurs just when one would expect it in the maturation of the novel's prepubescent hero. Soon after the primal scene of his encounter with Magwitch in the graveyard, still stunned by the fear of it, and a long way from knowing what it means, Pip lifts a slice of bread-and-butter from his sister's table and hides it for later delivery to the convict.[4] Pip, the Dodger might say, thus becomes a prig. And like Oliver's truncated definition of "prig," which in refusing the signified turns us back upon the phoneme (thus stimulating, as Roland Barthes would suggest, the desire to eroticize—if not to frig—the sign), Pip's language also abjures denotation: "Conscience is a dreadful thing," he states, "when it accuses man or boy; but when, in the case of a boy, that secret burden co-operates with another secret burden down the leg of his trousers, it is (as I can testify) a great punishment."[5] Pip carefully avoids a definition of that "secret burden"; his ambiguity, now semantic instead of phonemic, allows the bread-and-butter to function as an alibi for the arousal that he is—as anyone familiar with the perturbations of male adolescence can attest—at such pains to conceal.

Having secreted the morsel down his pants leg, Pip continues to be harassed by his "wicked secret" (55) through the novel's early scenes. When he undertakes the chore of stirring the Christmas pudding, he finds himself altogether discomfited: "I tried it with the load upon my leg (and that made me think afresh of the man with the load on *his* leg), and found the tendency of exercise to bring the bread-and-butter out at my ankle, quite unmanageable. Happily, I slipped away, and deposited that part of my conscience in my garret bedroom" (45). Stealing the meager repast does not merely coincide ("co-operate") with the primary arousal ("another secret burden down the leg of his trousers"): it literalizes the economic metaphor, by which masturbation is classically imagined, of counterproductive labor. Likewise, while the load of which Pip relieves himself surreptitiously in his bedroom signals the irresistible culmination of such titillation, it also completes the analogy between masturbation and theft through a common charge of wastefulness. The trail of butter down his leg points further toward that scene in which, on his first night in London, a now-idle gentleman—Pip claims to detect in his bed "much of [a boiled fowl's] parsley and butter in a state of congelation when I retired for the night" (202).[6] Whether through the profligacy of moneyed leisure or the degeneracy of desperate theft, autoeroticism is figured as wasteful sexual energy.

If the discovery of these suspiciously buttery emissions in Pip's bedrooms suggests an excessively lubricious reading strategy, disavowal of this discovery would itself partake of the very paranoia that structures Pip's response. For in the scene we have been examining, Pip is quick to identify himself with the criminal. First, through corporeal metonymy (that oedipal limp) he links himself to the shackled Magwitch. Further, in abetting the convict, Pip fears he may *become* a convict, by virtue of the paranoiac imagination that affiliates his crime (and his body) with an illegality whose discipline is materialized almost immediately in the soldiers on the doorstep. Victorian proscriptions of self-abuse and the concomitant vigilance in preventing their infringement notoriously inspired the kind of guilt this passage bespeaks among habituated onanists.[7] Not least in an effort to resist the continuing allure of the prohibitions against a practice otherwise thoroughly banalized today, this reading will insist that *Great Expectations* is imbued with lessons about the erotic dispositions of bodies. Rather than recapitulate the protagonist's phobic recoiling against sexual possibilities, I will, in what follows, propose to locate at the very heart of the Victorian literary canon a deeply saturated perversity. One of the nineteenth-century novel's principal accomplishments is to formulate a literary language that expresses eroticism even as it designates sexuality the supremely unmentionable subject. While the regulatory, often punitive dimension of these articulations cannot be overestimated, there is a comparable danger in recognizing nothing other than their prohibitive aspect, thereby merely relocating the critical institutions that have traditionally prevented readers from identifying erotic pleasures—call them perversions—within so respectable a text as *Great Expectations*. The novel both arouses and coerces its readers' desires; tracing the productive interplay of pleasure and power allows not only a reconception of this classic work but a charting of Victorian sexual ideology's formidable operations.[8]

Thanks to the Victorian novel's renowned loquaciousness, the subjects it cannot utter generate particularly nagging silences. How can we make these silences speak? Precisely through attention to the rhetoric of unspeakability: such tropes as periphrasis, euphemism, and indirection give rise to signifying practices that fill in these enforced absences.[9] Even as sexuality is unspeakable, it—or what was, historically, coming to be designated "it"—is everywhere being spoken. The novel, we will see, encrypts sexuality not in its plot or in its announced intentions, but in its margins, at the seemingly incidental moments of its figurative language, where, paradoxically, it is so starkly obvious as to be invisible. The novel directs our attention to its visibly invisible surface with its manifest interest in the materiality of the sign; it offers a model for such reading in, for instance, young Pip's assumption that "the shape of the letters" (35) on the tombstones conveys the physical appearance of his parents, or in the silenced Mrs. Joe's ideogram for Orlick—the hammer—which everyone misreads as a letter (150-51).[10] If the very letters that constitute its matter bear meanings beyond the literal, then by analogy we can detect other sorts of hidden information in aspects of the novel's surface usually considered so conspicuous as to be undeserving of comment. The arena of the unnoticeable (or what it comes down to, the unnoteworthy) shelters what can hardly be thought, much less articulated, in the novel; here instantiated in a specifically literary register is the institutionalization of the unspeakability of sex, which has, as Foucault demonstrates, been generative, not repressive, of discourses on sexuality.

The placement of hand on genitals remains a secret in the Victorian novel, but like all secrets it wants to be told. The scene with which we have been concerned, of masturbation's near exposure, is only the most explicit instance of a pattern that runs throughout *Great Expectations*, a pattern which figures the sexual caress not in the genitals that are handled but in the hands that do the touching. From this early point, at which the boy's bulge virtually speaks its own name, the narrative quickly relegates such unutterable instances of provocation and arousal to the commonplace, benign, and unblushing representation of characters' hands. In a genre that forbids direct observation of genitals in action, this manual code gives voice to what otherwise cannot be spoken.

The sexual secrets of the Victorian novel, that is to say, have not been silenced, but are audible instead in a different key.

Why hands? An account of their place in Victorian culture would consider the wealth of tracts on chirology, palmistry, and graphology from the period, as well as such anatomo-spiritual works as Sir Charles Bell's popular treatise *The Hand; Its Mechanism and Vital Endowments, as Evincing Design*.[11] The fact is not simply that the hand was paid a great deal of attention, but that—given the extent of Victorian self-regulation, both literary and sartorial—it was one of the few anatomical parts regularly available *for* attention: the usual costume of middle-class English adults in the nineteenth century covered all of the body but the head and the hands. Much has been made of the former body part, the head, both in literary representation and in those famous Victorian pseudo-sciences, phrenology and physiognomy. But critics have had little to say about the other part of the body that could be examined—the hand.[12] Nineteenth-century observers felt the hand to be fully saturated with information about its possessor's character; a book entitled *The Hand Phrenologically Considered: Being a Glimpse at the Relation of the Mind with the Organisation of the Body* (1848) exemplifies the Victorian investment in readings of the hand, the technicist discourse of the work enabling it to sidestep the dubiety of palmistry:

> The hand not only affords us characters by which the age and sex may be determined, it is likewise an index of the general habit of body, of the kind of temperament, and of the mental tendency and disposition. . . . A soft, thick hand, loaded with fat, denotes little energy of character, and a soft, yielding, inactive disposition; while, on the contrary, a thin, bony, or muscular hand indicates a rough, active, energetic nature.[13]

Whether through its physiology, the lines that mark it, or the writing with which it is synonymous, the hand is so freighted with significance as to reveal all the vital information about the body and mind behind it.

For the Victorian reader, the hand would immediately be available both as a site of sexual signification and as a dangerous sexual implement. Hands are particularly important to any rendering of masturbation, as the putative etymology of the word suggests: *manus* (hand) + *stuprare* (to defile).[14] Preferring a Greek derivation, urologist William Acton suggests "chiromania" as a synonym for onanism, which he states, in *The Functions and Disorders of the Reproductive Organs* (1857), "can be properly applied, in the case of males, only to emission or ejaculation induced by titillation and friction of the virile member with the hand." In his account of the usual symptomatology of the onanist, Joseph W. Howe argues in *Excessive Venery, Masturbation and Continence* (1887) that hands deserve the special attention of "the experienced eye": "The superficial veins of the integument covering the hands and feet on the dorsal aspect, are very much enlarged or dilated. . . . The hands are often moist and clammy. While the patient is sitting, his shoulders stoop, and both hands are generally placed on the inside of the thighs."[15] Despite anti-onanists' attempts to constrain hands, their resistance to being covered (one can manage, as Miss Skiffins demonstrates, only so far with gloves on) marks their importance: the hand is the only exposed site of sexual communication below the neck.[16]

I cite Victorian manual and medical authorities not to establish any specific resonance with *Great Expectations* but instead to demonstrate the kinds of attention that the hand received in the period. We need not show that, say, Dickens was familiar with *Onania* in order to prove Pip a masturbator; we hardly want to, in fact, for the novel nowhere delivers the reified identity of "the onanist." The history of masturbation is both institutional *and* private (however oblique our access to the latter), and its story is one of both proscription and excitation. Given the novel's implication in both efforts—warning against and encouraging solitary vice—my interest here is in tracing the enfolding of that erotic/somatic practice in particular literary structures, specifically in linguistic formations of codification, connotation, and euphemism. These rhetorical strategies, it must be emphasized, are not intentional reactions to sexual prohibitions (the result of repression or censorship) but generative possibilities for sexual meanings that cannot yet recognize themselves: within a constellation of broader, including non-literary, discursive systems, such strategies contribute to the production of sexuality as the very category of the unspeakable. Rather than take the novel as a document in the institutional history of masturbation, then, my concern is to consider masturbation as a figure in the history of the novel.

When hands take on a specifically sexual meaning, I have suggested, they speak of masturbation; but their sexual qualities are also *generalizable*. The metonymic association of hands with autoeroticism functions as a conduit between representation and sexuality, but it does not restrict manual signification to a solitary sexual act. *Great Expectations* constructs its sexual taxonomy through its representation of hands, and while its master trope is therefore masturbation, the novel oversees a remarkably wide range of what will come—not least through the genre's own efforts at discriminating types—to be known as sexualities. I will consider the links between the overt representation of the manual, on the one hand, and the mystification of sexuality, on the other, first through the novel's thematics of male masturbation; I will then proceed to broaden the manual/erotic affiliation and examine the hand's capacity to signify non-solitary sexuality, specifically through its potential for both inciting and regulating male homoeroticism; finally, I will assess the novel's efforts at representing and managing women's sexuality through increasingly phantasmatic conjurations of the female hand. As exemplar, the novel trains the bodies of its characters—as instructor, those of its readers—in exceedingly particular lessons; it becomes, in this peculiar sense, a novel of manners.

* * *

Like many avid masturbators, Pip is deeply ashamed, and, just short of growing hair on his palms, he transfers his generalized sense of guilt onto the hands themselves. Pip is sorely touched by Estella's disdainful remark upon their first meeting: "'And what coarse hands he has!'" He responds, "I had never thought of being ashamed of my hands before; but I began to consider them a very indifferent pair. Her contempt for me was so strong, that it became infectious, and I caught it" (90). Pip's hands focus and localize the virulent shame that, articulated here in the register of social class, bears with it all the marks of a sexual embarrassment. What he learns from Estella, that is to say, is that embodied signs of labor are distasteful; the way in which he learns it, though, is through the shaming of a physical exposure, having his vulgar, vulnerable members seen by a girl. The disgrace that attaches to the hand would, to Dickens and his audience, as surely be coded for that other subject routinely repressed—work—as it would be for sex. Humiliation over the laboring (productive) hand converges on shame over the autoerotic (wasteful) one.[17]

Pip's rough appendages perennially trouble him, and the novel meticulously traces the coalescence between the laboring hand and the masturbatory one under the sign of embarrassment. When he tells his family tall tales of his first visit to Satis House—his initial step out of the working class—he strikes the pose of the guilt-ridden onanist: "They both stared at me, and I, with an obtrusive show of artlessness on my countenance, stared at them, and plaited the right leg of my trousers with my right hand" (98). Once he comes into his expectations, Pip's newfound riches—or is it his newly bulging body?—plague him with another kind of awkwardness: "I went circuitously to Miss Havisham's by all the back ways, and rang at the bell constrainedly, on account of the stiff long fingers of my gloves" (183). This manual erection coincides with Pip's rising expectations, as overt anxiety about class again takes the narrative form of a sexualized humiliation. The process of Pip's *Bildung* is an aggressive repudiation of the labor inscribed on his body: it tells the story of his refusal to *be* a hand.[18] Consequently, he takes the rowing master's compliment that he has "the arm of a blacksmith" (218) as the worst kind of insult.

In the logic of the plot, Pip can finally overcome the blackening of the forge—the shame of the laboring hand—with burns of another sort: after rescuing Miss Havisham, he notes, "When I got up, on the surgeon's coming to her with other aid, I was astonished to see that both my hands were burnt; for, I had no knowledge of it through the sense of feeling" (414). These burns finally serve as a badge of honor, not shame, for Pip, a mark of adult arrival that overwrites his adolescent humiliation. This trial by fire obliterates at once his infantilized relation to Satis House and the calloused hands of his youth: he is required to pass through it in order to locate the appropriate alloerotic, heterosexual object. In this developmental narrative, which the novel overtly endorses, Pip's desires are ultimately as self-regulating as the free market that Adam Smith had envisioned as being—or being ruled by—an invisible hand.

When masturbation and labor are supplemented with a third sense of the hand—writing itself—the manual shame embedded in the narrative discloses its profound effects. Unlike most first-person novels, *Great Expectations* lacks an explicit scene of writing—that scene before the beginning and after the end in which readers are offered an account of the text's genesis.[19] Like the worker, the writer is ashamed of his hand; he insists upon effacing (though perhaps succeeds only in displacing) the signs of his own manual labor at bringing the novel into being. Though we never witness the inscription of the novel itself, the narrative obsessively renders the exertions of the writing hand: from Pip's early problems learning to cipher ("getting considerably worried and scratched by every letter" [75]) down to his final scrivening labor for the Firm whose name merely embellishes that of his occupation— "I was clerk to Clarriker and Co." (489)—the hero writes throughout the story.[20] We would expect the writer's hand, like the productive one of the laborer, to exhibit the telltale marks of its toil (callouses, ink stains, cramps)—to bear witness to the work of what Melville dubs "a poor be-inked galley-slave, toiling with the heavy oar of a quill, to gain something wherewithal to stave off the cravings of nature"—but the narrator never displays his laboring hand.[21] Only when he lives as a gentleman does Pip have the leisure to read, and he then does little else; writing is thus as much a mark of the protagonist's class descent (the economic necessity of writing) as of his rise (the intellectual ability to do so). We are prohibited from seeing Pip write this fiction for reasons both economic and sexual: on one side, the writing of this life is itself the signal of a fall in class terms, which must be occluded; on the other, any exposure of himself in the act of imagining his life would violate the autoerotic scene with which the solitary reverie, accompanied by manual manipulation, has already been aligned.[22] Writing, like masturbation, cannot be narrated outright—yet it also *needn't* be, for it has already left its mark (spilled its ink) everywhere; it too is made shameful, so chastened by that interiorized conduct manual, the conscience, that it is evident only in its traces.[23] Whether it covers work, writing, or sex, the coy hand thus seems to signal displacement itself.

The young Pip conforms most nearly to the identity of the onanist not because, as in some historical narrative, he evinces characteristics typical of the contemporary pathology, but because in his case hands take over the expression of emotions such as shame, self-assurance, arousal, or dejection more usually affiliated with sexuality.[24] If Pip's hands encode certain features of autoeroticism, we might inquire how they became so accomplished. The narrative offers an initial, ontogenetic explanation: from the first, Pip avers that his sister "had established a great reputation with herself and the neighbours because she had brought me up 'by hand,'" and that he knows "her to have a hard and heavy hand, and to be much in the habit of laying it upon her husband as well as upon me" (39). Here is one source, then, for so total a cathexis of the hand: it is both the punished and the punisher, the organ that sins and the one that disciplines. And while Pip's hands designate him a masturbator, Mrs. Joe's serve rather unambiguously to phallicize her (particularly through their tool, Tickler)—at least until her penchant for dealing blows is dealt a stronger one and she is silenced "by some unknown hand" (147), which unsurprisingly turns out to be Orlick's "murderous hand" (438).

To the muscular femininity of his surrogate mother's "bad cop," Pip's father-figure correspondingly exhibits the sentimental masculinity of a "good" one:

> Joe laid his hand upon my shoulder with the touch of a woman. . . . O dear good Joe, whom I was so ready to leave and so unthankful to, I see you again, with your muscular blacksmith's arm before your eyes, and your broad chest heaving, and your voice dying away. O dear good faithful tender Joe, I feel the loving tremble of your hand upon my arm, as solemnly this day as if it had been the rustle of an angel's wing! (168)

The portrayal of Joe is in keeping with the usual representation of male sentimentality; the class signification of bodily attributes provides that the very "muscular blacksmith's arm" which could so humiliate Pip on the Thames crew team functions, in the forge from which it derives, as the sign of an unimpeachably wholesome and regenerate masculinity. The antithesis of his wife's hand, the "woman's touch" that characterizes Joe's paradoxically serves to fortify, not to destabilize, the edifice of his virility, even as it threatens Pip, the precarious arriviste, whose feminized masculinity has an entirely different class valence. Where Mrs. Joe's hand trains Pip's through violence and terror, Joe's works more subtly, as a nostalgic—but for all that, no less thoroughly repudiated-negative exemplar. The child is always in danger of being slapped by "mother" for touching himself; the gentleman is always in danger of becoming as manly as "father"—and thus losing his class standing—or seeming as womanly as him—and thus losing his manhood.

Though Pip's body is schooled in a gender curriculum whose first instructors are, by virtue of their class status, comically reversed, the simplicity of this role reversal ensures that the inculcation will do its work all the same. It might be imagined that in such a scheme, Pip's early assimilation to a masturbatory erotics functions in keeping with a developmental narrative, so that his discovery of an interest in Estella can sweep over the adolescent vice and mature heterosexuality install itself. In fact, the presence in the novel of several other immature male characters with a predilection for self-abuse suggests the very normality of Pip's habit, if not of its persistence in his story. Instances of what teenage boys still term pocket-pool abound: young Pip "religiously entertained" the belief that his deceased "five little brothers . . . had all been born on their backs with their hands in their trousers-pockets, and had never taken them out in this state of existence" (35); Orlick typically "would come slouching from his hermitage, with his hands in his pockets" (140); and Bentley Drummle "sat laughing in our faces, with his hands in his pockets" (238). The model of normative development we will wish to call seriously into question, but for now we shall consider the challenge offered by the fact that the behavior of at least one adult character in the novel is equally, though in different ways, coded for autoeroticism.

The characteristics we associate most with the body of Pip's guardian, Jaggers, are those of touching himself—his trademark "biting the side of his great forefinger"—and otherwise drawing attention to his unaccountably large hands (Pip notes the solicitor has "an exceedingly large head and a corresponding large hand" [111-12]). His classic pose: "The strange gentleman . . . with a manner expressive of knowing something secret about every one of us . . . remained standing: his left hand in his pocket, and he biting the forefinger of his right" (163). Even if we overlooked the finger he keeps in his mouth, we could hardly avoid noticing the one stashed in his pocket—for Pip's isn't the only pants leg found bulging with secret burdens. "[Jaggers] pushed Miss Havisham in her chair before him, with one of his large hands, and put the other in his trousers-pocket as if the pocket were full of secrets" (262). Jaggers's case is somewhat more profound than that of the boys who pocket their hands, both because he is the only adult to do so and because the secrets in his pockets connote the other reason for keeping one's hands there: to lay hold of money. Both Pip (309) and

Drummle (238) keep their wealth so concealed, and, as Pip executes the pun on the family name, he relies on our knowledge that while money is kept in pockets, it is not in the Pockets: "Both Mr. and Mrs. Pocket had such a noticeable air of being in somebody else's hands, that I wondered who really was in possession of the house and let them live there, until I found this unknown power to be the servants" (213). Jaggers is famous for ensuring that, as he says, "the secret was still a secret" (425), and it is his skill at keeping secrets in his pocket that makes him so adept at getting money (even if not spending) there as well.[25] Through Jaggers, the novel lends vivid materiality to the familiar Victorian analogy—condensed in the theory of "spermatic economy"—between male sexuality and a money economy.[26]

If Jaggers's version of autoeroticism functions in one sense as that which is sublimated by his acquisitiveness and in another as, say, the bodily inscription of his propensity for taking charge of others' secrets, in a third sense it registers the consistent pattern of his solipsistic withdrawal from scenes of potential erotic engagement. Again taking hands as our clue, we first recognize his distaste for human contact in his Pilate-like hygiene mania:

I embrace this opportunity of remarking that he washed his clients off, as if he were a surgeon or a dentist. He had a closet in his room, fitted up for the purpose, which smelt of the scented soap like a perfumer's shop. It had an unusually large jack-towel on a roller inside the door, and he would wash his hands, and wipe them and dry them all over this towel, whenever he came in from a police-court or dismissed a client from his room. (233)

Jaggers's approach is often signaled by the advance guard of this scented soap (112, 261)—a redolence perhaps attributable to the massive surface area of the organs in question. Jaggers's attention to others' hands amounts to no less a form of self-involvement than his fastidiousness about his own. In one instance, he takes a peculiar interest in Bentley Drummle: before the dinner party he throws for Pip and his "intimate associates" (227), Jaggers remarks, upon first laying eyes on Drummle's form, "'I like the look of that fellow'" (234); "'I like the fellow, Pip; he is one of the true sort'" (239), he repeats after dinner. In an effort to get a better look at the body of "the Spider," Jaggers stages a competition among the boys by provoking Pip's future rival to demonstrate the strength of his arm:

> [Drummle] informed our host . . . that as to skill he was more than our master, and that as to strength he could scatter us like chaff. By some invisible agency, my guardian wound him up to a pitch little short of ferocity about this trifle; and he fell to baring and spanning his arm to show how muscular it was, and we all fell to baring and spanning our arms in a ridiculous manner. (236)

Like the comparison of equipment usual in any high-school boys' locker room, this scene belies the pretense of romantic rivalry (it predates Bentley's interest in Estella) with its own gleeful erotics. Yet for all the zeal of his "invisible agency," Jaggers's taste for Drummle—and in particular, for his arm—is "quite inexplicable" (236). The plot never sufficiently rationalizes it, except through some vague notions of the solicitor's perverse contrariety. Likewise, the occasion that this arm-wrestling provides for showing off Molly's superior strength—"'Very few men have the power of wrist that this woman has'" (237)—remains largely unexplained, as does the sadomasochistic dramatization of this master/servant relationship. Wemmick's later explanation—"'She went into his service immediately after her acquittal, tamed as she is now'" (406)—merely asserts its own insufficiency; surely if all Jaggers wanted was a domestic servant he needn't have taken in "a wild beast tamed" (224). Though they work according to the novel's usual manual semiotics, these sites of Jaggers's prospective erotic interest rapidly lose their motivation; the plot abandons them as false leads, and Jaggers seems finally more interested in keeping his hands to himself than in pursuing others'.

If the lawyer appears to suffer from an unaccountable withholding, he can at least be said to have made professional use of this attribute, as Pip testifies in describing one of his most effective litigious techniques:

> He always carried (I have not yet mentioned it, I think) a pocket-handkerchief of rich silk and of imposing proportions, which was of great value to him in his profession. I have seen him so terrify a client or a witness by ceremoniously unfolding this pocket-handkerchief as if he were immediately going to blow his nose, and then pausing, as if he knew he should not have time to do it before such client or witness committed himself, that the self-committal has followed directly, quite as a matter of course. (261-62)

Jaggers's large-handed handkerchief trick gives bodily, objective form to the particular erotic disposition we have identified with him: auto-eroticism as a mode of refusing alloeroticism. Not unlike the flirtation between "prig" and "Master Bates" in *Oliver Twist*, this spectacle—in the context of Jaggers's finger-biting and pocketed secrets—textually codes the sexualization of refusal that it cannot name. And while Pip's frigs result in sticky messes (butter down the pants leg, butter in the bed), Jaggers turns refusal—here, to allow the phlegm to come—into *ars erotica*. Through the representation of an adult character coded for onanistic behavior, Dickens gives literary form not so much to a Victorian pathology or sexual identity as to a particular "perverse" sexual practice. Though Pip and Jaggers both bespeak autoeroticism, they personify two very different modalities of it, neither in an especially proximate relation to the classic onanist of Tissot or Acton: Pip's practice is guilty, excessive, uncontrolled, a sexualized strategy for repudiating the manual labor he abhors; Jaggers's is manipulative, parsimonious, recoiling, a performance and extension of his economic motivations. To insist upon the conformity of literary characters to the genuinely repressive models of medical authorities may itself be to fall victim to a coercively normative, normalizing sexuality; instead, without obliging ourselves to abandon the postulate that all sexuality is shot through with ideology, can we imagine that the novel engages sexualities unaccounted for by official pathologies?

* * *

The solitary hands we have observed thus far in *Great Expectations* are marked, via a metonymic connection, for male masturbation: when hand and genital organ touch, the former (speakable) can connote the latter (unspeakable). The novel's erotic investment in hands is so general, however, as to allow for metaphoric links as well, so that sexual practices less directly managed by the hand may nonetheless be imagined as manual. We now shift our attention from singular hands to redoubled ones in order to read sexuality: the moments at which two men's hands are engaged arise first, in the most highly socialized form of male hand-holding—the handshake—and then, in the other shape they principally assume in the novel, pugilism. Returning to Jaggers, we again find his mode of refusal striking. While he is frequently "throwing his finger at [one] sideways" (165), and is quick to lay a hand on Pip's shoulder or arm (163, 190-91, 424), he rarely takes the young man in hand. Indeed, Jaggers is all but unwilling to extend his hand—and the largeness of his endowment makes the fact of his withholding all the more disappointing:

> It was November, and my guardian was standing before his fire leaning his back against the chimney-piece, with his hands under his coat-tails.
> "Well, Pip," said he, "I must call you Mr. Pip to-day. Congratulations, Mr. Pip."
> We shook hands—he was always a remarkably short shaker—and I thanked him. (305)

A man who has so noticeably large a hand and yet is such a "remarkably short shaker" will always fail to satisfy.[27] As Pip comes to learn, however, handshaking in the world of this novel has a curiously negative valence in any case.

The handshake is the one social ritual by which men—most especially those who are strangers—routinely touch each other. It functions to draw people together by holding them apart: it interposes hands between other body parts as a safe form of contact. Why, then, this shortness on the part of Jaggers's shaker? Why, even more pertinently, the castigation of this ritual in the form of Pumblechook's unctuous insistence on it? One recalls how the seedsman, after learning that Pip has come into his expectations, clings to the boy with an obsequiousness as oppressive as the proverbial cheap suit that Pip has just come from being fitted for by Trabb.

"But do I," said Mr. Pumblechook, getting up again the moment after he had sat down, "see afore me, him as I ever sported with in his times of happy infancy? And may I–*may* I—?"

This May I, meant might he shake hands? I consented, and he was fervent, and then sat down again.

"Here is wine," said Mr. Pumblechook. "Let us drink, Thanks to Fortune, and may she ever pick out her favourites with equal judgment! And yet I cannot," said Mr. Pumblechook, getting up again, "see afore me One—and likewise drink to One—without again expressing—May I–*may* I—?" (180)

Pumblechook's sycophancy is insatiable, at least so long as Pip stays in the money; once Pip is "brought low," however, the hand is extended "with a magnificently forgiving air," and Pip notes "the wonderful difference between the servile manner in which he had offered his hand in my new prosperity, saying, 'May I?' and the ostentatious clemency with which he had just now exhibited the same fat five fingers" (483). Here is the novel's signal instance of a hand freighted with meaning, yet what it bespeaks is not the efficacy of gestural communication. Instead, at the moment it raises the possibility that in the most familiar code of manual conduct—the handshake—something might supervene upon the literal, the narrative can be nothing but derisive (as if to confirm that hands are evocative only where they are not, in the novel's conscious terms, meant to be so). At the point where connotations of the manual—including but not limited to the erotic—seem most likely to proliferate, the mode of parodic excess preempts all meanings but the most repugnant hypocrisy.[28]

Though Pip's hand may remain insufficiently chafed by Pumblechook's grip, in the progressive tale of his body's schooling it receives a final chastening lesson. Jaggers's second, Wemmick, is noted for parodically representing the schizophrenic divide between the office persona of the bureaucratic modern man and his home life ("'the office is one thing, and private life is another'" [231]). While on the job, Wemmick faithfully emulates the withholding posture of his employer: "Something of the state of Mr. Jaggers hung about him too, forbidding approach beyond certain limits" (281). And like Jaggers, Wemmick finds distasteful Pip's provincial penchant for handshaking:

> "As I keep the cash," Mr. Wemmick observed, "we shall most likely meet pretty often. Good day."
> "Good day."
> I put out my hand, and Mr. Wemmick at first looked at it as if he thought I wanted something. Then he looked at me, and said, correcting himself,
> "To be sure! Yes. You're in the habit of shaking hands?"
> I was rather confused, thinking it must be out of the London fashion, but said yes.
> "I have got so out of it!" said Mr. Wemmick—"except at last. Very glad, I'm sure, to make your acquaintance. Good day!" (197)

The perplexity that Wemmick evinces at Pip's quaint amiability here is only elucidated later. For the man of business, handshaking is shown to have practical purposes: besides the exhibition of the "portable property" (224) he has acquired from condemned prisoners ("he wore at least four mourning rings" [195]), he reserves demonstrative use of his hands for its utility *as* a sign. As he leads Pip on a tour of Newgate prison, the narrator notes: "He turned to me and said, 'Notice the man I shall shake hands with.' I should have done so, without the preparation, as he had shaken hands with no one yet." After the brief conversation between Wemmick and the designated man, "They shook hands again, and as we walked away Wemmick said to me, 'A Coiner, a very good workman. The Recorder's report is made to-day, and he is sure to be executed on Monday'" (281-82). Wemmick hopes to land a bit of portable property from the condemned man, and reserves his embrace to satisfy this materialistic impulse. His handshake, like Pumblechook's, foregrounds its own function as coded behavior; divested of any erotic significance, Wemmick's secret handshake holds no secret (except so far as the unwitting Coiner is concerned) because its code is transparent. No wonder he is so reluctant to take up Pip's hand when they first meet: to do so would, in Wemmick's bodily lexicon, be tantamount to marking him for the gallows.

While the handshake routinizes and sublates manual contact among characters, the other context in which hands regularly meet—fisticuffs—tends in a rather different direction. Unlike the ostentatious signification with which the text loads handshaking (a system of meaning, I have argued, so manifest that it paradoxically empties itself out), the novel's most fully embodied moments of physical violence are either so curiously undermotivated or so thoroughly overdetermined as to proliferate the meanings available to a manual semiotics. Although in the logic of the novel's plot, fights interpose at junctures of fierce romantic rivalry, the *narration* of the battles consistently provides the occasion for the playing out of erotic contact, both homo- and heterosexual, between combatants.[29] Insofar as this precipitate collapse of the pugilistic into the erotic becomes a problem for Victorian masculinity, we might take John Sholto Douglas, Marquess of Queensberry, as the figure effectively to drive a wedge between them. By dint of historical "accident," the very man who, in 1867, codified the rules of "fair play" in boxing—thereby regulating and legitimating the procedures for homosocial sparring—was destined to initiate the century's most notorious legal proceedings for homoerotic touching—thereby taking the lead in the fin-de-siècle anathematization of homosexuals.[30]

At Pip's first encounter with Herbert Pocket, for instance, the relationship is one of immediate and unmediated physical aggression: "'Come and fight,' said the pale young gentleman." As Herbert's provocation appears wholly unmotivated, he soon supplies the incitement it is felt to require: "'I ought to give you a reason for fighting, too. There it is!' In a most irritating manner he instantly slapped his hands against one another, daintily flung one of his legs up behind him, pulled my hair, slapped his hands again, dipped his head, and butted it into my stomach" (119). To such ungentlemanly conduct the gentleman's reaction—that is, the bellicosity Herbert desires—itself must be reconfigured, albeit in hindsight, as a form of chivalrous combat for feminine affections. Thus, Pip's payoff for sparring with Herbert is the opportunity to kiss Estella, the scene's unseen observer. Yet even if this putative erotic aim were capable of sustaining a state of arousal, it would nonetheless function only retrospectively and defensively as the alibi for the more provoking touches elaborated in the battle with Herbert. In fact, Pip feels as a result that he has prostituted himself, "that the kiss was given to the coarse common boy as a piece of money might have been, and that it was worth nothing" (121). In compensation for the tussle's lack of motivation, then, the text supplies a series of rationales—ranging from insult to romance to monetary recompense—whose insufficiency is demonstrated by the very rapidity of their deployment.

However persuasive the pretext for pugnacity in the novel may be (in this case, hardly at all), it thus functions primarily as the occasion for physical contact between adversaries—contact whose cathexes evince a logic quite different from the plot's. And while the sensory modality of the novel's eroticism is primarily tactile, there is a peculiarly embodied form of the visual—an assaultive kind of looking—which also partakes of these haptic significations. In the present scene, the bout between Herbert and Pip is preceded by both narrator-Pip's account of Herbert's awkward frame (he later discreetly terms it "a little ungainly" [201]) and Herbert's somewhat more suspect examination of Pip's physique. In a remarkable description of his adversary's seminudity, Pip recounts:

> [Herbert] fell to pulling off, not only his jacket and waistcoat, but his shirt too, in a manner at once light-hearted, businesslike, and bloodthirsty.
>
> Although he did not look very healthy—having pimples on his face, and a breaking out at his mouth—these dreadful preparations quite appalled me. . . . He was a young gentleman in a grey suit (when not denuded for battle), with his elbows, knees, wrists, and heels, considerably in advance of the rest of him as to development.
>
> My heart failed me when I saw him squaring at me with every demonstration of mechanical nicety, and eyeing my anatomy as if he were minutely choosing his bone. (120)

The investment of Pip's narration in looking at and rendering the repulsive particulars of his antagonist's body is strangely at odds with the character's professed distaste for the figure that Herbert cuts.[31] And at the moment that Pip, almost despite himself, catalogues the corners of the pale young gentleman's frame, Herbert returns the gaze. The fight then proceeds from this curiously cruising scrutiny; from sizing up to feeling up, we will see, the novel's pattern is here established.

The striptease that Pip witnesses at his introduction to Herbert enacts a form of male-male perusal not uncommon in Dickens's work. Such an androphilic once-over is most fully elaborated in the following passage in *The Old Curiosity Shop* (1840-41):

> Mr. Swiveller looked with a supercilious smile at Mr. Cheggs's toes, then raised his eyes from them to his ankle, from that to his shin, from that to his

knee, and so on very gradually, keeping up his right leg, until he reached his waistcoat, when he raised his eyes from button to button until he reached his chin, and travelling straight up the middle of his nose came at last to his eyes, when he said abruptly, "No, sir, I didn't."[32]

The point at which one man can no longer anatomize another's body—"and so on very gradually"—is always telling. But as if to rectify Herbert's enticing literalization of that familiar gaze ("he undressed me with his eyes"), the revelation moves in the opposite direction when the two meet again, now grown up. As Pip first espies the mature Herbert mounting the stairs, he reverses the striptease both by clothing his friend and by moving this time from the head downward: "Gradually there arose before me the hat, head, neckcloth, waistcoat, trousers, boots, of a member of society of about my own standing" (198). Here the progressive dressing (of a nude ascending a staircase) ensures their rivalry is at an end; proleptically asserting a Freudian developmental mythology, it insists that a more happily socialized and sublimated relation will ensue.[33]

The relationship most thoroughly structured around hand-to-hand combat, of course, is not finally Pip's friendship with Herbert but his enmity with Orlick. This conflict too originates in an aggressive looking: "I had leisure to entertain the retort in my mind, while [Orlick] slowly lifted his heavy glance from the pavement, up my legs and arms, to my face" (254). Even in the midst of Orlick's climactic attack on Pip, he pauses for a leisurely gander at his victim—a glance that can afford to be less furtive than earlier: "'Now,' said he, when we had surveyed one another for some time, 'I've got you.' . . . 'Now, wolf,' said he, 'afore I kill you like any other beast—which is wot I mean to do and wot I have tied you up for—I'll have a good look at you and a good goad at you. Oh, you enemy!' . . . Then, he took up the candle, and shading it with his murderous hand so as to throw its light on me, stood before me, looking at me and enjoying the sight" (435-38).

Violence is visualized before it is actualized; but Orlick's is of a specially ferocious variety, requiring not only specular conjuration but verbal confirmation as well. For however violating this staring-down may be, its narration is always coy in the elision of certain body parts. The linguistic analogue to the so-far-and-no-farther gaze is a device (comparable to the "prig" from *Oliver Twist*, the "secret burden" from Pip's childhood) by which the novel evokes, while still refusing to denote, terms for male sexuality around Orlick. "He pretended that his christian name was Dolge—a clear impossibility—but he was a fellow of that obstinate disposition that I believe him to have been the prey of no delusion in this particular, but wilfully to have imposed that name upon the village as an affront to its understanding" (139-40). With no other objection than this—that in its inscrutability the name simply *feels* obscene—Pip implies that a lack of definition itself signifies a transgression against propriety. Pip's assertion of this name's "impossibility" aims to bolster the straightness and clarity of his own narrative, a species purportedly remote from the obscenity of Orlick's indirection; yet the proximate impossibility of his own name belies this effort, as the novel's opening words attest: "My father's family name being Pirrip, and my christian name Philip, my infant tongue could make of both names nothing longer or more explicit than Pip. So, I called myself Pip, and came to be called Pip" (35). The case for the perversity of connotation becomes unequivocal in the next instance:

> "Well then," said [Orlick]), "I'm jiggered if I don't see you home!"
> This penalty of being jiggered was a favourite supposititious case of his. He attached no definite meaning to the word that I am aware of, but used it, like his own pretended christian name, to affront mankind, and convey an idea of something savagely damaging. When I was younger, I had had a general belief that if he had jiggered me personally, he would have done it with a sharp and twisted hook. (158)

Here the insistent non-meaning of the word redounds upon the victimized body with a sexual signification that cannot otherwise be uttered.

The denotative refusal entailed in the "supposititious case" functions as a place-holder for sexual meanings, not simply by obliterating some other, straightforward language (as in this example, by eliding the term "buggered"), but by producing those meanings as inarticulable.

Orlick's visual and verbal pugnacity toward Pip issues in the inevitable corporal confrontation between them, at the sluice-house by the limekiln at novel's end. In returning to characters' bodies, the scene naturally refers us, through its usual synecdochal route, to their hands. Throughout the final chapters Pip is sorely disabled by the burns his arms received at Satis House; Orlick's attack is so effective in part because it exacerbates Pip's condition. As the lights go down Pip finds himself pinned to the wall:

> Not only were my arms pulled close to my sides, but the pressure on my bad arm caused me exquisite pain. Sometimes, a strong man's hand, sometimes a strong man's breast, was set against my mouth to deaden my cries, and with a hot breath always close to me, I struggled ineffectually in the dark, while I was fastened tight to the wall. "And now," said the suppressed voice with another oath, "call out again, and I'll make short work of you!"
>
> Faint and sick with the pain of my injured arm, bewildered by the surprise, and yet conscious how easily this threat could be put in execution, I desisted, and tried to ease my arm were it ever so little. But, it was bound too tight for that, I felt as if, having been burnt before, it were now being boiled. (434)

If the hand of Pip's that touches his own body is regularly subject to rebuke, the one that feels (and is felt by) other men is even more thoroughly penalized. Yet here the brutal ferocity of "a strong man's hand" and its arousing caress are absolutely coterminous. Fearsomely violent as this assault is, its erotic sensations are manifest: the "strong man's breast" set against Pip's mouth, and, in return, the attacker's own "hot breath" against him, serve to literalize the lickerish "kiss" inhering in Orlick's surname.[34] As if to draw on Pip's youthful training matches with Herbert and Bentley—as if to dramatize the tantalizing prospect of being "jiggered"—this serious adult business with Orlick enacts all the erotic potential of murderous male combat. The particular correspondence that the novel has established between the manual and the genital only barely prepares us for the scene's concatenation of terror and tenderness, of the one hand that savors to inflict pain and the other that anguishes to endure it.[35]

At this point we can identify—though, as I will suggest, only prematurely—what might be termed the novel's homophobia. On the one hand, it denies the handshake any of the erotic valence we might well expect to attend this ritual: either because of the refusal of others (Jaggers or Wemmick) or because of Pip's own repulsion (at Pumblechook), this manual contact is insufficient to bring men together. On the other hand, Pip's pugilistics with Herbert, Drummle, and Orlick (as well as Magwitch's with Compeyson) represent a form of contact too close for comfort: however ecstatically and erotically charged one may suspect these passages of being, the form they take—of increasingly savage violence—must sit uneasily with any gleefully homotropic reading. If, that is to say, the cost of men touching men is that one of them be pummeled, we must recognize a certain ideological resistance in the text to such an erotics. To this apparent dead end, however, the novel proposes several alternate routes. Thanks largely to the fluidity with which *Great Expectations* structures the thematic of hands, we are left not with an antithesis between homophobic and homophilic, but rather with an apparatus that ultimately brings these two terms—not to mention their hetero counterparts—into a relatively stable and consolatory relation of mutually reinforcing regulation.

For one instance, let us, in pursuing our investigation of pugilism, witness the novel's strenuous effort to redeem it for normative heterosexuality. Earlier I ascribed Wemmick's refusal to shake Pip's hand as much to the single-mindedness of his economic motives in the workaday world as to any phobic pathology. When turning to his erotic interests at home, however, we find Wemmick himself must overcome another's refusal, in the resistance of his fiancée, Miss Skiffins, to yield to his hands. Upon meeting her, Pip "might have pronounced her gown a little too decidedly orange, and her gloves a little too intensely green"; he notes further that "Miss Skiffins . . . retained her green gloves during the evening as an outward and visible sign that there was company" (313).[36] Like her suitor, Miss Skiffins knows full well the hand's capability to signify: these gloves ensure her genteel incapacity for domestic labor as much as they conceal her dishpan hands (she "washed up the tea-things, in a trifling lady-like amateur manner that compromised none of us. Then, she put on her gloves again" [315]). But while the gloves afford Miss Skiffins an "outward and visible sign" of *class* propriety, their verdancy promises a *sexual* steaminess as surely as her unwillingness to remove them withholds it.

The elaborate charade by which Wemmick makes a pass at his inamorata confirms this dynamic; it is his hands now that her gloves must peel off:

> As Wemmick and Miss Skiffins sat side by side, and as I sat in a shadowy corner, I observed a slow and gradual elongation of Mr. Wemmick's mouth, powerfully suggestive of his slowly and gradually stealing his arm round Miss Skiffins's waist. In course of time I saw his hand appear on the other side of Miss Skiffins; but at that moment Miss Skiffins neatly stopped him with the green glove, unwound his arm again as if it were an article of dress, and with the greatest deliberation laid it on the table before her. Miss Skiffins's composure while she did this was one of the most remarkable sights I have ever seen, and if I could have thought the act consistent with abstraction of mind, I should have deemed that Miss Skiffins performed it mechanically.
>
> By-and-by, I noticed Wemmick's arm beginning to disappear again, and gradually fading out of view. Shortly afterwards, his mouth began to widen again. After an interval of suspense on my part that was quite enthralling and almost painful, I saw his hand appear on the other side of Miss Skiffins. Instantly, Miss Skiffins stopped it with the neatness of a placid boxer, took off that girdle or cestus as before, and laid it on the table. (316)

By contrast with the performances of sexual excitation we've previously observed, this one can afford to be frankly erotic. Yet even as this pantomime of heterosexual courtship struggles to establish a relation to the normative, it repeatedly collapses into the realm of proscribed sexuality. Even—perhaps especially—when the flavor of eroticism is most vanilla (heterosexual, monogamous, genital), its pungency does not diminish against the palate; through the very nearness of its *exposure* in the narration, the representation of sexuality here continues to sting the readerly tongue. The "slow and gradual elongation of Mr. Wemmick's mouth" and the collateral distention of his arm, for example, only barely keep under wraps the other turgidity to which they give rise. The "mechanical" procedure of Miss Skiffins's resistance itself is metaphorized as *déshabillement* (she "unwound his arm again as if it were an article of dress, and . . . took off that girdle"), as though to confirm that so hot a refusal functions as an enticement to arousal. Furthermore, however superficially normative this passage's sexual thematics may be, the *mise en scène* returns us to a spectacle of sexual impropriety: unusual in the novel, Pip is here positioned as observer of others' erotic play, and his "interval of suspense . . . that was quite enthralling and almost painful" bespeaks a more-than-passive relation to the scene. Indeed, the pas de deux between Wemmick's arm and Miss Skiffins's gloves titillates Pip into a state of voyeuristic autoeroticism no different from that which novels themselves had been accused of arousing.

Finally, the contest between "his hand" and her "green glove" drifts irresistibly toward an allegory of fisticuffs. The narrative alignment of the modest maiden to "a placid boxer" installs the scene among those of intermasculine, androphilic pugilism; at its most explicit moment of heterosexual pursuit, then, the novel's erotic language modulates into the definitionally male and homosocial. For all that Miss Skiffins boxes with kid gloves on, it seems to say, she throws her punches with determination. Yet if in one sense the current of fistic homoeroticism unsettles the characters most preoccupied with bourgeois propriety, the

Wemmick-Skiffins match, as we'll see, also works in the other direction (not unlike the Marquess of Queensberry) toward the reform and sanitization of boxing itself.

Indeed, the novel works arduously to redirect the erotic divagations set loose here. Lest the state of premarital arousal prove unsustainable, Miss Skiffins eventually removes her green gloves (still fully cognizant of their utility as signifiers) as a means of marking a new order of conjugally sanctioned eroticism. Arriving at church with Wemmick, Pip observes: "That discreet damsel was attired as usual, except that she was now engaged in substituting for her green kid gloves, a pair of white" (463).[37] Refusal having been abandoned as an erotic mode, domesticity triumphs in the Castle at Walworth: "It was pleasant to observe that Mrs. Wemmick no longer unwound Wemmick's arm when it adapted itself to her figure, but sat in a high-backed chair against the wall, like a violoncello in its case, and submitted to be embraced as that melodious instrument might have done" (464). The spur to desire is now so fully normalized by the institution of marriage that it loses its edge: although Wemmick evinces no sign of disappointment, one need only set an ungirdled boxer beside an encased cello to determine which woman—Miss Skiffins or Mrs. Wemmick—is the more enticing. In the miniature, mechanical, businesslike form that the Wemmicks lend it, the marriage plot's usual propensity for damage is made starkly evident: characters' bodies are disciplined into conformity, domesticity cancels eros, married life instantly obliterates memories of the prior excitation requisite for having brought it about. Here proven in its punishing aspect is a cardinal rule of the novel genre: that nuptials represent the end, not the beginning of things.

The fights we have examined illustrate different modes of repression, in varying degrees of punitiveness, for managing and disciplining the play of hands. In each instance, the sexual possibilities generated by hands are expunged from the plot—from the register of articulated representation—by means of violence, only to resurface in the contours of the narrative voice, where they can pass by virtue of going unheard inside the novel. Male homosocial desire is expressed as brutality, while premarital sex is narratable only insofar as it fuels the hegemony of matrimony. But in addition to these transformations of errant manual desire accomplished through battle, the novel manages other, less violently chastening ones. As against the compulsions of the handshake and the fistfight, we will want now to consider the *consensual* modality of male manual regulation in the novel.

Through the shift from denuding to redressing, I have suggested, Herbert's youthful belligerence is rehabilitated as properly sublimated, adult male homosociality. Following his adolescent ineptitude in the boxing ring, moreover, Herbert's mastery of the hand correspondingly matures as well. Although we learn surprisingly little about his grown-up appendages, this lack is more than compensated by the peculiar knack he develops for tending to Pip's hands—a taste initiated, perhaps, in those first moments of "eyeing [Pip's] anatomy as if he were minutely choosing his bone" (120). Indeed, Herbert's proclivity is confirmed both by his impulse, almost immediately upon becoming reacquainted with Pip, to christen him "Handel" and by his own surname, Pocket, the usual receptacle for hands in the novel. At their first dinner in town, Herbert interlards his conversation with a course in table manners for the newly arrived Pip, instructing him in the proper handling of utensils and other matters of the body's polite disposition at table ("'the spoon is not generally used over-hand, but under,'" etc. [203-6]). Herbert interjaculates this manual conduct lesson (as if to literalize a parody of the silver-fork novel) through his recounting of Miss Havisham's history. In the second installment of this tale—when Pip realizes that Magwitch is Estella's father—Herbert is again preoccupied with the condition of his friend's hands, this time changing the bandages that cover Pip's burns ("'Lay your arm out upon the back of the sofa, my dear boy, and I'll sit down here, and get the bandage off so gradually that you shall not know when it comes'" [416-19]). Through both stories, then, the narrative interpolates information about Pip's hands, as though, at these crucial moments of the protagonist's overt erotic interest, the novel's encrypted sign of that desire need literally be close at hand.

The story that Herbert tells in the midst of his bodywork on Pip is not merely incidental: significantly, this narrative concerns the conspiracy of Miss Havisham's half-brother, Arthur, with her fiancé, Compeyson, to defraud her:

> "It has been supposed that the man to whom she gave her misplaced confidence, acted throughout in concert with her half-brother; that it was a conspiracy between them; and that they shared the profits."
>
> "I wonder he didn't marry her and get all the property," said I.
>
> "He may have been married already, and her cruel mortification may have been a part of her half-brother's scheme," said Herbert. "Mind! I don't know that."
>
> "What became of the two men?" I asked, after again considering the subject.
>
> "They fell into deeper shame and degradation—if there can be deeper—and ruin." (205-6)

The implication of a debased, presumably homosexual criminality in this last line derives its force from contrast with the scene of its narration. Compeyson's story functions as a cautionary tale about the dangers of excessive intimacy between two young men; conversely, Pip's and Herbert's is the comfortably homosocialized relation, where eros is sublimated as pugilism, camaraderie, bachelor-marriage, and eventually marriage brokering. While in the boys' earlier encounter (the adolescent sparring match) eroticism was registered only as a "supposititious case," their newfound intimacy (the now far gentler touching) can be more frankly denoted. In forming the frame of an interpolated tale (which itself has an antithetical disciplinary moral) the hand-holding dispersed throughout the present scenes is rendered explicitly—it is the scene of narration—by virtue of being more highly socialized.

For Magwitch, the other figure given to excessive handling of Pip, socialization again requires a transposition of eros from narrative discourse to plot, though in his case the change is accomplished through more radical means. From the first, Magwitch embodies a certain pedophilia: the novel's opening, showing his combined aggression and affection for Pip, suggests a species of man-boy love, and it is primarily through his man-handling of Pip that we come to register such pederastic impulses. At their initial encounter, "The man, after looking at me for a moment, turned me upside down, and emptied my pockets" (36); and, "After darkly looking at his leg and me several times, he came closer . . . took me by both arms, and tilted me back as far as he could hold me" (37). The recognition scene between patron and protégé stages the climax of the touching here initiated, in the form of an erotic ballet performed by the hands:

> I saw, with a stupid kind of amazement, that he was holding out both his hands to me. . . . He came back to where I stood, and again held out both his hands. Not knowing what to do—for, in my astonishment I had lost my self-possession—I reluctantly gave him my hands. He grasped them heartily, raised them to his lips, kissed them, and still held them. . . . At a change in his manner as if he were even going to embrace me, I laid a hand upon his breast and put him away. . . . I stood, with a hand on the chair-back and a hand on my breast, where I seemed to be suffocating—I stood so, looking wildly at him, until I grasped at the chair, when the room began to surge and turn. He caught me, drew me to the sofa, put me up against the cushions, and bent on one knee before me: bringing the face that I now well remembered, and that I shuddered at, very near to mine. . . . The abhorrence in which I held the man, the dread I had of him, the repugnance with which I shrank from him, could not have been exceeded if he had been some terrible beast. . . . I recoiled from his touch as if he had been a snake. . . . Again he took both my hands and put them to his lips, while my blood ran cold within me. . . . He laid his hand on my shoulder. I shuddered at the thought that for anything I knew, his hand might be stained with blood. (332-39)

This narration has a perilously overt sexual charge: one need hardly cite the bended knee, the kissing of hands, the prostration on the couch, the insistent caresses, to locate the courtship conventions of which it partakes. Pip's gag reflex serves to bolster, not to diminish the eroticism of the episode, for it demonstrates his revulsion to be as highly cathected as the convict's attraction. The narrative attention to Magwitch's manipulation, in its root sense, empowers his cataclysmic revelation even as it threatens to run out of control through a homoeroticism we are made to feel and, through Pip, to feel repulsed by.[38] But like his former partner, Molly, this "terrible beast" must be tamed as well.

How does the novel recuperate Magwitch's erotic palpation and Pip's corresponding palpitation? For Pip, the immediate antidote to the fearsome caress of the grizzled convict's "large brown veinous hands" (333) arrives in the form of his companion's reassuring embrace: "Herbert received me with open arms . . . got up, and linked his arm in mine" (356-58). Through the developments of the plot, moreover, Pip is capable of turning Magwitch's lecherous pawing back upon him, lending it a normalized, moralized signification. On his deathbed, Magwitch again feels Pip's hands, now silently communicating through a sentimentalized hand-holding. "He had spoken his last words. He smiled, and I understood his touch to mean that he wished to lift my hand, and lay it on his breast. I laid it there, and he smiled again, and put both his hands upon it" (469). Then, as if to repay Magwitch for the earlier episode, Pip makes his own revelation:

> "You had a child once, whom you loved and lost. . . . She is living now. She is a lady and very beautiful. And I love her!"
>
> With a last faint effort, which would have been powerless but for my yielding to it and assisting it, he raised my hand to his lips. Then, he gently let it sink upon his breast again, with his own hands lying on it. (470)

Pip is at last able to translate his benefactor's uncomfortable stroking into heterosexual terms, now giving that touch a proper meaning *in* the plot: he transposes it onto the heterosexual economy by lending it the valence of the "consent of a beloved's father to a suitor's entreaty." Much as he has had to endure Magwitch's caress, that is to say, the hand he now can own to wanting is Estella's, in marriage. Those earlier, less fully accountable hand-squeezings are now available to him reworked retrospectively as the beneficence of a future father-in-law. Pip can afford to be "yielding" and "assisting" to the old man's supplications by virtue of his knowledge that whatever homoerotic force they might once have had has been defused and rewritten—written into the story proper—as straight desire.

* * *

Both Magwitch and Herbert partake of a homoerotic handling of Pip and both must be retrofitted in order to discipline those desires. Whether through visceral repugnance or progressive socialization, the novel attempts to school the men's bodies in normative heterosexual touching. It is not only through other men that Pip learns these lessons, however, for the women in his story must also undergo dramatic transformations in order to rectify the manual problems they present. The two modes of regulating sexuality that we have identified for the men—the violently coercive and the consensual—also structure female eroticism. While Biddy submits to her training for respectable femininity, Molly resists domestication to the utmost; Estella, meanwhile, never has the option of choosing because she never properly has any desires that require management. The novel, moreover, makes a distinction between male and female sexuality broadly conceived, through its phantasmatic construction of the latter, which functions largely in the service of a solitary male dream of its own sexual capacity. In situating erotic subject and object in the same body, autoeroticism, as we have seen, alienates the onanist from himself, thereby paradoxically constituting him *as* a subject.[39] Rarely more than fantasy objects, the female characters buttress the narrative's masturbatory mode, for the novel's sexual architectonics bars them from sustaining a position as desiring subjects.

Biddy and Pip start out as perfect counterparts, their as-yet un-gendered identities equally oriented around the manual. "She was an orphan like myself," says Pip; "like me, too, had been brought up by hand" (74). Also like Pip, Biddy exhibits a hand replete with the dirty-ing signs of both manual labor and onanistic indulgence: "Her hands always wanted washing" (74), Pip notes early on; and at one point, to reassure him, "she put her hand, which was a comfortable hand though roughened by work, upon my hands, one after another" (156). For all their youthful likeness, however, the specter that Biddy presents of fe-male masturbation and of an affirmative female desire is more than Pip can abide. The novel manages the anxiety Biddy inspires by ascribing to her all the dreariness of provincial working-class life, the ignominy of which is routed specifically through the femininity of her touch. The uncleanliness of her hands distresses Pip rather vividly at the point he repudiates her: while they converse, Biddy is shown "plucking a black-currant leaf," "looking closely at the leaf in her hand," and "having rubbed the leaf to pieces between her hands—and the smell of a black-currant bush has ever since recalled to me that evening in the little garden by the side of the lane" (175). Like Jaggers's, Biddy's hands generate a characteristic aroma; but where "scented soap" indicates a fastidious mysophobia, the provocative image of Biddy's "black-currant bush" bespeaks an *odor di femina* that sends Pip running. If we didn't already suspect this hedge of signaling a demonstrative and menacing female sexuality, two other references would ensure that we do so. One: the alibi that Jaggers provides for Molly's wrist ("much disfigured—deeply scarred and scarred across and across" [236]), the sign of a more fearsome—and therefore more severely chastised—feminine sexuality: "She had struggled through a great lot of brambles which were not as high as her face; but which she could not have got through and kept her hands out of; and bits of those brambles were ac-tually found in her skin and . . . the brambles in question were found on examination to have been broken through, and to have little shreds of her dress and little spots of blood upon them here and there" (406). Two: the image Pip conjures up for his youthful acquiescence to Biddy's guidance through the thicket of language: "By the help of Biddy . . . I struggled through the alphabet as if it had been a bramble-bush; getting considerably worried and scratched by every letter" (75). The women who navigate these pungent, puncturing bushes offer more of an affront to male sexuality and authority than the novel cares to sustain.

If in Pip's imagination Biddy represents a distressing (all too available, all too appropriate) sexual possibility, whatever desires she herself can be said to express finally appear thoroughly managed and manageable. Her feminine pliancy is evident from the first in her concern for others' hands: when they are children, Biddy tutors Pip, remedying his early orthographic troubles (75); when, with no apparent discomposure, she eventually transfers her affections from nephew to uncle, she also trains Joe's maladroit hand (473-74). Through a disturbing but not unfamiliar bit of Dickensian sleight of hand, the minimal degree of erotic errancy that Biddy has displayed is fully recuperated in the redirection of her interest toward Joe. He, for one, can identify with having dirt under the nails ("'No, don't wipe it off—for God's sake, give me your blackened hand!'" Pip cries to him [304]), though upon moving into the Gargery household, Biddy concomitantly improves her personal hygiene: "I became conscious of a change in Biddy . . . her hands were always clean" (152). Ultimately the new Mrs. Joe exhibits a hand fully accommodated to matrimonial-maternal orthodoxy: "Biddy looked down at her child, and put its little hand to her lips, and then put the good matronly hand with which she had touched it, into mine. There was something in the action and in the light pressure of Biddy's wedding-ring, that had a very pretty eloquence in it" (490). Light though it may be, the wedding ring exerts sufficient pressure to remind Pip of the female trajectory parallel to, but divergent from, his own.

Unlike Miss Skiffins, who requires combat—however figurative—

to bring about the bliss of connubial sterility, Biddy accedes willingly to marital hegemony. Molly, by contrast with both, perpetrates the story's only interfemale bout, and she is consequently subject to an even more violent form of correction. Intervening in the boys' dilettantish display of arm-wrestling aptitude, Jaggers reveals Molly to be the real heavyweight among the novel's prize-fighters: "'There's power here,' said Mr. Jaggers, coolly tracing out the sinews with his forefinger. 'Very few men have the power of wrist that this woman has. It's remarkable what mere force of grip there is in these hands. I have had occasion to notice many hands; but I never saw stronger in that respect, man's or woman's, than these'" (237). While the boys' sparring connotes a certain homoeroticism, the sexual provocation of Molly's violence is identifiable only through the extraordinary means requisite to its suppression. Even the titillating gaze we've come to associate with such manual displays is here rendered paralyzing, as the Medusa one cannot but look upon: "We all stopped in our foolish contention. . . . When she held her hands out, she took her eyes from Mr. Jaggers, and turned them watchfully on every one of the rest of us in succession" (236). Seduction here amounts to a rage kept in check by its ritual humiliation. No mere "placid boxer" in drag (unlike Miss Skiffins's, these hands are always available for viewing), Molly exhibits a savagery that the narrative's libidinal economy can barely contain.

Wemmick later comes to narrate Molly's story, explaining the source of those mysterious scars and that "force of grip":

"[Molly] was tried at the Old Bailey for murder, and was acquitted. . . . The murdered woman—more a match for the man, certainly, in point of years—was found dead in a barn near Hounslow Heath. There had been a violent struggle, perhaps a fight. She was bruised and scratched and torn, and had been held by the throat at last and choked. Now, there was no reasonable evidence to implicate any person but this woman, and, on the improbabilities of her having been able to do it, Mr. Jaggers principally rested his case. You may be sure," said Wemmick, touching me on the sleeve,

Critical Insights

"that he never dwelt upon the strength of her hands then, though he sometimes does now. . . . [Molly] was so very artfully dressed from the time of her apprehension, that she looked much slighter than she really was; in particular, her sleeves are always remembered to have been so skilfully contrived that her arms had quite a delicate look. She had only a bruise or two about her—nothing for a tramp—but the backs of her hands were lacerated, and the question was, was it with finger-nails?" (405-6)

In form, Molly's battle with her rival differs little from the other bouts of jealousy in the novel; the fact, however, of the players' gender-reversal (here two women fight for the love of a man), as well as the fight's more serious consequences (the death of one combatant, the other's loss of her child), makes a difference. Pugilism, as we've seen, even when heterosexual, relies on intermasculine codes of conduct to generate its eroticism; when two women fight, crossing the border to sexuality is a more perilous prospect. To fight *as a woman*, this narrative suggests, is a deadly undertaking, because it threatens normative femininity so radically: the possibility of an *avant la lettre* lesbian eroticism here is rapidly chastened and expunged, for female sexuality undergoes the most rigorous surveillance.

Instead of demonstrating pure animus, then, Molly represents so high-voltage a current of sexual violence that its erotic charge must be defused through the most repressive means conceivable. The punishment she suffers for her manual conduct is a life-sentence of "taming" at Jaggers's hands, but more is at stake in her representation than a wholesale denial of female eroticism: she exemplifies the way in which repression functions as a vigilant and perpetual *management* of eros. Jaggers, as we've noted, exhibits a sadistic pleasure in displaying and exercising the "wild beast tamed" (224) to the cohort of young men he gathers for dinner:

"If you talk of strength," said Mr. Jaggers, "I'll show you a wrist. Molly, let them see your wrist."

Her entrapped hand was on the table, but she had already put her other hand behind her waist. "Master," she said, in a low voice, with her eyes attentively and entreatingly fixed upon him. "Don't."

"*I'*ll show you a wrist," repeated Mr. Jaggers, with an immovable determination to show it. "Molly, let them see your wrist."

"Master," she again murmured. "Please!"

"Molly," said Mr. Jaggers, not looking at her, but obstinately looking at the opposite side of the room, "let them see *both* your wrists. Show them. Come!"

He took his hand from hers, and turned that wrist up on the table. She brought her other hand from behind her, and held the two out side by side. (236)

This sadomasochistic tableau is the taming technique to which Wemmick has alluded—a performance Jaggers clearly must stage with some regularity in order to keep his handmaid in line. The sheer power of Molly's hands requires the sheer coercion of Jaggers's discipline; his delight at showing her off derives not from admiration of her strength but from pride in having controlled it.

In the magnetic field of the novel's eroticism, Molly occupies the negative pole; what, then, ought we to make of the connection between her and Estella, so clearly designated the protagonist's sexual cathode? Pip first suspects their relationship when, shortly after Jaggers's exhibition of Molly, he has an uncanny feeling upon meeting the grown-up Estella:

What was it that was borne in upon my mind when she stood still and looked attentively at me? . . . As my eyes followed her white hand, again the same dim suggestion that I could not possibly grasp, crossed me. My involuntary start occasioned her to lay her hand upon my arm. Instantly the ghost passed once more, and was gone.

What *was* it? (259)

Pip regards Estella's pointing finger and, following the novel's usual exchange, his inability literally to "grasp" his feeling is transferred onto, and compensated by, Estella's laying *her* hand on him. At their next meeting, Estella's hand again disturbs him: as he sees "her face at the coach window and her hand waving," he is once more startled by an ineffable likeness: "What *was* the nameless shadow which again in that one instant had passed?" (284). In being designated "nameless," this relation—unlike those other terms ("secret burden," "jiggered") whose namelessness remains implicit—ceases to be so: the novel of course finally can name it, denominating this uncanniness *maternity*. And as soon as namelessness is articulable, it has consequences in the plot.

Pip at last lights upon the "one link of association" (403) that confirms the affiliation he suspects: having witnessed "the action of Estella's fingers as they worked" (373) at knitting, he then finds "a certain action of [Molly's] fingers as she spoke arrested my attention. . . . The action of her fingers was like the action of knitting. . . . Surely, I had seen exactly such eyes and such hands, on a memorable occasion very lately! . . . I had passed by a chance swift from Estella's name to the fingers with their knitting action, and the attentive eyes. And I felt absolutely certain that this woman was Estella's mother" (403). More surprising than the revelation of Molly as Estella's mother is the suggestion that Pip could establish that relationship based on the appearance of their hands—for other than this "action of knitting," they have nothing in common. The very attempt to align these two sets of hands by force of uncanny conjunction only points up the antithesis between them: Molly's are marked while Estella's are blank; Molly's signify (even if what they designate is sexuality held in check) while Estella's do not. For Estella is so insistently the object of erotic denotation that her depiction virtually evacuates the connotative register in which we have located sexuality elsewhere in the novel.

The link to Molly persists in interfering with Estella's appropriateness as Pip's amorous desideratum, but the novel sufficiently manages this taint to keep it from tarnishing the daughter even as it continually condemns the mother. In a rare moment of offering advice, Jaggers discourages Pip from revealing Estella's pedigree, arguing, "'Add the case that you had loved her, Pip, and had made her the subject of those "poor dreams" . . . then I tell you that you had better—and would much sooner when you had thought well of it—chop off that bandaged left hand of yours with your bandaged right hand, and then pass the chopper on to Wemmick there, to cut *that* off, too'" (426). For Pip "to establish her parentage" would be "to drag her back to disgrace," and consequently to annihilate his own "dreams"; in Jaggers's image, it would amount to amputation—or, by the logic of hands in the novel, castration. This exposure would associate Estella with Molly, whose brutally inscribed flesh has always engendered castration anxiety; the Estella whom Jaggers counsels Pip not to reveal is thus in a true sense Molly's daughter—one with fantastically disabling sexual powers.

Pip of course resists the impulse to disclose Estella's origins, and in so doing he both protects her from "disgrace" and saves himself from the threat of dismemberment. In fact, Estella has never seemed particularly dangerous, for while her mother is perpetually and actively tamed, Estella is so almost by definition. Her irascible demeanor, and the sexual frigidity that accompanies it, have less to do with serving her own desires than with her fashioning as a suitably impossible object for the male characters captivated by her looks. To the extent that Estella appears as a desiring subject, she does so as the "mere puppet" (288) of her guardian, Miss Havisham; and as if to ensure that the willfulness evident in her aggressive passivity will be utterly disarmed, she receives a decisive pummeling at the hands of her husband, Drummle (490-91). Unlike those of the other female characters we have considered, Estella's hands are virtually maintenance-free; there is little of interest to say about them, except that little is said of them. Since she signals the overt representation of the subject's desire, Estella's appearances in the narrative obviate the necessity for sex appeal to reside wholly in the linguistic timbre.[40] As if to amplify the silence of her own desire, Estella is shown simply to have a "white hand" (259); and although Pip can fondle it, hers is possibly the least erogenous hand in the book:

> "I am beholden to you as the cause of [Miss Havisham's relatives] being so busy and so mean in vain, and there is my hand upon it."
>
> As she gave it me playfully—for her darker mood had been but momentary—I held it and put it to my lips. "You ridiculous boy," said Estella, "will you never take warning? Or do you kiss my hand in the same spirit in which I once let you kiss my cheek?"
>
> "What spirit was that?" said I.
>
> "... A spirit of contempt for the fawners and plotters." "If I say yes, may I kiss the cheek again?"
>
> "You should have asked before you touched the hand. But, yes, if you like."
>
> I leaned down, and her calm face was like a statue's. (287-88)

Estella succeeds as Pip's proper erotic object by the very thoroughness of her de-eroticization in the narrative; she does not simply represent the refusal ordinarily requisite to provoke desire but is *constitutively phantasmatic*. Though we are meant to register Pip's arousal at the alluring sight of her, the narrative voice—otherwise so rich in provocative periphrasis—becomes laryngitic around her "beauty," relying on such tropes as "indescribable majesty and . . . indescribable charm" (491). While the novel elsewhere registers eroticism in a combination of denotative refusal and connotative titillation, at the points of Pip's greatest official erotic interest, these strategies are reversed: in asserting *fortissimo* Pip's desire for Estella, the narrative need no longer marshal its battery of *sotto voce* techniques. At the moment desire's tale can be told, the narrative modulates into abstract diction, abandoning all of its prior engagement with corporeality: "She was so much changed, was so much more beautiful, so much more womanly, in all things winning admiration had made such wonderful advance, that I seemed to have made none" (256).[41]

For those who take the singular voicing *in* the plot of Pip's feelings for Estella to indicate the text's only genuine eroticism, the novel reads as a conventional romance. Such readers, however, are obliged to account for the fact that, even in its famously revised ending, *Great Expectations* resists bringing about the usual novelistic resolution in matrimony. As though to clear the space necessary for sanctioned, sanctified heterosexual romance, male homoeroticism is finally repudiated and female subjectivity thoroughly thwarted; yet we are left wondering why, despite these preparations, the romance plot is not more emphatically accomplished. One might, of course, point to the final version of the novel's ending, where Pip records the sensation of "what [he] had never felt before . . . the friendly touch of the once insensible hand" (491). If the novel does, as Bulwer-Lytton wished, conclude in happy domesticity, then its last sentence—"I took her hand in mine, and we went out of the ruined place. . . ." (493)—would provide a coherent resolution for its manual thematics. Yet the suspended animation entailed not only by the preservation of the original ending but by the ambiguity of the final version itself ("I saw no shadow of another parting from her") makes so smug a termination precarious.[42] Despite critical attestations of its plot's "perfection," the fact that the story is waylaid *before* the threshold has left readers notoriously unsettled about its ultimate outcome.[43]

Why should a novel with such copious erotic investments finally fail to resolve the most basic romance plot? One answer is that its strategies for regulating the vagaries of sexual desire simply prove *too* effective: they discipline all sexuality, even the most orthodox, quite out of existence. Not only are female domination, male homosexuality, onanism, and sadomasochism eliminated, but genitally oriented, maritally legitimated heterosexual monogamy itself comes to seem impossible.[44] Though the novel entertains a range of sexual designations, exchanges, developments, and diffusions, the sexual hegemony in which it issues becomes so powerful as finally to suspend not only that order's own ideal—institutionalized heterosexual monogamy—but anything that exceeds the fantasy of the solitary subject.

Yet despite the apparent elimination of all erotic possibilities, this sole remainder—the solitary imagination—suggests that bodily self-regulation may generate its own rewards. For even as the novel inculcates lessons about sexual continence in its audience, it agitates and incorporates the erotogenic pleasures of solitary reading. Indeed, the very irresolution of the ending offers an alternative to erotic abjuration, one that animates the oscillation between the hegemony of the marriage plot and the violence of its refusal. Rather than resolving all the previous travails of hands through the story, the novel's ultimate ambivalence may instead reinscribe the mode of sexual deferral by which it has operated from the first: in the manner of an imaginary object held perpetually at bay by autoerotic reverie, its eroticism can persist precisely by being suspended as undecidable. Just as Estella can never be more to Pip than a "poor dream"—the object of solitary sexual fantasy—so the residuum of the novel's ending finally demonstrates the sustainability, rather than the complete evacuation, of the masturbatory thematic that has mobilized its eroticism throughout. The ambiguity of the ending thus accomplishes a shift in the location of the novel's erotics that I have already suggested: in its finality it extinguishes the evocative narration through which sexuality has been connoted; but in the irresolution of its plot—its denotative practice—it now preserves those concerns as strictly undecidable. Even as it draws to an end, the novel resituates masturbation—sustains it, that is to say, by refusing closure.[45] The originary sexuality that enables the novel's flood of erotic potentials, masturbation also serves as the remainder left behind when all other possibilities have been forsworn.

From *English Literary History* 60, no. 1 (1993): 217-259. Copyright © 1993 by The Johns Hopkins University Press. Reprinted with permission of The Johns Hopkins University Press.

Notes

1. On the history of masturbation, see E. H. Hare, "Masturbatory Insanity: The History of an Idea," *Journal of Mental Science* 108 (January 1962): 2-25; R. P. Neuman, "Masturbation, Madness, and the Modern Concepts of Childhood and Adolescence," *Journal of Social History* 8 (Spring 1975): 1-27; Robert R. Hazelwood et al., *Autoerotic Fatalities* (Lexington, MA: D.C. Heath, 1983); Michel Foucault, *The History of Sexuality*, vol. 1, trans. Robert Hurley (New York: Vintage, 1978); *A History of Private Life*, vol. 4, ed. Michelle Perrot (Cambridge: Harvard Univ. Press, 1990), 494-96; and Eric Trudgill, *Madonnas and Magdalenes: The Origins and Development of Victorian Sexual Attitudes* (New York: Holms & Meier, 1976), 49-55. The most widely available Victorian medical materials on masturbation are: William Acton, *The Functions and Disorders of the Reproductive Organs* (1857; London: Churchill, 1875 [6th ed.]); Joseph W. Howe, *Excessive Venery, Masturbation and Continence* (1887; reprinted, New York: Arno, 1974); and *The Secret Vice Exposed! Some Arguments Against Masturbation* (New York: Arno, 1974), which reprints five works from 1723 to 1858, including the famous founding text of masturbation, *Onania; or, the Heinous Sin of Self-Pollution* (10th ed., 1724), and S. A. Tissot's *Treatise on the Diseases Produced by Onanism* (1832 ed.).

2. I take the links between the novel and masturbation that concern stimulating and regulating the imagination from Thomas W. Laqueur, to whom I am grateful for showing me his unpublished essay, "Onanism, Sociability, and the Imagination," which traces the historical dimensions of this conjunction fully. See also Walter Kendrick, *The Secret Museum: Pornography in Modern Culture* (New York: Viking, 1987), 88-92. On the charges of wastefulness and immorality that punctuated the early history of the novel, see John Tinnon Taylor, *Early Opposition to the English Novel* (New York: King's Crown, 1943); cited in Laqueur.

3. Charles Dickens, *Oliver Twist* (London: Penguin, 1966), 109; further references will be made parenthetically to this edition.

4. Peter Brooks designates the "scene" as such; *Reading for the Plot: Design and Intention in Narrative* (New York: Knopf, 1984), 110.

5. Charles Dickens, *Great Expectations* (London: Penguin, 1965), 44; further references will be made parenthetically to this edition.

6. In still another instance, Pip and his friends display a nearly postcoital serenity at being smeared with the butter from their tea and toast: "The Aged prepared such a haystack of buttered toast, that I could scarcely see him over it. . . . We ate the whole of the toast, and drank tea in proportion, and it was delightful to see how warm and greasy we all got after it. The Aged especially, might have passed for some clean old chief of a savage tribe, just oiled" (315).

7. Robert Newsom, "The Hero's Shame," *Dickens Studies Annual* 11 (New York: AMS, 1983): 1-24, convincingly charts the dynamics of guilt and shame in Dickens's writing using a psychoanalytic model. As if to validate those pathologies, however, Newsom preempts a full treatment of sexual thematics: "It is easy to feel in reading this novel [*Oliver Twist*] a real streak of perversity or at least sense of perversity in it, but just because it is so easy to interpret these scenes, one may leave it to the imagination to

determine exactly what activities pocket-picking, oyster-eating, and so on, may represent" (16). Also relevant, from the same volume, is Elliot L. Gilbert, "'In Primal Sympathy': *Great Expectations* and the Secret Life" (89-113), which argues that the "secret vice" under scrutiny in the novel is *selfishness*; the latter might reasonably serve as a figure for masturbation if one excised all considerations of sexuality and the body.

8. This is to argue with Foucault (note 1), who writes: "Pleasure spread to the power that harried it; power anchored the pleasure it uncovered. . . . The power that lets itself be invaded by the pleasure it is pursuing; and opposite it, power asserting itself in the pleasure of showing off, scandalizing, or resisting. . . . These attractions, these evasions, these circular incitements have traced around bodies and sexes, not boundaries not to be crossed, but *perpetual spirals of power and pleasure*" (45; emphasis in original).

9. On the enticements and concomitant hazards of reading connotation generally, and homosexual meanings in particular, I am indebted to D. A. Miller, "Anal *Rope*," *Representations* 32 (Fall 1990): 114-33.

10. Michel Foucault writes, "Fiction consists not in showing the invisible, but in showing the extent to which the invisibility of the visible is invisible" (*Foucault/ Blanchot* [New York: Zone, 1990], 24). The assumption that the materiality of writing bears some organic relation to its semantic content is hardly unique to *Great Expectations*. The notion of a writing that holds the key to the hand (and by extension, the personality) which inscribed it was reinvigorated in 1872 by Abbé Hypolite Michon's *Le mystère de l'écriture* (which invented the term "graphology") and by the numerous derivative guides to interpreting penmanship. Exemplary among these is Edward Lumley, *The Art of Judging the Character of Individuals from Their Handwriting and Style* (London: John Russell Smith, 1875), and Don Felix de Salamanca (pseud. John H. Ingram), *The Philosophy of Handwriting* (London: Chatto & Windus, 1879).

11. Fourth in the Bridgewater series on "the power, wisdom and goodness of God, as manifested in the creation" (first published in 1833 and reprinted throughout the century). For histories of chiromancy and chirology including but not limited to the rage for such work in the nineteenth century, see N. Vaschide, *Essai sur la psychologie de la main* (Paris: Rivière, 1909); Géza Révész, *The Human Hand: A Psychological Study*, trans. John Cohen (London: Routledge, 1958); and Walter Sorell, *The Story of the Human Hand* (Indianapolis: Bobbs-Merrill, 1967).

12. Notable exceptions include "Class and Gender in Victorian England: The Diaries of Arthur J. Munby and Hannah Cullwick," *Feminist Studies* 5 (1979): 86-141, in which Leonore Davidoff discusses Munby's eroticization of Cullwick's hands as a class crossing that reverses gender roles (111-13); and "'Descend, and Touch, and Enter': Tennyson's Strange Manner of Address," *Genders* 1 (Spring 1988): 83-101, in which Christopher Craft suggests the specifically homoerotic aspect of hands in Victorian culture (91-92). Craft's parenthetical proposal—"imagine, for instance, counting the handshakes in Dickens"—exercised an earlier generation of critics. Most thorough of these is Charles R. Forker, whose "The Language of Hands in *Great Expectations*," *Texas Studies in Language and Literature* 3 (1961): 280-93, substantially catalogues a "*leitmotif* of plot and theme—a kind of unifying symbol or natural metaphor for the book's complex of human interrelationships and the values and attitudes that motivate them" (281). In the same spirit, of seeking to prove through the representation of hands

what the novel's plot and characterization have already made clear, see M. H. Levine, "Hands and Hearts in *Great Expectations*," *Ball State University Forum* 6 (Autumn 1965): 22-24; Jack B. Moore, "Hearts and Hands in *Great Expectations*," *Dickensian* 61 (Winter 1965): 52-56; and Bert G. Hornback, *Great Expectations: A Novel of Friendship* (Boston: Twayne, 1987), 83-93. Walter L. Reed, *An Exemplary History of the Novel* (Chicago: Univ. of Chicago Press, 1981), 269-70, briefly treats the theme, as does Elaine Showalter, *Sexual Anarchy: Gender and Culture at the Fin de Siècle* (New York: Viking, 1990), 114-15; Helena Michie, *The Flesh Made Word: Female Figures and Women's Bodies* (New York: Oxford Univ. Press, 1987), 97-102, considers the Victorian novel's synecdochal mode of representing female bodies more generally.

13. *The Hand Phrenologically Considered: Being a Glimpse at the Relation of the Mind with the Organisation of the Body* (London: Chapman and Hall, 1848), 56-58.

14. Though its origin remains obscure, the supposition that the etymology of *masturbation* collapses ideas about hands with those about sex is all the more telling if invented to fit the apparent facts. According to the *OED*, the word's origin is either **mazdo-* (virile member) + *turba* (disturbance), or *manus* (hand) + *stuprare* (to defile). Seventeenth- and eighteenth-century writers tend to rely on the latter etymology: from *manual stupration* to *manustupration* to *mastupration*; see Hare (note 1), 20, n. 5.

15. Acton (note 1), 38; Howe (note 1), 72-73. For instances of binding the hands to prevent self-abuse, see Neuman (note 1), citing cases in which muffles and strait-jackets are used to prevent the vice (12); see also Acton (52) and Howe (209). By the advent of psychoanalysis, such manual discipline is taken to hypostatize the threat of castration attendant upon the little boy's discovery of the genital orientation of his eroticism. In "The Dissolution of the Oedipus Complex" (1924), Freud writes: "When the (male) child's interest turns to his genitals he betrays the fact by manipulating them frequently; and he then finds that the adults do not approve of this behaviour. More or less plainly, more or less brutally, a threat is pronounced that this part of him which he values so highly will be taken away from him. . . . [Adults] mitigate the threat in a symbolic manner by telling the child that what is to be removed is not his genital, which actually plays a passive part, but his hand, which is the active culprit" (*The Standard Edition of the Complete Psychological Works of Sigmund Freud*, ed. James Strachey, 24 vols. [London: Hogarth Press, 1953-74], 19:174-75).

16. While the hand arguably bears a less organic metonymic relation to female than to male masturbation, its utility as a sign for autoeroticism derives from its *lack* of gender designation. It is worth noting that "digitate" is a nineteenth-century term for specifically female masturbation (John S. Farmer, *Dictionary of Slang* [1890; reprinted, Ware, Hertfordshire: Wordsworth, 1987], s.v. *frig*, 73-74). Nineteenth-century anti-onanist literature fully treats both male and female cases, making progressively greater distinctions between the two.

17. Though it might be argued that labor is as ineffable as sex, the former's unspeakability can at any rate be explicitly denominated: after Estella's initial rejection, Pip designates his class shame "the smart without a name" (92). Even if only as "nameless," class can be denoted; sex, by contrast, signifies only through connotation. In "Work and the Body in Hardy and Other Nineteenth-Century Novelists," *Representations* 3 (Summer 1983): 90-123, Elaine Scarry writes: "As in the literature of desire

the genitals become the spoken or unspoken locus of orientation, so throughout the literature of creation the hands become the most resonant and meaning-laden part of the human anatomy" (110). The difficulty of distinguishing the hand that signifies "desire" from the one that stands for "creation" (that is, work) in *Great Expectations* suggests a distinction less absolute than the one that Scarry's terms propose.

18. This is the laboring hand whose plight Dickens could alternately decry and idealize. From *Hard Times* (1854): "Among the multitude of Coketown, generically called 'the Hands,'—a race who would have found more favour with some people, if Providence had seen fit to make them only hands, or, like the lower creatures of the seashore, only hands and stomachs—lived a certain Stephen Blackpool, forty years of age" (New York: Norton, 1966), 49. From *Bleak House* (1852-53): "Some of Rouncewell's hands have just knocked off for dinner time, and seem to be invading the whole town. They are very sinewy and strong, are Rouncewell's hands—a little sooty too" (Boston: Houghton Mifflin, 1956), 640.

19. Dickens's other first-person novels—*The Old Curiosity Shop, David Copperfield, Bleak House*—all do, to a lesser or greater degree, present such explanations. See Brooks (note 4), on the site of narration: "Repetition speaks in the text of a return which ultimately subverts the very notion of beginning and end, suggesting that the idea of beginning presupposes the end, that the end is a time before the beginning, and hence that the interminable never can be finally bound in a plot" (109).

20. On Pip's writing, see Robert Tracy, "Reading Dickens's Writing," *Dickens Studies Annual* 11 (note 7): 37-59. The classic deconstructive account of the affinity between writing and masturbation is Jacques Derrida, "'. . . That Dangerous Supplement . . .'" in *Of Grammatology*, trans. Gayatri Chakravorty Spivak (Baltimore: Johns Hopkins Univ. Press, 1976), 141-64. The most sophisticated recent grammatological study of the hand is Jonathan Goldberg, *Writing Matter: From the Hands of the English Renaissance* (Stanford: Stanford Univ. Press, 1990).

21. Herman Melville, *Pierre; or, the Ambiguities* (1852; New York: Grove Press, 1957), 362.

22. At its end, the novel generates the usual Dickensian mystification of social class, with Pip vacillating between claims for his poverty and those for his wealth—as if, in the aggregate, we will simply feel him to occupy that ambiguous middle: "I must not leave it to be supposed that we were ever a great House, or that we made mints of money. We were not in a grand way of business, but we had a good name, and worked for our profits, and did very well" (489).

23. The false hands of the forge and the forger ultimately converge in Orlick: an indolent laborer in Joe's smithy, he also joins forces with Compeyson, the counterfeiter. "'I've took up with new companions, and new masters. Some of 'em writes my letters when I wants 'em wrote—do you mind?—writes my letters, wolf! They writes fifty hands; they're not like sneaking you, as writes but one'" (438). As the opposite of Pip's manual formulation—where writing and labor collapse into shame—Orlick's is the negative moment, where deceptive writing and resistance to work are linked through anger, with Orlick's sexual violence as the correlate to Pip's guilty masturbation. See Eve Kosofsky Sedgwick, *Between Men: English Literature and Male Homosocial Desire* (New York: Columbia Univ. Press, 1985), 132.

24. For an argument that does, by contrast, discover the pathological "erotic identity" of the onanist in a nineteenth-century novel, see Eve Kosofsky Sedgwick, "Jane Austen and the Masturbating Girl," *Critical Inquiry* 17 (1991): 818-37.

25. Pip and Estella asseverate Jaggers's propensity for keeping secrets: "'Mr. Jaggers,' said I . . . 'has the reputation of being more in the secrets of that dismal place [Newgate] than any man in London.' 'He is more in the secrets of every place, I think,' said Estella, in a low voice" (289).

26. Laqueur (note 2) argues against scarcity theories of sexuality, claiming that masturbation is, on the contrary, perceived as threatening because of its seeming *limitlessness*. Whether masturbation is imagined as unproductive or excessively productive, however, its association with the hand would in any case set it in a conflictive relation to "genuinely" productive manual labor.

27. Jaggers offers a hand in one other place (352). When it fails to issue its olfactory warning, this appendage is capable of inciting Pip's paranoiac delusions through an approach from the rear: "I had strolled up into Cheapside, and was strolling along it, surely the most unsettled person in all the busy concourse, when a large hand was laid upon my shoulder, by some one overtaking me. It was Mr. Jaggers's hand, and he passed it through my arm" (400). The "large hand" that claps Pip on the shoulder gives fleshy form to the fantasies that so often "unsettle" him.

28. Dickens exploits the handshake's erotic possibilities in, for instance, the following reunion in *The Mystery of Edwin Drood* (1870; London: Mandarin, 1991): "The two shook hands with the greatest heartiness, and then went the wonderful length—for Englishmen—of laying their hands on each other's shoulders, and looking joyfully each into the other's face. 'My old fag!' said Mr. Crisparkle. 'My old master!' said Mr. Tartar" (242-43). In "The Pursuit of Homosexuality in the Eighteenth Century: 'Utterly Confused Category' and/or Rich Repository?'" in *'Tis Nature's Fault: Unauthorized Sexuality during the Enlightenment*, ed. Robert Purks Maccubbin (Cambridge: Cambridge Univ. Press, 1987), 132-68, G. S. Rousseau suggests that, at least in the mid-eighteenth century, handshaking was felt to provoke (rather than to sublimate) closer erotic encounters between men. He cites a 1749 tract: "'Tho many Gentlemen of Worth, are oftentimes, out of pure good *Manners*, obliged to give into it [squeezing of the hand]; yet the Land [England] will never be purged of its *Abominations*, till this *Unmanly, Unnatural* Usage be totally abolish'd: For it is the first Inlet to the detestable Sin of *Sodomy*" (150).

29. Sedgwick (note 23), chaps. 9-10, writes persuasively of the murderous anal erotics that pervade male-male combat—"male rape"—in late Dickens novels. Even in its reliance on the minimal "alibi" of heterosexual motives, however, Sedgwick's assessment of the Magwitch/Compeyson and Pip/Orlick violence may overstate the case.

30. Dennis Brailsford, in *Bareknuckles: A Social History of Prize-Fighting* (Cambridge: Lutterworth Press, 1988), explains how, by the middle of the nineteenth century, barefisted pugilism in England had come to be considered vulgar, excessively violent, and insufficiently regulated; it was associated with the lower classes, with the United States and Australia, and with black men. Queensberry initiated the effort to rehabilitate pugilism's declining popularity among the respectable classes by limiting

the length and number of rounds and by introducing boxing gloves. In Queensberry, then, the new regulatory system for boxing dovetails with other mid- and late-century efforts at disciplining male-male touching; in all instances, hitting below the belt is clearly forbidden.

31. This is not the only instance of Pip's noticing—and then blanching at having noticed—another man's all-too-visible body under the banner of revulsion. At the theater one night he notes, "I found a virtuous boatswain in his Majesty's service—a most excellent man, though I could have wished his trousers not quite so tight in some places and not quite so loose in others" (396). When Pip meets with the "secret-looking man . . . with an invisible gun," who seems inexplicably to be making a pass at him, he notes: "The strange man, after glancing at Joe, and seeing that his attention was otherwise engaged, nodded to me again when I had taken my seat, and then rubbed his leg—in a very odd way, as it struck me" (103-4). In each case, the euphemism is so startling as to beg decoding.

32. Charles Dickens, *The Old Curiosity Shop* (London: Penguin, 1972), 115-16.

33. Other intermale relationships mediated by erotically charged fights could be adduced here as well: the two scenes of Magwitch and Compeyson fighting, as well as Pip's confrontations with Drummle. Besides the arm-wrestling cited above, the following scene exemplifies the high-voltage wire that delineates hostile looking from tantalizing touching: "I had to put my hands behind [Drummle's] legs for the poker. . . . Here Mr. Drummle looked at his boots, and I looked at mine, and then Mr. Drummle looked at my boots, and I looked at his. . . . I felt here, through a tingling in my blood, that if Mr. Drummle's shoulder had claimed another hair's breadth of room, I should have jerked him into the window; equally, that if my own shoulder had urged a similar claim, Mr. Drummle would have jerked me into the nearest box" (369-70).

34. To "lick" the "or": Latin *os, ora,* "mouth"; thus, "I could only see his lips" (434).

35. We learn the following precise details about the placement of the men's hands—phrases which, strung together, relate the plot of the scene in brief: "I quickened my pace, and knocked at the door with my hand"; "I tried the latch. It rose under my hand"; "I could see his hands"; "He sat with his arms folded on the table"; "He put his hand into the corner at his side"; "He leaned forward staring at me, slowly unclenched his hand and drew it across his mouth as if his mouth watered for me"; "'I know'd you at Gargery's when you was so small a wolf that I could have took your weazen betwixt this finger and thumb'"; "His hands hanging loose and heavy at his sides . . ." ; "The last few drops of liquor he poured into the palm of his hand, and licked up"; "'I have no hurt but in this throbbing arm'" (433-41).

36. On the class and proprietary signals conveyed by gloves, see Richard D. Altick, *The Presence of the Present: Topics of the Day in the Victorian Novel* (Columbus: Ohio State Univ. Press, 1991), 795-98.

37. On the wedding day, the narrative's cathexis of gloves is curiously transferred from Miss Skiffins—deeroticized the moment she steps up to the altar—to a "comic" attack on Wemmick's father: "The old gentleman . . . experienced so much difficulty in getting his gloves on, that Wemmick found it necessary to put him with his back against a pillar, and then to get behind the pillar himself and pull away at them, while I

for my part held the old gentleman round the waist, that he might present an equal and safe resistance. By dint of this ingenious scheme, his gloves were got on to perfection" (463). As if to overcome the sexual barriers of decrepitude and infirmity, the two younger men here assault the Aged Parent in a scene less vivid than Orlick's attack on Pip only for being sanctioned by place (the church) and occasion (the wedding).

38. By comparison with Pip's relation to Miss Havisham, it might be argued that this eroticism has more to do with age than gender, but a careful examination of the touches between Pip and his "fairy godmother" indicates a cathexis far less entailed upon physical contact than his relation with Magwitch. At his departure for London (when he believes Miss Havisham to be his benefactress), Pip reverses and naturalizes the choreography of supplication that will later (with Magwitch) become so suggestive: "She stretched out her hand, and I went down on my knee and put it to my lips. I had not considered how I should take leave of her; it came naturally to me at the moment, to do this" (184). At his final interview with Miss Havisham, a series of touches fail their mark: "She stretched out her tremulous right hand, as though she was going to touch me; but she recalled it again before I understood the action, or knew how to receive it" (408); "Her hand . . . trembled again, and it trembled more as she took off the chain to which the pencil was attached, and put it in mine. All this she did, without looking at me" (410). Finally she manages, like Magwitch, to go down on bended knee before Pip: "She turned her face to me . . . and, to my amazement, I may even add to my terror, dropped on her knees at my feet; with her folded hands raised to me. . . . I entreated her to rise, and got my arms about her to help her up; but she only pressed that hand of mine which was nearest to her grasp, and hung her head over it and wept" (410). No revulsion and retreat here, only an embrace in return for the one she offers.

39. In his remarkable study *La main et l'esprit* (Paris: Presses Universitaires de France, 1963), Jean Brun suggests that the hand, as the primary organ of touching (as against merely being touched), constitutes the subject of desire: "Par elle-même la peau est beaucoup plus touchée qu'elle ne touche; seule la main est à la fois touchante et touchée car elle constitue une sorte de micro-organisme chargé de nos désirs, de nos craintes, de nos espoirs et de nos émotions, partant à l'aventure pour sonder la distance qui sépare chacun de nous de ce qu'il n'est pas" (97). (By itself the skin is touched much more than it touches; only the hand is at one and the same time touching and touched, for it constitutes a sort of microorganism full of our desires, our fears, our hopes, and our feelings, setting out randomly to sound the distance that separates each of us from what he is not.) If we keep in mind the Dickensian hand coded for masturbation, then Brun's discussion of the "reciprocity" entailed in any manual contact would evoke a sense of the closed circuit through which autoeroticism produces its practitioner as simultaneously subject and object of desire: "Lorsque de sa main l'homme touche, il tente d'émigrer hors de sa corporéité pour aller à la rencontre de l'autre, et cette expérience s'achève par on retour sur lui-même, retour chargé d'affectivité et peut-être de drames dans la mesure où, par le toucher, l'homme est sans cesse renvoyé à son moi. Car le toucher est le seul de nos sens à être chargé de ce que E. Minkowski appelle «un élément de réciprocité», toucher c'est être en même temps touché par ce que l'on touche; l'oeil peut voir sans être vu, l'oreille écoute sans être entendue, mais la main ne peut toucher sans être elle-même touchée. . . . Par la main qui touche, le moi va vers

---

l'autre; par sa main touchée il revient vers soi" (102). (When man touches with his hand, he tries to move outside of his corporeality to encounter the other, and this experience concludes with a return to himself, a return full of emotion and perhaps drama insofar as, by touching, man is unceasingly thrown back upon his ego. For touch is the only one of our senses to be full of what E. Minkowski calls "an element of reciprocity," to touch is at the same time to be touched by what one touches; the eye can see without being seen, the ear hears without being heard, but the hand cannot touch without itself being touched. . . . Through the hand that touches, the ego approaches the other; by the touched hand it returns to itself.)

40. George Bernard Shaw registers this sentiment in writing, "The notion that [Pip] could ever have been happy with Estella: indeed that anyone could ever have been happy with Estella, is positively unpleasant" (*Critical Essays on Charles Dickens's Great Expectations*, ed. Michael Cotsell [Boston: G. K. Hall, 1990], 41).

41. The narrative here relies on what Roland Barthes identifies as the trope for beauty, which "cannot assert itself save in the form of a citation": *catachresis*, the "rhetorical figure which fills this blank in the object of comparison whose existence is altogether transferred to the language of the object to which it is compared" (*S/Z*, trans. Richard Miller [New York: Hill and Wang, 1974], 33-34). Catachresis evokes that which has *no name* (still in a denotative register), unlike the tropes for unspeakability (associated with connotation), which designate that which *must not be named*.

42. On the ambiguity of the novel's ending, D. A. Miller, *Narrative and Its Discontents: Problems of Closure in the Traditional Novel* (Princeton: Princeton Univ. Press, 1981), writes: "In both endings, evidence of closure coexists, overlaps, and often coincides undecidably with counter-evidence of the narratable" (275). I take undecidability—whether, for instance, Pip drops or hangs onto Estella's hand after the tale is told—to be one of the novel's techniques for sustaining the masturbatory erotics that have impelled it.

43. On the novel's "perfection," Shaw (note 40), for instance, writes: "Dickens did in fact know that *Great Expectations* was his most compactly perfect book" (34); and J. Hillis Miller, *Charles Dickens: The World of His Novels* (Cambridge: Harvard Univ. Press, 1958), asserts: "*Great Expectations* is the most unified and concentrated expression of Dickens' abiding sense of the world, and Pip might be called the archetypal Dickens hero. In *Great Expectations* Dickens' particular view of things is expressed with a concreteness and symbolic intensity he never surpassed" (249).

44. One is reminded of Freud's ironic account of the strictures fostered by bourgeois sexual ideology in *Civilization and Its Discontents* (1930; New York: Norton, 1961): "As regards the sexually mature individual, the choice of an object is restricted to the opposite sex, and most extragenital satisfactions are forbidden as perversions. The requirement, demonstrated in these prohibitions, that there shall be a single kind of sexual life for everyone, disregards the dissimilarities, whether innate or acquired, in the sexual constitution of human beings; it cuts off a fair number of them from sexual enjoyment, and so becomes the source of serious injustice. The result of such restrictive measures might be that in people who are normal—who are not prevented by their constitution—the whole of their sexual interests would flow without loss into the channels that are left open. But heterosexual genital love, which has remained exempt from

outlawry, is itself restricted by further limitations, in the shape of insistence upon legitimacy and monogamy. Present-day civilization makes it plain that it will only permit sexual relationships on the basis of a solitary, indissoluble bond between one man and one woman, and that it does not like sexuality as a source of pleasure in its own right and is only prepared to tolerate it because there is so far no substitute for it as a means of propagating the human race" (60).

45. This is to argue that the oft-discussed "problem" of the novel's ending be seen as *productive*. It is precisely the resistance to closure that makes *Great Expectations* such a peculiar choice as exemplar for Brooks's (note 4) discussion of plottedness: "We have at the end what could appropriately be called a 'cure' from plot, in Pip's recognition of the general forfeiture of plotting, his renunciation of any attempt to direct his life. Plot comes to resemble a diseased, fevered state of the organism caught in the machinery of a desire which must eventually be renounced. Plot, we come to understand, was a state of abnormality or deviance.... Deviance is the very condition for life to be 'narratable': the state of normality is devoid of interest, energy, and the possibility for narration" (138-39). I understand the reinscription of "deviance" (particularly if we allow the word its historical sense as sexual deviance) to unsettle the novel's closure, and the attempt to "cure" it—however unsuccessful—as an effect of its sexual ideology's "machinery."

Gender and Class in Dickens:
Making Connections

Peter Scheckner

Charles Dickens preferred workers the way he preferred Victorian women: grateful for favors received, humble, patient, and passive. Conversely, although he understood the profound inequality and exploitativeness of Victorian society, Dickens feared the consequences of workers—among the most oppressed of these were women—taking their social destiny into their own hands. This paper attempts to make these points and to suggest that for the most part women in Dickens function as a close metaphor for workers. It was important for the author that male workers and their mates be saved from themselves. As we reached a degree of gender parity at the end of this end of this century, it is appropriate to make these gender and class connections.

Great Expectations is Dickens's thirteenth and next-to-last completed novel and, unlike *Hard Times*, published seven years earlier (in 1854), social class is not its central focus. Nevertheless, the genealogies in this work show that virtually everyone is a victim of oppressive circumstances, if not of economics, then of a sexual or domestic disaster. Pip is from a family of five brothers, all deceased while they were still infants. Joe Gargery's father beat his wife. Pip, Biddy, and Estella were orphaned or abandoned by their parents. Miss Havisham's mother died when the girl was quite young. In this novel only Biddy appears to have emotionally survived a less-than-nurturing childhood. Molly, Jaggers's housekeeper and Estella's mother, as a youth had become a nasty girl when she strangled a rival in love.

In such a pathological male world it is no wonder most of the women in *Great Expectations* don't sit by the hearth darning their men's socks. The sympathetic reader will come to understand and eventually forgive the craziness, coldness, or callousness of such troubled women as Mrs. Joe, Miss Havisham, Molly, and Estella. For these characters are no match for the novel's true villains: Joe's father,

Compeyson, Drummle, and Orlick are genuine bad guys. They beat, abuse, or kill other people, usually women. The remainder of the men, while not nice people, notably Uncle Pumblechook, Jaggers, and Abel Magwitch, are nonetheless more humane; certainly they are not in the same league with Orlick and company.

Nevertheless, when it came to the portrayal of women and madness, Dickens reveals many of the contradictions the author was little able to resolve. In his portrayal of women in *Great Expectations*, Dickens saw the world with almost the same unbalanced perspective as does Pip when Magwitch turns him upside down in the churchyard. *Great Expectations*, for example, contains four truly interesting women, "interesting," that is, in their separate pathologies. Two are rather on the masculine side: Georgiana Maria "Mrs. Joe" (who raises Pip and often her husband "by hand") and Molly (whose chief physical characteristic is her powerful—homicidal?—wrists, not her womanly charms). The two others are the witch-like Miss Havisham and the emotionally impoverished Estella. Biddy, the fifth major female character, is the novel's one truly virtuous, patient, domestic woman, but as a character she is by contrast bland, like most "good" women in Dickens.

Crazy or crazed, cold, calloused, or criminal start to describe Miss Havisham, Estella, Mrs. Joe, and Molly in that order. Biddy is, well, *custodial*. In any event these adjectives don't add up to a well-rounded portrayal of women. As early as June, 1841, thirteen years before the publication of *Hard Times*, at least one critic observed Dickens's sexual stereotyping. That year the writer made a trip to Scotland. During a dinner in Dickens's honor, John Wilson, a writer for *Blackwood's Magazine*, remarked that the only flaw in Dickens's works was his failure to portray the female character in all its fullness and complexity.

"Great" expectations include "repressed" as well as social and class expectations in this book, and when the women fall victim to such expectations they go nuts. The thwarted sexual passions of Molly and Miss Havisham and the sexually repressed Mrs. Joe and Estella begin to explain why these women are unhappy. This fundamental contradiction in *Great Expectations*, between a passionate nature and a social life which frustrates this passion, has a biographical basis in the author's own life.

Although Dickens clearly means no maliciousness to women in this work or in any other, the great Victorian marital upheaval of June, 1858, is illustrative of Dickens's ambivalent attitude towards women, especially toward strong women.

On that date Dickens sent a deed of separation to his wife of twenty-two years—Catherine Hogarth—who had borne him no fewer than ten children. Dickens's marriage ended in disaster and public humiliation for everyone, most of all his wife. Dickens told his side, only his side, of the separation in a statement published in the *London Times* and later in his periodical *Household Words*.

The breakup took a series of nasty turns. Dickens forbade his wife to see her own children, and when their son Walter died suddenly in 1864, Dickens did not even send Catherine a note. Even Dickens's death in 1870 did not ease his wife's pain and exile: no one apparently thought to invite her to the funeral. Perhaps the most definitive observation made about this famous marital disaster was made by Phyllis Rose in her study of five famous Victorian marriages, *Parallel Lives*. "For us," Rose concludes, Dickens "provides a fine example of how *not* to end a marriage" (191).

Nevertheless, Dickens cannot be easily stereotyped about gender or class issues. At the height of his own fame Dickens helped further the career of at least three women writers, among whom was the prominent Elizabeth Gaskell, the author of *North and South* and *Mary Barton*, which incidentally are about strong, un-Dickensian women. Dickens published her works in *Household Words*. Although the infamous playwright Oscar Wilde thought that Dickens's sentiment regarding women was overly sentimental and even phony ("it would take a heart of steel *not* to laugh at the death of Little Nell," Wilde said), most of us probably do shed tears for her and for Little Dorrit. Little Dorrit and her family spent time in the same jail—the Marshalsea prison—as did Dickens and his family for four months when Charles was only eleven.

Crying over lost women, repentant prostitutes, and dying impoverished girls—provided none of these women were wives or political reformers—were causes Dickens loved to champion and did. In 1847 Dickens organized for the millionaire Baroness Angela Burdette-Coutts Urania Cottage, a home intended for reforming prostitutes.

But how will Dickens be read in the beginning years of this century given *au currant* nationwide curriculum transformations that seek, in the words of a New Jersey state-sponsored project, "to integrate issues of women and gender, race/ethnicity, class, and sexuality into the curriculum"?

Held up to the light of class and gender considerations, Dickens will probably fare contradictorily. As to the politics of social class, Dickens feared social upheavals and the organized working class more than anything else. In *The Old Curiosity Shop* (1840-41), *Barnaby Rudge* (1841), *Hard Times* (1854), and *A Tale of Two Cities* (1859) Dickens makes clear that for him the only thing worse than social oppression is the dreadful spectacle of Chartists, Gordon rioters, trade unionists, or French revolutionaries taking to the streets. On the race question Dickens was at best conservative towards the natives of color in the British empire, especially when they rebelled, as they did in India and in Jamaica; and on the question of gender, things get more complicated and sometimes rough.

Here are the arguments that Dickens was, as a male novelist, both typical and rather conservative of his day: First, Dickens wrote as if he believed a woman's place was mostly in the home, doing domestic things and supporting her husband. Mrs. Joe Gargery is an example of what happens when a woman tries to boss a man. Even though Mrs. Joe stays home by the hearth, when she gets too assertive she becomes very unattractive and may even deserve a strong smack on the head—which she gets, as we know, from Orlick. Biddy, on the other hand, is exactly the kind of woman needed to end this troubled book: she's gentle and kind; she bears children she loves; and she takes good care of her man.

Second, Dickens is unsympathetic with women who socially rebel and who have public causes. Such women become either terrible (Dickens gives us the example of Joan of Arc in his *Child's History* or the "tigress" revolutionary Madame Defarge in *A Tale of Two Cities*) or ludicrous (Mrs. Jellyby in *Bleak House*, who educates the natives in Africa but neglects her own family).

Third, as to female sexuality, Dickens's women are passive (for example, Biddy) or, as in the case of Miss Havisham, Mrs. Joe, and Molly, they have raging hormones and spell trouble. For a variety of reasons, women in Dickens who exhibit passion of any kind are tortured by other women or abused by men, perhaps because Dickens himself began to become more and more a misogamist as his marriage to Catherine fell apart.

In *Great Expectations* Miss Havisham is jilted by a man, driven mad, and then dies in a type of auto da fe. She spends her adult life with near-perfect success teaching her pupil Estella to hate all men. Perhaps the darkest example of this inexplicable torture of women, especially of women as would-be lovers, occurs with Mr. Jaggers's housekeeper Molly (Estella's criminal mother). Molly is too physically strong and too passionate for her own good. Loving too well, Estella's mother strangled her rival, probably had great sex with Magwitch (aka Provis), but now, given Dickens's strict morality in these matters, must be punished by being Mr. Jaggers's servant.

Fourth, some women in Dickens's novels just get in the way—of men, that is. We see a few of these women in *Hard Times*. Possibly because she is too dull to utter an intelligible thought, Mrs. Gradgrind is made miserable by her husband; their daughter Louisa (not unlike Estella in *Great Expectations*) is deprived of any chance to enjoy love and sex with any man other than her brother. In the same novel Mrs. Sparsit is totally humiliated when she becomes too meddlesome in the affairs of men. Interesting, too, that Sparsit is one of the few women in Dickens who actually have a full-time, out-of-the house job. And of course Mr. Bounderby's mother is just a doormat for her overly ambitious, capitalist son. The one woman who ultimately survives everyone else's hard times is, of course, Sissy Jupe. She alone, like Biddy, is allowed to prosper—primarily by being fertile and very family oriented—probably because like Dickens she was "in art"; her father ran a circus.

Fifth, apparently Dickens believed that a man's nature, his psychological, emotional, and intellectual makeup, differs inherently from that of a woman. That is, men are rough and injurious; women are capable of healing. This is what *Hard Times* is largely about and explains Biddy's role in *Great Expectations*. Gradgrind and his son Tom, Josiah Bounderby, M'Choakumchild, James Harthouse, and Bitzer hurt the three most vulnerable groups in Dickens: women, children, and the poor. The three angels of mercy in *Hard Times* are Rachel, Mrs. Pegler, and Sissy Jupe. Rachel, a spiritual healer and a worker, is fairly canonized. She is described as "a woman working, ever working, but content and preferring to do it as her natural lot, until she should be too old to labour any more" (298). Rachel is Dickens's perfect heroine: giving, self-sacrificing, and with rarely a thought in her head.

To be fair, however, neither Dickens's male nor female characters have profound inner intellectual lives. The perfect example of this in *Great Expectations* is Biddy, who rather passively falls in and out of love with Pip and then effortlessly moves on to Joe, who can never be more than a father figure to her.

Which of these five accusations against Dickens applies in particular to *Great Expectations*? Actually a lot, since it is impossible to read Dickens and not realize that two major threads running through *Great Expectations* and most of his other fifteen novels are class—specifically class differences, class aspirations, and class exploitation—and gender, relationships between the sexes, and the emotional and sexual plight of women in mid-nineteenth century industrial England. What, in addition, is the relationship between Dickens's treatment of social class and his portrayal of women?

Our understanding of Dickens has matured a great deal since the

1930's when the Marxist critic T. A. Jackson declared in an ideological paroxysm that Dickens was almost a Communist revolutionary. Still, in 1986 the popular novelist John Irving wrote an Introduction to *Great Expectations* in which he states, quite correctly, that Dickens was ever "the champion of the *un*-championed," and that "vice and cruelty were not randomly bestowed on individuals at birth but were the creations of society." Understanding that social and political institutions were to blame for human misery and not the poor themselves must have been fairly strong stuff in 1986 when the Reagan administration was busy installing bigotry, greed, and an aggressive get-rich-quick way of life.

Yet, as George Orwell pointed out over fifty years ago in his 1939 essay on Dickens, the great irony is that "Dickens seems to have succeeded in attacking everybody and antagonizing nobody. Naturally this makes one wonder whether after all there was something unreal in his attack upon society" (49). Perhaps also, something may have been unreal about his portrayal of the two kinds of characters Dickens felt were the most abused in his time—workers and women (children of course fell into both categories).

Orwell advises us to start defining Dickens by what the latter was *not*. First and foremost Dickens was decidedly *not* radical or subversive, either in his characterization of women as sexually or socially oppressed, or of workers as an exploited class. As a matter of fact, Dickens rarely wrote about industrial or agricultural workers. The majority of England's men, women, and children who labored in the fields or in factories and who produced all of England's food, clothing, and everything else for that matter rarely hold center stage. When laborers do find themselves "between the covers of a book," Orwell observes, "it is nearly always as objects of pity or as comic relief" (50).

What is true in *Great Expectations* is generally true of Dickens's novels: his characters are mainly middle or lower-middle class types—lawyers (as in Jaggers), shopkeepers, innkeepers, artisans (a blacksmith like Joe Gargery), servants (Molly), clerks (most of Pip's friends), and criminals (like Magwitch). Stephen Blackpool in *Hard Times*—he is a worker in a mill—is a notable exception. But blacksmiths, lawyers, clerks, and criminals were hardly representative of the English working class during the 1840's and 50's when Dickens wrote most of his novels.

In the whole of his works Dickens portrays no agricultural worker who is a major character. However, Stephen Blackpool is a significant character, not because Dickens created a strong willed, socially conscious, or politically aware person not, for a change, from the middle or upper classes. Just the opposite is true. Blackpool, like virtually all of Dickens's female characters, is the very opposite of being socially subversive. He hasn't a clue as to why the world as he knows it is in such "a muddle." Since Dickens was always guided by the principle that neither workers nor women should rebel against their oppression, Blackpool turns to his worst oppressor, Josiah Bounderby, and says (and I am paraphrasing Stephen's heavy dialect), "I can't be expected to know how to end my suffering. Don't look to me for a solution. Its up to my betters to figure that out" (150).

In some ways Stephen Blackpool is a prototype of the Dickensian worker and of a certain type of female character. The poor are best when they suffer or pass their days passively, quietly, and in a state of stupefaction. This is the way Dickens most prefers them because, in extreme contrast, the working poor act out control. In the 1840's Dickens portrayed rampaging agricultural workers in *The Old Curiosity Shop* (1841) and in his Christmas Book, *The Chimes* (1844), and drunken, anarchic workers in *Barnaby Rudge* (1841), an historical novel about the Gordon Riots which took place in London in 1780.

In *A Tale of Two Cities* (1859, Dickens's only other historical novel), insurrectionary workers and women as harpies are combined. Both are portrayed as lunatic as and possibly even more malevolent than the aristocracy they are trying to pull down. "The men were terrible in [their] bloody-minded anger with which they looked down into the streets," but, writes Dickens, "the women were a sight to chill the boldest. . . . They ran out with streaming hair, urging one another, and themselves, to madness with the wildest cries and actions" (212).

Novels like *Barnaby Rudge*, *Hard Times*, and *A Tale of Two Cities* represent Dickens's response to the actual and violent class warfare raging in England until, roughly, the 1850's. In these works the poor had abandoned Dickens's central moral message, applicable to both workers and to women. It is an appeal expressed both ironically and seriously in *The Chimes* by Sir Joseph Bowley, Baronet, Member of Parliament, and "Friend and Father of the Poor," to the destitute laboring class:

> The one great moral lesson which that class requires . . . is entire Dependence on myself. They have no business whatever with—with themselves. If wicked and designing persons tell them otherwise, and they become impatient and discontented, and are guilty of insubordinate conduct and black-hearted ingratitude. . . . I am their Friend and Father still. It is so Ordained. It is in the nature of things. (106-7)

Presented as caricature, Sir Joseph's sentiments are precisely what Dickens novels end up articulating. Workers and women—with some exceptions—stand and should stand dependent before the governing class of righteous men. At the end of *The Chimes*, Will Fern, an out-of-work field hand, makes an appeal to One in Authority, in this case an Alderman, because to whom can the oppressed turn?—certainly not to themselves:

> Give us, in mercy, better homes . . . better food . . . kinder laws . . . and don't set Jail, Jail, Jail afore us, everywhere we turn. There an't a condescension you can show the Laborer then, that he won't take, as ready and as grateful as a man can be; for he has a patient, peaceful, willing heart. But you must put his rightful spirit in him first . . . [for] his spirit is divided from you at this time. Bring it back, gentlefolks, bring it back! Bring it back, afore the day comes when even his Bible changes in his altered mind, and the words seem to him to read . . . thy people are Not my people; Nor thy God my God! (133)

"Nowhere," as George Bernard Shaw observed in his "Introduction to *Hard Times*," "does [Dickens] appeal to the working classes to take their fate into their own hands and try the democratic plan." Workers should appeal to the ones in authority to save them from themselves, from the fires of rebellion which rage in their hearts sometimes out of control. So, too, should women be counseled by understanding men.

Although women in Dickens present a more psychologically complex case than do workers, the former too have their place in society and need to stay in it. "Bad" women in Dickens appear to get their just desserts. When women deviate from a sexual norm, when they overreach themselves, or become too intense about anything, the social status quo for Dickens is threatened. When women are too passionate, they go completely crazy like Miss Havisham, or are everlastingly punished, like Molly. When Mrs. Joe assumes a masculine role, she is critically injured by a man insecure about his own masculinity—that is, Orlick. Taught to be a man hater, Estella is only "saved" for society when she is punished by her brutish husband, Bentley Drummle. When women aren't downright angelic (and only women without husbands qualify for angelhood), like Rachel and to a lesser extent Louisa by the end of *Hard Times*, or Little Nell in *The Old Curiosity Shop*, they need to bear their disappointments stoically, in relative quiet, as does Biddy in *Great Expectations*.

The end of the passage in *Tale of Two Cities* about the rampaging revolutionary women contains within it a small moral. "Numbers of the women," Dickens writes, "lashed into blind frenzy, whirled about, striking and tearing at their own friends until they dropped into a passionate swoon, and were only saved by the men belonging to them from being trampled under foot" (213). The men may have "belonged" to these overly-passionate women, but it was the men who ultimately had to save their wives and sisters from their own self-destructiveness.

In *Great Expectations* we learned that female passion can only lead to disaster of one form or another. When Orlick justifiably calls Mrs. Joe "a foul shrew," Pip's sister begins to shriek, and rather than take her side against Orlick, Pip remarks:

I must remark of my sister, what is equally true of all the violent women I have ever seen, that passion was no excuse for her, because it is undeniable that instead of lapsing into passion, she consciously and deliberately took extraordinary pains to force herself into it, and became blindly furious by regular stages. (107)

Ultimately, Molly, Mrs. Joe, and even Estella are tamed or softened by men, though most often brutally. Miss Havisham, too far gone in her throes, is consumed by that which nourished her madness. In the absence of workers, rebellious or otherwise, in *Great Expectations*, Dickens had no need to ridicule them as he did when he attacked their efforts at organizing through Dickens's only union organizer—the satirical character Slackbridge in *Hard Times*. Nevertheless, the earlier novel and *Great Expectations* are instructive about gender and class in Dickens, and both works point to a fundamental irony.

Perhaps no other writer of Dickens's generation more consistently and convincingly expressed the sexual and social outrages perpetrated against workers and women as a direct result of nineteenth-century predatory capitalism. In *The Chimes* Dickens showed the nature of class outrages, especially as they affected the daughters of the working class. In this, the most bleak and politically satiric of Dickens's Christmas tales, Lilian and Margaret have seen their health and youth robbed from them by impoverishment:

Such work, such work [Meg tells her friend]! So many hours, so many days, so many long, long nights of hopeless, cheerless, never-ending work—not to heap up riches, not to live grandly or gaily, not to live upon enough, however coarse; but to earn bare bread; to scrape together just enough to toil upon, and want upon, and keep alive in us the consciousness of our hard fate! How can the cruel world go round, and bear to look upon such lives! (127)

Dickens never more sharply and less apologetically expressed the fundamental contradictions of capitalism as he did in this tale. "I believe I have written a tremendous book. . . . It will make a great uproar, I have no doubt," Dickens wrote to Thomas Mitton on November 5, 1844. He was right: the Chartists made a big fuss over it, but the Liberal *Morning Chronicle* (December 17, 1844) said that Dickens had "gone into the very opposite extreme of ranging party against party and class against class." As Alderman Cute said in *The Chimes* "It's almost enough to make one think, if one didn't know better, that at times some motion of a capsizing nature was going on in things which affected the general economy of the social fabric" (130).

The Chartists must have been drawn to the open class warfare in *The Chimes*. In a rare reference to a Chartist activity, Will Fern tells Margaret:

> There'll be a Fire tonight. There'll be Fires this winter-time, to light the
> dark nights, East, West, North, and South. When you see the distant sky
> red, they'll be blazing . . . think of me no more; or, if you do, remember
> what a Hell was lighted up inside of me. (147-48)

He is referring to rick-burning, a practice in the late 1830's and early 40's in which agricultural workers took revenge against farmers who paid them starvation wages. These same fires of rage blazed before among the harridans of *A Tale of Two Cities*.

Dickens obviously was drawn to women like Lilian and Margaret and workers like Will Fern and Trotty as portrayed in *The Chimes*. They are not so much towers of strength and resistance are they are victims and proponents of great endurance, patience, humility, and passivity. Most of the tale is a vision of young workers' lives "sinking lower and lower; [the wife] enduring, poor thing, miseries enough to wear her life away" (143). Lilian achieves near sainthood by dying young, a penitent woman who had been forced into prostitution. As she expires she tells Meg, "He suffered her to sit beside His feet, and dry them with her hair" (137), a reference to Mary Magdalene, the patron saint of repentant prostitutes.

Toward the end of this work, Trotty sums up what lessons he has drawn from the long nightmares he has had of his family and friends who live, when they are able, merely to work. It is a speech of great emotion, but of equally great disempowerment:

> I know that our Inheritance is held in store for us by Time. I know there is a Sea of Time to rise one day, before which all who wrong us or oppress us will be swept away like leaves. I see it, on the flow! I know that we must trust and hope, and neither doubt ourselves, nor doubt the Good in one another! Oh Spirits, merciful and good, I am grateful! (151)

The Chimes ends the way Dickens often liked to end his works which illustrate irreconcilable social and class differences—with an outburst of domestic joy: the men tamed, the women in a maternal mode. In his 1912 introduction to *Hard Times*, Shaw wrote that the novel "is Karl Marx, Carlyle, Ruskin, Morris, Carpenter, rising up against civilization itself as a disease, and declaring that it is not our disorder but our order that is horrible; that it is not our criminals but our magnates that are robbing and murdering us."

Nevertheless, the genuine radicalness of the novel is undercut by Dickens's equally fixed bourgeois conservatism. *Hard Times*, which in most respects takes an unflinching look at capitalist antihumanitarian values, ends with a romantic and irrelevant tableau of Sissy Jupe and her family: "Herself again a wife—a mother—lovingly watchful of her children" (298). Dickens pleads with the reader, presumably a middle-class audience which could effect social change, "It rests with you and me whether, in our two fields of action, similar things shall be or not. Let them be!" he entreats (299).

With this same idealism, Dickens concludes *The Chimes*. Richard and Meg get married. The music of a band, the chimes "in lusty operation," and dancing couples fill up the background. Again an appeal is made, this time to the Listener, to "try to bear in mind the stern realities from which these shadows come [of Trotty's nightmares, which make up most of *The Chimes*]; and in your sphere—none is too wide, and none too limited for such an end—endeavor to correct, improve, and soften them" (154). The working poor and women—"not the meanest of our brethren or sisterhood," Dickens writes—should not be "debarred their rightful share in what our Great Creator formed them to enjoy" (154).

The Chimes and *Hard Times* are explicitly critical of workers taking matters into their own hands. The union organizer Slackbridge in *Hard Times*, as Shaw pointed out in his introduction, "is a mere figment of the middle-class imagination. No such man would be listened to by a meeting of English factory hands." Women fare a lot better than do labor leaders, probably because they are all better victims. Rachel, Louisa, and all the mothers in this novel—Bounderby's, Bitzer's, Louisa's—are tormented to one degree or another. Not showing any aggressiveness, they are treated kindly. Sissy shows strength, but it is of a private, close-to-home nature, and she is the book's undeniable heroine.

In *The Chimes* social class and gender are similarly linked: those destitute men and women who stay close to home, even when they temporarily stray like Lilian, deserve our mercy. Will Fern has, he explains to Margaret, "a Hell . . . lighted up inside of me." He doesn't really want to do what he's doing. In both works, Time, Fate, and the goodness of the Masters are the forces to which Dickens ultimately makes his great appeal.

From *The Midwest Quarterly* 41, no. 3 (2000): 236-250. Copyright © 2005 by *The Midwest Quarterly*, Pittsburg State University. Reprinted by permission of *The Midwest Quarterly*.

Bibliography

Dickens, Charles. *Barnaby Rudge*. New York: Oxford University Press, 1996.

_____. *Bleak House*. New York: Oxford University Press, 1991.

_____. *A Child's History of England*. New York: Oxford University Press, 1996.

_____. "The Chimes." *Christmas Books*. New York: Oxford University Press, 1996.

_____. *Great Expectations*. New York: Oxford University Press, 1996.

_____. *Hard Times*. New York: Oxford University Press, 1996.

_____. *The Old Curiosity Shop*. New York: Oxford University Press, 1994.

Gaskell, Elizabeth. *Mary Barton*. Ed. Stephen Gill. New York: Penguin, 1970.

_____. *North and South*. Ed. Angus Easson. New York: Oxford University Press, 1982.

Jackson, Thomas. *Charles Dickens: Progress of a Radical*. New York: International Publishers, 1987.

Orwell, George. *A Collection of Essays*. New York: Harcourt Brace, 1991.

Rose, Phyllis. *Parallel Lives: Five Victorian Marriages*. New York: Random House, 1984.

RESOURCES

1812	Born Charles John Huffam Dickens, the second of eight children, on February 7 to John and Elizabeth Dickens.
1813	Alfred Allen Dickens (brother) is born.
1814	John Dickens, a clerk in the Navy Pay Office, is transferred from Portsea to London. During these early years, Dickens is schooled by his mother and takes a strong interest in reading the fiction classics found in his father's library. Alfred Allen Dickens dies.
1816	Letitia Mary Dickens (sister) is born.
1817	John Dickens moves the family to Chatham. Charles attends Dame School with his sister Fanny.
1819	Harriet Dickens (sister) is born.
1820	Frederick Dickens (brother) is born.
1821	Dickens begins studying at the Rev. William Giles School. He remains at this school, even after his family moves back to London in 1822.
1822	Composes his first tragedy, *Misnar, the Sultan of India*. Alfred Lamert Dickens (brother) is born.
1824	John Dickens is arrested for debt and imprisoned at Marshalsea Prison. Charles begins working at Warren's Blacking Factory and moves into a poor neighborhood. His father is released three months later.
1824-1826	Dickens attends Wellington House Academy in London but is forced to leave when his father is evicted from his home.
1827	Dickens studies at Mr. Dawson's school and works as a law clerk and spends time reading in the British Museum. Augustus Dickens (brother) is born.

1830	Meets Maria Beadnell, the daughter of George Beadnell, a prosperous banker.
1831	Becomes a reporter for the *Mirror of Parliament*.
1832	Works as a staff writer for the *True Sun*.
1833	Dickens publishes his first piece, "A Dinner at Poplar Walk," in *Monthly Magazine* under the pen name Boz. Maria Beadnell ends relationship with Dickens.
1834	Dickens works as a staff writer on the *Morning Chronicle*. His "street sketches" begin to appear in the *Evening Chronicle*. Dickens meets Catherine Hogarth. John Dickens is arrested for debt.
1836	*Sketches by Boz*, illustrated by George Cruikshank, is published. Dickens and Catherine Hogarth marry in April. Two plays are produced, *The Strange Gentleman* and *The Village Coquettes*, both at the St. James's Theatre. Dickens starts work as the editor of *Bentley's Miscellany*. Dickens meets John Forster.
1836-1837	*Pickwick Papers* is published in monthly installments.
1837	*Pickwick Papers* is published in book form; *Oliver Twist* begins to appear in *Bentley's Miscellany*. Dickens moves to 48 Doughty Street in Bloomsbury (now home of the Charles Dickens Museum). *Is She His Wife?*, a play, is produced at the St. James's Theatre. Dickens's first child, Charles Culliford Boz Dickens, is born. Catherine's sister Mary dies.
1838	*Nicholas Nickleby* is published in installments and is completed in October of 1839. Dickens's first daughter, Mary, is born.
1839	The Dickenses move to Devonshire Terrace. Daughter, Kate Macready Dickens, is born. *Nicholas Nickleby* appears in book form.
1840	Dickens edits *Master Humphrey's Clock*; publishes *The Old Curiosity Shop*.
1841	*Barnaby Rudge* is published in *Master Humphrey's Clock*. Son Walter Landor Dickens is born.

1842	Dickens and his wife travel to America. Dickens publishes *American Notes* and begins work on *Martin Chuzzlewit*.
1843	*Martin Chuzzlewit* appears in monthly installments. *A Christmas Carol* is published.
1844	Dickens travels to Italy. *The Chimes* is completed. Son Francis Jeffrey Dickens is born.
1845	Dickens produces and acts in Jonson's *Every Man in His Humour*. *The Cricket on the Hearth* is written, and Dickens begins work on *Pictures from Italy*. A fourth son, Alfred D'Orsay Tennyson Dickens, is born.
1846	Dickens creates and edits the *Daily News* but resigns shortly afterward. Begins *Dombey and Son*. Travels to Switzerland. *The Battle of Life: A Love Story* appears.
1847	Son Sydney Smith Haldimand Dickens is born. Dickens begins managing a theatrical company.
1848	Older sister Frances (Fanny) dies. Dickens's theatrical company performs for Queen Victoria. Dickens publishes his last Christmas book, *The Haunted Man*.
1849	Dickens begins work on *David Copperfield*. A sixth son, Henry Fielding Dickens, is born.
1850	Dickens begins publishing *Household Words*, a weekly journal. Daughter Dora Annie Dickens is born and dies.
1851	Dickens's father dies.
1852	*Bleak House* begins appearing in monthly installments. The first bound volume of *A Child's History of England* appears. Dickens's last child, Edward Bulwer Lytton Dickens, is born.
1854	*Hard Times* is published in *Household Words* and later appears in book form.

1855	*Little Dorrit* appears in monthly installments. The Dickens family travels to Paris.
1856	Dickens purchases Gad's Hill Place. Rehearses Wilkie Collins's *The Frozen Deep*.
1857	Dickens performs in *The Frozen Deep*. Meets Ellen Ternan. Hans Christian Andersen visits Gad's Hill.
1858	Dickens begins a series of paid public readings. Separates from Catherine and tries to dispel rumors of an affair with Ellen Ternan.
1859	Dickens begins a new weekly, *All the Year Round*. *A Tale of Two Cities* is published.
1860	Dickens begins writing the series *The Uncommercial Traveller*. *Great Expectations* appears in weekly installments.
1861	First installment of *Great Expectations* is published in *Harper's Weekly*, New York, in November.
1863	Dickens continues his readings in Paris and London. His daughter Elizabeth dies and his own health is in serious decline.
1864	*Our Mutual Friend* appears in installments.
1865	Dickens and Ellen Ternan survive a train crash in Kent. *Our Mutual Friend* appears in book form. The second collection of *The Uncommercial Traveller* is published.
1866	Despite poor health, Dickens continues to give readings in the English provinces.
1867	Dickens travels to America and gives readings in Boston and New York. Meets President Andrew Johnson.
1869	Begins *The Mystery of Edwin Drood*.
1870	On June 9, Charles Dickens dies at age fifty-eight.

Works by Charles Dickens

Short Fiction

"A Dinner at Poplar Walk," 1833
Sketches by Boz, 1836
A Christmas Carol, 1843
The Chimes, 1844
The Cricket on the Hearth, 1845
The Battle of Life: A Love Story, 1846
The Haunted Man, 1848
Reprinted Pieces, 1858
The Uncommercial Traveller, 1860
George Silverman's Explanation, 1868
Christmas Stories, 1871

Long Fiction

Pickwick Papers, 1836-1837
Oliver Twist, 1837-1839
Nicholas Nickleby, 1838-1839
The Old Curiosity Shop, 1840-1841
Barnaby Rudge, 1841
Martin Chuzzlewit, 1843-1844
Dombey and Son, 1846-1848
David Copperfield, 1849-1850
Bleak House, 1852-1853
Hard Times, 1854
Little Dorrit, 1855-1857
A Tale of Two Cities, 1859
Great Expectations, 1860-1861
Our Mutual Friend, 1864-1865
The Mystery of Edwin Drood, 1870

Drama

The Strange Gentleman, pr. 1836
The Village Coquettes, pr., pb. 1836
Mr. Nightingale's Diary, pr., pb. 1851 (with Mark Lemon)
No Thoroughfare, pr., pb. 1867 (with Wilkie Collins)

Children's Literature

A Child's History of England, 1852-1854

Nonfiction

American Notes, 1842
Pictures from Italy, 1846

Bibliography

Ackroyd, Peter. *Dickens*. London: Sinclair-Stevenson, 1990.

Alexander, Doris. *Creating Characters with Charles Dickens*. University Park: Penn State University Press, 1991.

Barickman, Richard, Susan MacDonald, and Myra Stark. *Corrupt Relations: Dickens, Thackeray, Trollope, Collins and the Victorian Sexual System*. New York: Columbia University Press, 1982.

Bloom, Harold, ed. *Charles Dickens's Great Expectations*. Philadelphia: Chelsea House, 2000.

Bolton, Philip H. *Dickens Dramatized*. London: Mansel, 1987.

Brinton, Ian. *Dickens's Great Expectations*. Reader's Guides 52. New York: Continuum International Publishing Group, 2007.

Brooks, Peter. "Repetition, Repression, and Return: The Plotting of *Great Expectations*." In *Great Expectations*, ed. Edgar Rosenberg. New York: W.W. Norton, 1999. 679-689.

Brown, Ivor. *Dickens in His Time*. London: Nelson, 1963.

Campbell, Elizabeth. *Fortune's Wheel: Dickens and the Iconography of Women's Time*. Athens: Ohio University Press, 2003.

Carey, John. *The Violent Effigy: A Study of Dickens' Imagination*. London: Faber and Faber, 1979.

Carlisle, Janice. *The Sense of an Audience: Dickens, Thackeray and George Eliot at Mid-Century*. Athens: University of Georgia Press, 1981.

Clayton, Jay. *Charles Dickens in Cyberspace: The Afterlife of the Nineteenth Century in Postmodern Culture*. Oxford: Oxford University Press, 2003.

Collins, Philip, ed. *Dickens and Crime*. London: Macmillan, 1962.

Connor, Steven, ed. *Charles Dickens*. London: Longman, 1996.

Coolidge, Archibald C., Jr. *Charles Dickens as Serial Novelist*. Ames: Iowa State University Press, 1967.

Cotsell, Michael, ed. *Critical Essays on Charles Dickens's Great Expectations*. Boston: G. K. Hall and Co., 1990.

Dabney, Ross. *Love and Property in the Novels of Charles Dickens*. Berkeley: University of California Press, 1967.

Daldry, Graham. *Charles Dickens and the Form of the Novel*. Totowa, NJ: Barnes & Noble, 1987.

Davies, James A. *The Textual Life of Dickens's Characters*. London: Macmillan, 1989.

Davis, Paul B. *Charles Dickens A to Z: The Essential Reference to His Life and Work*. New York: Facts on File, 1998.

Dessner, Lawrence Jay. "*Great Expectations:* The Ghost of a Man's Own Father." *PMLA* 91, no. 3 (1976): 436-449.

_____. "*Great Expectations:* The Tragic Comedy of John Wemmick." *Ariel: A Review of International English* 6, no. 2 (1975): 65-80.

Epstein, Norrie. *The Friendly Dickens: Being a Good-Natured Guide to the Art and Adventures of the Man Who Invented Scrooge.* New York: Viking, 1998.

Ford, George H. *Dickens and His Readers: Aspects of Novel Criticism Since 1836.* Princeton, NJ: Princeton University Press, 1955.

Ford, George H., and Lauriat Lane, Jr., eds. *The Dickens Critics.* Ithaca, NY: Cornell University Press, 1961.

Forker, Charles R. "The Language of Hands in *Great Expectations.*" *Texas Studies in Language and Literature* 3 (1961): 280-293.

Garis, Robert. *The Dickens Theatre: A Reassessment of the Novels.* Oxford: Clarendon Press, 1965.

Ginsburg, Michal Peled. "Dickens and the Uncanny: Repression and Displacement in *Great Expectations.*" *Dickens Studies Annual* 13 (1984): 115-124.

Gissing, George. *Charles Dickens: A Critical Study.* New York: Dodd, Mead, and Co., 1904.

Hagan, John. "Structural Patterns in Dickens's *Great Expectations.*" *ELH* 21 (1954): 54-66.

Hardy, Barbara. *The Moral Art of Charles Dickens.* London: Athlone Press, 1970.

Hawes, Donald. *Who's Who in Dickens.* New York: Routledge, 1998.

Herst, Beth F. *The Dickens Hero: Selfhood and Alienation in the Dickens World.* New York: St. Martin's Press, 1990.

Hobsbaum, Philip. *A Reader's Guide to Charles Dickens.* Syracuse, NY: Syracuse University Press, 1998.

Hori, Masahiro. *Investigating Dickens's Style.* Basingstoke: Palgrave Macmillan, 2004.

Hornback, Bert G. *Great Expectations: A Novel of Friendship.* Boston: Twayne, 1987.

Jacobson, Wendy S., ed. *Dickens and the Children of Empire.* New York: Palgrave, 2000.

Johnson, Edgar. *Charles Dickens: His Tragedy and Triumph.* 2 vols. New York: Simon & Schuster, 1952.

Jordan, John O., ed. *The Cambridge Companion to Charles Dickens.* New York: Cambridge University Press, 2001.

Kaplan, Fred. *Dickens: A Biography.* Baltimore: Johns Hopkins University Press, 1998.

Kelly, Mary Ann. "The Functions of Wemmick of Little Britain and Wemmick of Walworth." *Dickens Studies Newsletter* 14 (1983): 145-149.

Kincaid, James R. *Dickens and the Rhetoric of Laughter.* Oxford: Clarendon Press, 1971.

Leavis, F. R., and Q. D. Leavis. *Dickens: The Novelist.* London: Chatto & Windus, 1970.

Lerner, Laurence. *Angels and Absences: Child Deaths in the Nineteenth Century.* Nashville: Vanderbilt University Press, 1997.

Levine, Richard A. "Dickens, the Two Nations, and Individual Possibility." *Studies in the Novel* 1, no. 2 (1969).

Lucas, John. *The Melancholy Man: A Study of Dickens's Novels.* London: Methuen, 1970.

Meckier, Jerome. *Hidden Rivalries in Victorian Fiction: Dickens, Realism and Revaluation.* Lexington: University Press of Kentucky, 1987.

Miller, J. Hillis. *Charles Dickens: The World of His Novels.* Cambridge, MA: Harvard University Press, 1958.

Mitchell, Sally. *Daily Life in Victorian England.* Westport, CT: Greenwood Press, 1996.

Moore, Grace. *Dickens and Empire: Discourses of Class, Race and Colonialism in the Works of Charles Dickens.* Montpelier, VT: Ashgate, 2004.

Morgantaler, Goldie. "Meditating on the Low: A Darwinian Reading of *Great Expectations.*" *Studies in English Literature 1500-1900* 38 (1998): 701-721.

Moshe, Ron. "Autobiographical Narration and Formal Closure in *Great Expectations.*" *Hebrew University Studies in Literature* 5 (1977): 37-66.

Newlin, George, ed. and comp. *Every Thing in Dickens: Ideas and Subjects Discussed by Charles Dickens in His Complete Works—A Topicon.* Westport, CT: Greenwood Press, 1996.

Newsom, Robert. *Charles Dickens Revisited.* New York: Twayne, 2000.

Paroissien, David. *A Companion to Charles Dickens.* Oxford: Blackwell, 2008.

Pykett, Lyn. *Charles Dickens.* New York: Palgrave, 2002.

Rosenberg, Edgar, ed. *Great Expectations: Authoritative Texts, Backgrounds, Contexts, Criticism.* New York: Norton, 1999.

Sadrin, Anny. *Great Expectations.* London: Unwin Hyman, 1988.

Schad, John. *The Reader in the Dickensian Mirror: Some New Language.* New York: St. Martin's Press, 1992.

Schlicke, Paul. *Dickens and Popular Entertainment.* London: Allen and Unwin, 1985.

Scott, P. J. M. *Reality and Comic Confidence in Charles Dickens.* London: Macmillan, 1979.

Smiley, Jane. *Charles Dickens.* New York: Viking, 2002.

Smith, Grahame. *Charles Dickens: A Literary Life.* New York: St. Martin's Press, 1996.

Spenko, James L. "The Return of the Repressed in *Great Expectations.*" *Literature and Psychology* 30, nos. 3/4 (1980): 133-146.

Stoehr, Taylor. *Dickens: The Dreamer's Stance.* Ithaca, NY: Cornell University Press, 1965.

Stone, Harry. *Dickens and the Invisible World: Fairy Tales, Fantasy, and Novel-Making.* London: Macmillan, 1980.

_____. *The Night Side of Dickens: Cannibalism, Passion, Necessity*. Columbus: Ohio State University Press, 1994.

Traill, Nancy H. *Possible Worlds of the Fantastic: The Rise of the Paranormal in Fiction*. Toronto: University of Toronto Press, 1996.

Trudgill, Eric. *Madonnas and Magdalenes: The Origins and Development of Victorian Sexual Attitudes*. New York: Holms & Meier, 1976.

Vogel, Jane. *Allegory in Dickens*. Tuscaloosa: University of Alabama Press, 1977.

Walsh, Susan. "Bodies of Capital: *Great Expectations* and the Climacteric Economy." *Victoria Studies* 37 (1993): 73-98.

Waters, Catherine. *Dickens and the Politics of the Family*. New York: Cambridge University Press, 1997.

Welsh, Alexander. *The City of Dickens*. Cambridge, MA: Harvard University Press, 1986.

Westburg, Barry. *The Confessional Fictions of Charles Dickens*. De Kalb: Northern Illinois University Press, 1977.

Wilson, Angus. *The World of Charles Dickens*. New York: Viking Press, 1970.

Young, Melanie. "Distorted Expectations: Pip and the Problems of Language." *Dickens Studies Annual* 7 (1978).

CRITICAL INSIGHTS

About the Editor

Eugene Goodheart is the Edytha Macy Professor of Humanities Emeritus at Brandeis University. He has written extensively on nineteenth- and twentieth-century literature and modern literary and cultural theory. He is the author of eleven books, including *The Skeptic Disposition: Deconstruction, Ideology and Other Matters* (1984, 1991), *The Reign of Ideology* (1997), *Does Literary Studies Have a Future?* (1999), *Darwinian Misadventures in the Humanities* (2007), and a memoir, *Confessions of a Secular Jew* (2001). His many articles and reviews have appeared in, among other journals, *The Partisan Review*, *The Sewanee Review*, *New Literary History*, *Critical Inquiry*, and *Daedalus*.

About *The Paris Review*

The Paris Review is America's preeminent literary quarterly, dedicated to discovering and publishing the best new voices in fiction, nonfiction, and poetry. The magazine was founded in Paris in 1953 by the young American writers Peter Matthiessen and Doc Humes, and edited there and in New York for its first fifty years by George Plimpton. Over the decades, the *Review* has introduced readers to the earliest writings of Jack Kerouac, Philip Roth, T. C. Boyle, V. S. Naipaul, Ha Jin, Jay McInerney, and Mona Simpson, and published numerous now classic works, including Roth's *Goodbye, Columbus*, Donald Barthelme's *Alice*, Jim Carroll's *Basketball Diaries*, and selections from Samuel Beckett's *Molloy* (his first publication in English). The first chapter of Jeffrey Eugenides's *The Virgin Suicides* appeared in the *Review*'s pages, as well as stories by Edward P. Jones, Rick Moody, David Foster Wallace, Denis Johnson, Jim Shepard, Jim Crace, Lorrie Moore, Jeanette Winterson, and Ann Patchett.

The Paris Review's renowned Writers at Work series of interviews, whose early installments include legendary conversations with E. M. Forster, William Faulkner, and Ernest Hemingway, is one of the landmarks of world literature. The interviews received a George Polk award and were nominated for a Pulitzer Prize. Among the more than three hundred interviewees are Robert Frost, Marianne Moore, W. H. Auden, Elizabeth Bishop, Susan Sontag, and Toni Morrison. Recent issues feature conversations with Salman Rushdie, Joan Didion, Stephen King, Norman Mailer, Kazuo Ishiguro and Umberto Eco. (A complete list of the interviews is available at www.theparisreview.org.) In November 2008, Picador will publish the third of a four-volume series of anthologies of *Paris Review* interviews. The first two volumes have received acclaim. *The New York Times* called the Writers at Work series "the most remarkable and extensive interviewing project we possess."

The Paris Review is edited by Philip Gourevitch, who was named to the post in

2005, following the death of George Plimpton two years earlier. Under Gourevitch's leadership, the magazine's international distribution has expanded, paid subscriptions have risen 150 percent, and newsstand distribution has doubled. A new editorial team has published fiction by Andre Aciman, Damon Galgut, Mohsin Hamid, Gish Jen, Richard Price, Said Sayrafiezadeh, and Alistair Morgan. Poetry editors Charles Simic, Meghan O'Rourke, and Dan Chiasson have selected works by Billy Collins, Jesse Ball, Mary Jo Bang, Sharon Olds, and Mary Karr. Writing published in the magazine has been anthologized in *Best American Short Stories* (2006, 2007, and 2008), *Best American Poetry*, *Best Creative Non-Fiction*, the Pushcart Prize anthology, and *O. Henry Prize Stories*.

The magazine presents two annual awards. The Hadada Award for lifelong contribution to literature has recently been given to William Styron, Joan Didion, Norman Mailer, and Peter Matthiessen in 2008. The Plimpton Prize for Fiction, given to a new voice in fiction brought to national attention in the pages of *The Paris Review*, was presented in 2007 to Benjamin Percy and to Jesse Ball in 2008.

The Paris Review won the 2007 National Magazine Award in photojournalism, and the *Los Angeles Times* recently called *The Paris Review* "an American treasure with true international reach."

Since 1999 *The Paris Review* has been published by The Paris Review Foundation, Inc., a not-for-profit 501(c)(3) organization.

The Paris Review is available in digital form to libraries worldwide in selected academic databases exclusively from EBSCO Publishing. Libraries can contact EBSCO at 1-800-653-2726 for details. For more information on *The Paris Review* or to subscribe, please visit: www.theparisreview.org.

Contributors

Eugene Goodheart is the Edytha Macy Professor of Humanities Emeritus at Brandeis University. He is the author of eleven books of literary and cultural criticism as well as a memoir, *Confessions of a Secular Jew* (2004).

Charles E. May is Professor Emeritus of Literature at California State University, Long Beach. He is the author and editor of seven books and over 500 articles and reviews in books, reference works, journals, and newspapers.

Elizabeth Gumport is an M.F.A. candidate in fiction at Johns Hopkins University. Her writing has appeared in *n+1*, *Canteen*, and *Slate*.

Gurdip Panesar earned his M.A. and Ph.D. degrees in English literature from the University of Glasgow, Scotland. Dr. Panesar has contributed various entries to literary reference works and teaches in the Department of Adult Education at the University of Glasgow.

Shanyn Fiske is an Assistant Professor of English and director of the Classical Studies Minor at Rutgers University (Camden). She is the author of *Heretical Hellenism: Women Writers, Ancient Greece, and the Victorian Popular Imagination* (Ohio, 2008). She has published articles on Charles Dickens, Charlotte Brontë, Alicia Little, and other nineteenth-century writers.

Mary Ann Tobin teaches composition and literature at Triton College in River Grove, Illinois. She is also a dual member of the Chicago, Illinois, and Pittsburgh, Pennsylvania, branches of the International Dickens Fellowship, serving as the latter branch's newsletter editor and webmaster. She has presented numerous papers before both local and international gatherings of the Fellowship and has had an article appear in its journal, *The Dickensian*.

Eiichi Hara is Professor of English Literature at Tohoku University. He is the author of *Comparative Culture through Fairy Tales* and co-author of *The Gordian Knot: The Discourse of Marriage in English Renaissance Drama*. In 2005 he was elected the president and honorary secretary of the Japan Dickens Fellowship.

Peter Brooks is Sterling Professor of Comparative Literature at Yale University. His books include *Realist Vision* (2005), *Troubling Confessions: Speaking Guilt in Law and Literature* (2000), *Psychoanalysis and Storytelling* (1994), *Body Work* (1993), *Reading for the Plot* (1984), *The Melodramatic Imagination* (1976), and *The Novel of Worldliness* (1969). His essays and reviews have appeared in *The New York Times*, *The New Republic*, *Times Literary Supplement*, *The Nation*, *London Review of Books*, and *Yale Law Journal*. He is a former Eastman Professor at Oxford University, and has been a visiting professor at Harvard University, the University of Copenhagen, the University of Bologna, and the Georgetown University Law Center. Between 2003 and 2006, he was University Professor at the University of Virginia.

Caroline Levine is Professor at the University of Wisconsin-Madison. Her books include *Provoking Democracy: Why We Need the Arts* (2007) and *The Serious Pleasures of Suspense: Victorian Realism and Narrative Doubt* (2003), which the 2004 Perkins Prize recognized as the year's best book in narrative studies. She is also the co-editor of *From Author to Text: Re-Reading George Eliot's "Romola"* (1998). Her articles have appeared in *Victorian Studies* and the *Journal of British Studies*.

Calum Kerr is a writer, lecturer, and reviewer living near Manchester in the United Kingdom. He has published a number of short stories and a series of essays regarding his Ph.D. rewriting of Robert Louis Stevenson's *The Strange Case of Dr. Jekyll and Mr. Hyde*. He is currently working on a number of projects, including a novel.

Elizabeth MacAndrew was Professor of English at Cleveland State University. Her books include *The Gothic Tradition in Fiction* (1980). Her articles have appeared in the *Journal of Popular Culture* and *Essays in Literature*.

John Cunningham is Professor Emeritus of English at Hollins College. He has published articles on *King Lear*, *A Handful of Dust*, John Donne, and T. S. Eliot, and is the author of *The Poetics of Byron's Comedy in "Don Juan"* (1982).

Samuel Sipe was Professor of English at Point Park College, now Point Park University.

William A. Cohen is Professor of English at the University of Maryland. He is the author of *Embodied: Victorian Literature and the Senses* (2008) and *Sex Scandal: The Private Parts of Victorian Fiction* (1996). His articles have appeared in the *Oxford Encyclopedia of British Literature*, *Nineteenth-Century Literature*, *Novel: A Forum on Fiction*, *South Atlantic Quarterly*, and *Victorian Studies*.

Peter Scheckner is Professor of Literature at Ramapo College of New Jersey. He is the author of *Class, Politics, and the Individual: A Study of the Major Works of D. H. Lawrence* (1985) and co-editor of *The Way We Work: Contemporary Writings from the American Workplace* (2008). His articles have appeared in *The Midwest Quarterly*, and his poetry in *The Tusculum Review*.

Acknowledgments

"The *Paris Review* Perspective" by Elizabeth Gumport. Copyright © 2008 by Elizabeth Gumport. Special appreciation goes to Christopher Cox and Nathaniel Rich, editors for *The Paris Review.*

"Stories Present and Absent in *Great Expectations*" by Eiichi Hara. From *English Literary History* 53, no. 3 (1986), pp. 593-614. Copyright © 1986 by The Johns Hopkins University Press. Reprinted with permission of The Johns Hopkins University Press.

"Repetition, Repression, and Return: *Great Expectations* and the Study of Plot" by Peter Brooks. From *New Literary History* 11, no. 3 (1980), pp. 503-523. Copyright © 1980 by The Johns Hopkins University Press. Reprinted with permission of The Johns Hopkins University Press.

"Realism as Self-Forgetfulness: Gender, Ethics, and *Great Expectations*" by Caroline Levine. From *The Serious Pleasures of Suspense: Victorian Realism and Narrative Doubt*, pp. 84-98. Copyright © 2003 University of Virginia Press. Reprinted by permission of University of Virginia Press.

"A Second Level of Symbolism in *Great Expectations*" by Elizabeth MacAndrew. From *Essays in Literature* 2, no. 1 (Spring 1975), pp. 65-75. Copyright © 1975 by Western Illinois University. Reprinted by permission of Western Illinois University.

"Christian Allusion, Comedic Structure, and the Metaphor of Baptism in *Great Expectations*" by John Cunningham. From *South Atlantic Review* 59, no. 2 (May 1994), pp. 35-51. Copyright © 1994 by South Atlantic Modern Language Association. Reprinted by permission of South Atlantic Modern Language Association.

"Memory and Confession in *Great Expectations*" by Samuel Sipe. From *Essays in Literature* 2, no. 1 (Spring 1975), pp. 53-64. Copyright © 1975 by Western Illinois University. Reprinted by permission of Western Illinois University.

"Manual Conduct in *Great Expectations*" by William A. Cohen. From *English Literary History* 60, no. 1 (1993), pp. 217-259. Copyright © 1993 by The Johns Hopkins University Press. Reprinted with permission of The Johns Hopkins University Press.

"Gender and Class in Dickens: Making Connections" by Peter Scheckner. From *The Midwest Quarterly* 41, no. 3 (2000), pp. 236-250. Copyright © 2005 by *The Midwest Quarterly*, Pittsburg State University. Reprinted by permission of *The Midwest Quarterly.*

Index

Cohen, Monica, 48
Collins, Philip, 43
Collins, Wilkie, 34-37, 50, 146, 193
Compeyson (*Great Expectations*); death, 121, 177, 184-185, 187, 265; engagement to Miss Havisham, 48; story, 246; villain, 19, 24, 62, 64, 209-210, 270
Confession. *See* Memory and confession in *Great Expectations*
Coolidge, Archibald, 35
Cornhill Magazine, 33
Cricket on the Hearth, A (Dickens), 9
Criticism of *Great Expectations*, 13, 15, 19, 26-27, 31, 34, 36-38, 41-42, 45, 48-51, 71, 87, 97-98, 128, 197, 213

Daleski, Herman, 202
Darwinism, 25, 31-32
David Copperfield (Dickens), 9, 13, 20, 33, 36; Agnes in, 66; David Copperfield in, 56, 71-72; Dora Spenlow in, 56, 66; narrative in, 56; social system in, 55-56; Tommy Traddles in, 61; Uriah Heep in, 6, 78
Day's Ride, A (Lever), 33
Death metaphors in *Great Expectations*, 179, 190-191
Defoe, Daniel, 22
De Saussure, Ferdinand, 149
Dickens, Catherine Hogarth, 8, 36, 271, 273
Dickens, Charles; death, 10, 38, 46, 271; early life, 8, 13, 20-21, 44, 48, 57; imagination, 6, 38-39, 46; letters, 33, 36, 50, 147; marriage, 8, 36, 273; maturity, 92; metaphors of education, 105; politics, 34, 40-42, 55-56, 174; public readings, 10; religion, 194; success, 8-9, 13, 34-35, 38, 43, 57, 196

Dickens, Charles, Jr., 50
Dickens, John (father), 8, 13, 20-21, 57
Dickens, Walter (son), 271
Dickens: A Collection of Critical Essays (Price), 46
"Dickens: The Two Scrooges" (Wilson), 43
Dickens and the Twentieth Century (Gross and Pearson), 46
Dickens and Women (Slater), 48
Dickens Critics, The (Ford and Lane), 46
Dickens Industry: Critical Perspectives 1836-2005, The (Mazzeno), 46
Dickens the Novelist (F.R. and Q.D. Leavis), 46
Dickens World, The (House), 43;
Dickensian, The, 38
Dombey and Son (Dickens), 9, 78
Dostoevsky, Fyodor, 38, 91, 95
Drummle, Bentley (*Great Expectations*), 157, 182, 228-230, 240; death, 30, 186, 188; marriage, 5, 14, 23, 153, 157-158, 278; villain, 23, 61, 158, 278
Dublin University Magazine, 37

Eco, Umberto, 129
Eliot, George, 20, 26, 35, 38
English Novel, The (Van Ghent), 45
Englishwoman's Domestic Magazine, 33
Erotic language in *Great Expectations*, 243
Estella. *See* Havisham, Estella
Excessive Venery, Masturbation and Continence (Howe), 222

Fairy tale in *Great Expectations*, 82-84
Fiction and the Reading Public (Leavis, Q.D.), 46

Film adaptations of *Great Expectations*, 51

Fire imagery in *Great Expectations*, 166, 170, 172-173, 185, 187-189, 191, 196-197

Fitzgerald, F. Scott, 4

Ford, George, 46

Forgiveness theme in *Great Expectations*, 178, 180, 185, 187-188, 190

Formalists, 72, 94, 97, 149

Forster, John, 33, 50, 86, 147-149, 153, 197

Fortune's Wheel (Campbell), 49

Foucault, Michel, 220, 261

Freud, Sigmund, 28, 38, 44, 98, 107-109, 113-114, 123, 238, 262, 267

Gargery, Joe (*Great Expectations*); apprentice, 21, 59, 78-79, 81, 151, 154; and Biddy, 23-25, 60, 65, 79, 85, 187, 192; childlike, 102; father, 269; kindness, 3, 5, 58, 66, 169, 172, 204, 227; language, 80; marriage, 65, 85-86, 187; pride, 136; realistic character, 39; reconciliation with Pip, 6, 63, 66, 170, 207; voice of reason, 58

Gargery, Mrs. Joe (*Great Expectations*); aphasia, 115, 146; attack, 206; cruelty, 45, 58-59, 74, 104, 134, 175, 226, 269-270; death, 106, 154, 162, 172, 181-182, 186, 188; origins, 48; signals, 137, 145-146

Garis, Robert, 202-203

Garnett, Robert R., 55, 59

Gaskell, Elizabeth, 35, 271

Gender in *Great Expectations*, 47-48, 270, 275

Genette, Gérard, 72

Gide, André, 99

Gilmour, Robin, 56, 60, 63

Ginsburg, Michal Peled, 44

Gissing, George, 39, 42, 50

Great Expectations (Dickens); allegory in, 161; apprentice stories in, 77-83, 87, 91; authorship problem, 71, 84; criticism, 13, 15, 19, 26-27, 31, 34, 36-38, 41-42, 45, 48-51, 71, 87, 97-98, 128, 197, 213; death metaphors in, 179, 190-191; erotic language, 243; fairy tale in, 82-84; film adaptations, 51; forgiveness theme, 180, 188; hands, 220-226, 228-230, 232-236, 240-242, 244-245, 247-248, 250-256, 259, 261, 263, 265-266; memory and confession in, 198, 201-202, 204-212, 214; narrative, 20, 26, 31; plot, 19, 31, 36, 43, 56, 73-77, 82-83, 85, 90, 99, 101-107, 111, 113-114, 118-125, 128, 146, 161, 165, 167, 171, 174, 220, 225, 230, 235-236, 244, 247-249, 255, 258-259, 262, 265, 268; publication of, 4, 19, 30, 33-36, 147-148, 152-153, 160, 269; stories present and absent in, 72-73, 75, 77, 81, 85, 87, 91-93; structure of, 71, 73, 77, 79, 84, 86, 90-91, 150, 152, 159, 177-178, 181, 191, 198, 213, 222-223, 241; symbolism in, 161-162, 164-168, 172-175; writing of, 5, 10, 32, 36, 55-56, 91, 94, 120, 149, 153

Great Gatsby (Fitzgerald); Daisy Buchanan in, 4; Jay Gatsby in, 4

Gregory, Marshall W., 196

Grob, Shirley, 82

Gross, John, 46

(Dickens); Francis Goodchild in, 78, 80; Tom Idle in, 78, 80

Lean, David, 25, 51

Leavis, F.R., 39, 46

Leavis, Q.D., 46, 50

Lever, Charles, 33, 35

Lewes, George Henry, 38

Lillo, George, 76

Little Dorrit (Dickens), 10, 23, 36

London Merchant, The (Lillo), 76-77, 81, 83

London Times, 271

Lucas, George, 150

Magwitch, Abel (*Great Expectations*); arrest, 4, 64, 151, 155; childhood, 209; confession, 63; criminal, 3-4, 19, 22, 25, 41, 63-64, 84-85, 101, 114, 145, 151, 153, 162, 167, 197, 203, 206, 208-209, 219, 275; death, 85, 121, 141, 155, 173, 177, 184-185, 187, 196-197, 204, 248; emissary, 107, 110; Estella's father, 4, 79, 96, 112, 245, 273; exile, 49, 51, 62, 64, 151; humanity of, 6, 30-31, 63-64, 270; manipulation, 248; Pip's double, 62-63; Pip's help to, 4, 6, 168, 171-173, 205, 217; Pip's second father, 84, 96, 112, 187, 192; wealth, 4, 22, 30, 41, 64, 79, 85, 114, 120, 151, 156, 166, 170, 209

Magwitch, Abel (Noonan), 51

Manual conduct in *Great Expectations*, 234, 245, 253

Martin Chuzzlewit (Dickens), 9, 36, 91

Marxism, 40-42, 45, 47, 275, 281

Mary Barton (Gaskell), 271

Mazzeno, Laurence, 46

Meckier, Jerome, 30

Melville, Herman, 225

Memory and confession in *Great*

Expectations, 198, 201-202, 204-212, 214

Mengel, Ewald, 63

Mill on the Floss, The (Eliot), 20

Miller, J. Hillis, 45, 58

Millett, Kate, 47

Millhauser, Milton, 86

Milton, John, 184, 197, 213

Mitchell, Sally, 22

Mitton, Thomas, 280

Molly (*Great Expectations*); past, 269; punishment, 278; sexual passion of, 270, 273; story, 93, 249, 252; trial, 172; wrist, 115, 250, 254

Moonstone, The (Collins), 129

Moore, Grace, 49

Morning Chronicle, 8

Morphology of the Folk Tale, The (Propp), 150

Morris, Christopher D., 29

Mots, Les (Sartre), 98

Moynahan, Julian, 78

Mystery of Edwin Drood, The (Dickens), 10, 129

Narrative Discourse (Genette), 72

Narrative of *Great Expectations*, 20, 26, 31; authorship, 71, 198, 202; conventional, 202, 208; failed, 72; historical, 226; logic, 5; models, 149

Narratology, 97

Nicholas Nickleby (Dickens), 92; publication of, 9

Noonan, Michael, 51

North and South (Gaskell), 271

Old Curiosity Shop, The (Dickens), 92, 237, 263; Little Nell in, 13, 278; publication of, 9, 13; Quilp in, 91; social oppression in, 272; workers in, 276

Oliphant, Margaret, 37, 47, 128

Oliver Twist (Dickens), 23-24, 43;
    Charley Bates in, 216, 231; Jonas
    Chuzzlewit in, 76, 91; Noah Claypole
    in, 78; Sykes in, 76, 91; Oliver Twist
    in, 8

Orlick, Dolge (*Great Expectations*);
    villain, 24, 26, 78, 137, 154, 157,
    171-172, 175-176, 182, 188-189,
    207, 239, 270, 272, 278

Orwell, George, 42, 275

Our Mutual Friend (Dickens), 10, 19,
    35, 38

Paltrow, Gwyneth, 51

Paradise Lost (Milton), 184, 197

Parallel Lives (Rose), 271

Passing (Larsen), 211

Pearson, Gabriel, 46

Pickwick Papers, The (Dickens), 8-9, 57,
    91-92

Pip (*Great Expectations*); alienation, 45-
    46, 72, 74, 80, 88, 110;
    apprenticeship to Joe, 21, 59, 78-79,
    81, 87, 151, 154, 203; baptism, 188-
    192, 194; childhood, 3-5, 14, 24, 45,
    102, 110-111, 121, 134, 164-166,
    169, 198-200, 203, 210, 239, 251,
    269; choices, 56, 64-65, 101;
    confession, 206, 208; consciousness,
    19, 24, 66, 100-101, 104, 110, 198,
    201, 206, 209; criminal career,
    74-75, 77, 81, 153, 201, 204-205;
    desire for Estella, 4, 6, 14, 27, 31,
    50, 56, 58-61, 63, 77, 90, 96, 111-
    112, 122, 140, 156-158, 181, 189,
    197, 210-211, 256-257; destiny,
    171; dream, 22, 25, 56, 58, 83-85,
    88, 93, 102, 110, 119, 132, 140,
    256, 259; ego, 106; false hopes, 72;
    fantasy, 5; father, 23, 71, 73, 76, 79,

84, 96, 100, 112, 114, 127, 227, 239,
    269; fear, 3, 5, 22, 26, 29, 61-62, 151,
    170-171, 175; gentlemanly
    aspirations, 4-5, 21, 25, 32, 40, 60-
    61, 226; guilt, 3, 5, 22, 27, 29, 59, 63,
    74, 76-77, 134, 154, 156, 164, 166-
    170, 177, 180-182, 190, 196, 205-
    206, 212, 219, 223-224, 231, 263;
    identity, 3, 58-59, 196-198;
    imagination, 251; inheritance, 3, 21-
    22, 63-64, 79, 151, 156, 209;
    knowledge, 118-119, 132, 134, 201;
    language, 79-80, 207, 212, 218;
    memories, 202, 205, 209-210, 213;
    moral maturity, 5, 56, 85, 161, 212;
    narrator, 3, 5-6, 19-20, 56, 73, 89,
    100, 111, 199, 201-203, 207-208,
    212, 214, 226, 235, 237; orphan, 3,
    56, 62-63, 74, 79, 93, 151; physique,
    237; redemption, 173; return, 134,
    181, 192, 204; roles, 83; self-
    possession, 5, 201; snobbery, 55, 65,
    154-155; spiritual maturity, 5-6, 56,
    161-162, 197-198, 212; suffering,
    196

Pirrip, Philip "Pip." *See* Pip

Plot in *Great Expectations*, 19, 31, 36,
    43, 56, 73-77, 82-83, 85, 90, 99,
    101-107, 111, 113-114, 118-125,
    128, 146, 161, 165, 167, 171,
    174, 220, 225, 230, 235-236,
    244, 247-249, 255, 258-259,
    262, 265, 268

Pocket, Herbert (*Great Expectations*),
    196; assault on, 156, 181, 236, 237;
    business venture, 22, 24, 29, 158;
    double for Pip, 61-62; fiancée, 23,
    186; financial security, 186;
    generosity to, 6, 171, 175; genteel
    judgment, 110; manners, 61, 105,
    245